PRAISE FOR BROOK BELLO

"It is difficult to think of anything more hellish than being trapped in the prison of sex trafficking. How could this be happening to so many all over the world? We have statistics that astound us, but it is the singular uniquely devastating stories of people like Brook Bello, that finally break through our physique and penetrate our hearts. With every passing page in Brook's book, she shares with heart wrenching honesty how it can happen to anyone. You will be deeply touched by this beautiful, brave woman that you will come to love and admire. But you will also be reminded, sadly, that she is just one of the many millions more still crying out in the darkness to be redeemed."
— *Kathy Lee Gifford*

"Dr. Brook Bello is a champion in my mind, and I know she is a champion to the minds of hundreds of women and girls she has rescued from sex trafficking in this country."
—*Diana Rowan Rockefeller, philanthropist, activist, founder and chair of Afghan Women Leaders CONNECT*

"With the explosion of technology, we're able to tell stories we never could before — in ways we never could. The great artists today are being raised with these tools, and they're the ones with the energy and the vision to go out and create something truly important. With these issues, only someone who has been there can truly understand what's going on. Brook is one of those people.
—*Jon Voight, Academy Award and Golden Globe Award-winning actor*

ALSO BY BROOK PARKER BELLO:

Living Inside The Rainbow:
Winning The Battlefield of the
Mind After Human Trafficking & Mental Bondage

Living Inside The Rainbow:
Workbook and Study Guide

To Soar Without Leaving the Ground

Fine Heart Tablebook

$S + C \times M = O$: *Space + Capacity x Measure = Capacity*
(Pocket Book Series 1)

Shame Undone
BROOK BELLO

with
MIKE YORKEY
and
MICHAEL B. KOEP

To God for all things
Mom and Dad, I love you forever

Foreword

In the darkest corners of the world, where unspeakable evils lurk, there are those who rise as beacons of hope, champions of justice, and warriors of light. Among these remarkable individuals, none shine as brightly as Brook Bello – a true luminary in the global fight against human trafficking while healing the subsequent trauma and shame suffered by its victims. It is with immense pride and admiration that I have the honor of introducing you to *Shame Undone*, Brook's profound and enlightening exploration of the human spirit's capacity to overcome the shackles of shame and mental health anguish.

Throughout my decades-long journey in the fight against human trafficking, I encountered countless remarkable souls who devoted their lives to combating this vile crime against humanity. Brook Bello stands tall among them, a paragon of compassion and courage, whose tireless efforts have left an indelible mark on thousands of lives across the world through her extraordinary work. Brook's relentless pursuit of justice and her unwavering commitment to empowering the oppressed have earned her international recognition and acclaim.

Here, in these pages and through her deeply personal story, you'll come to understand why Brook remains singular among those at the pinnacle of effectiveness in our struggle for human rights. In a world that often turns away from the uncomfortable truths, Brook's unflinching honesty challenges us to confront the shame that binds us collectively as a society. Her courage inspires us to be agents of change, advocates for justice, and champions of compassion.

Shame Undone is a testament to the resilience of the human spirit. In its pages, Brook bares her soul, sharing her own harrowing experiences and the insights gained from walking hand in hand with survivors on their journeys of healing and transformation. But she doesn't stop there, as Brook passionately teaches violators and men in prevention through her innovative education focusing on what she calls, the legacy of fatherhood. With profound wisdom, she shines a light on the insidious nature of shame, a force that can leave us imprisoned in the past, stifling our growth and hampering our ability to embrace life fully.

This book is not a mere memoir or a dry academic treatise; it is a roadmap to redemption. Drawing on her vast experiences in operating *More Too Life*, an anti-exploitation and trafficking prevention organization, Brook offers invaluable guidance on how to navigate the treacherous waters of shame, forging a path toward self-acceptance, forgiveness, and profound healing. Her words serve as a beacon of hope, illuminating the way for those who seek to break free from the chains of shame that threaten to consume them.

As I read *Shame Undone,* I found myself humbled by the strength of the human spirit and inspired by the extraordinary impact of Brook's work. Her ability to instill courage and hope in the hearts of survivors is unparalleled, and her unyielding dedication to creating a world free from exploitation and the mental and heart trauma it creates serves as an example for us all. Through her efforts, she has not only empowered survivors but has sparked a global movement for change, one that echoes far beyond the pages of this book.

When reflecting on my own experiences in combating trafficking and exploitation, I am reminded that the fight for freedom is not merely a battle fought in the streets or the corridors of power; it is waged within the hearts and minds of individuals. To those who may feel burdened by shame, or the emotional and mental pain it creates, Brook's voice serves as a soothing balm, whispering that you are not alone, and that healing is possible. Her experiences remind us that each of us possesses the power to rise above our past, to untangle the knots of shame, to get the help we need when suicide, a lack of mental heath balance and the ties of bondage that follows and to forge a future filled with boundless possibility.

Shame Undone is a testament to the triumph of the human spirit, and Brook Bello's journey stands as an enduring testament to the difference one person can make when armed with compassion, determination, and the unshakeable belief in the inherent worth of every individual.

I extend my deepest gratitude to Brook Bello for sharing her remarkable journey through the pages of *Shame Undone*. Also, for her new groundbreaking technology around mental health, A.I. and gaming simply to see others free regardless of who they are and what they are dealing with. Prevention is key, as Brook always says in exploitation and mental health challenges.

This book is a powerful instrument of change, a guide for all who seek liberation from the weight of shame, and a testament to the power of human kindness. Let us all stand together in support of this noble endeavor and join Brook in her unyielding pursuit of justice, compassion, and freedom for all.

—David Arkless, Tuscany, July 2023

David Arkless is Founder and Chairman of the ArkLight Consulting Group, former CEO of Manpower International, Founder of End Trafficking Now, Co-Founder of the World Economic Forum, Knight of the Order of Parte Guelfa, Professor at Durham University and Fellow of the Royal Society of Arts (FRSA.)

A Note to the Reader

What you are about to read is a true story. It's real, it's raw, and it's redemptive.

Shame Undone is based upon my memories, stories my parents and siblings told me, and research. I have changed the first names of my extended family to protect their privacy. I have also used pseudonyms for those who abused me and changed some of their identifying characteristics.

While parts of my story are sexually graphic, it is not my intention to cause offense to anyone. Beyond that, my greater hope is that by being frank with the depths of evil that I grew up with and experienced, the reader will better understand what it means to be sex trafficked and the harm this horrible and illegal practice does to individuals and societies.

Furthermore, it is my heartfelt desire that the reader will realize that there is hope, healing, and growth for anyone who has experienced the trauma of being sexually trafficked against his or her own will. We need to save these innocent individuals before their lives are destroyed or snuffed out, which is why I founded More Too Life, an organization committed to fighting human trafficking, and why I've written *Shame Undone*.

—Brook Parker Bello, 2022

Prologue

Los Angeles freeway gridlock.

I-10 is a parking lot stretching into the distance—all the way to the Santa Monica Pier and the wide blue sea. I'm caught between the broiling summer sun and the asphalt as my Jeep Wrangler struggles foot by foot toward a movie studio in Culver City. I am an aspiring actress, one of the thousands living in the Los Angeles area, on my way to an audition. I've not been cast in a feature film yet, but I hope this role, if I land it, will lead to an on-screen credit that will bolster my résumé and lead to bigger and better things. The Jeep inches forward and stops. I wonder how many other cars trapped around me carry similar dreams? I wish I could see the ocean from here.

Inhale. Exhale. Relax.

The audition calls for someone to play an attempted rape and kidnapping victim. I mentally rehearse my lines. My heart thumps nervously in my chest. I feel my hands tighten on the wheel. My eyes dart ahead, seeking some escape—some way to thread my way through this vexing, oppressive traffic. I whisper one of the lines—again and again.

I arrive at the auditorium in plenty of time to collect myself. When my name is called, I walk into the casting office. The room is plain with fluorescent lighting and no furniture save chairs for the producers and the film's director, Amy Goldstein. Amy has co-written a script about a top-secret hit-woman who hunts down —and kills—the leaders of a child-slave ring. The working title is *The Silencer*, and the role I am auditioning for is an attempted rape victim named Didi. I notice Amy's eyes staring into mine over the mauve rims of her glasses—weighing if I have what it takes to play this role—if I can act.

The casting director takes the role of the rapist. As he steps forward, I mentally review my lines again. I am given some direction.

The world around me blurs slightly. Closing my eyes, I see a trap door in the floor. I enter it. There are no windows below.

Then, I see her. A teenage girl who finds herself in the apartment of her high school science teacher, a male. She is supposedly there to study for her semester final with several other students, but she is alone with the teacher. And then, out of nowhere and without provocation, he pins her shoulders against the living room couch, unbuckles his belt—

"Are you ready, Brook?" asks Amy Goldstein, the director.

Am I ready?

There are no windows. There is only one door. I glance up through it and come back to reality, but only for a moment. I know I have to transfer cataclysmic emotions to the part I am auditioning for. I practice method acting, a technique in which I aspire to emotionally identify with the part I am playing. I become the character.

When the director calls out "Action," I have already disappeared, and so has my audience. I am down below, inside the trap door. I am in another time. I am a young girl. I have been here. I know what happens. It comes back—or it has never left.

I smell sweat—I taste tears—abject fury buried beneath the bulk of a hated memory as my heart bashes agains my ribs. Injustice. I let the fear unfold and build naturally in drama and intensity as I portray the girl being forcefully overpowered— broken—defiled. Me. It is me.

This is real. It is happening. It takes everything I have. I know this girl. I know this part.

I rise out of the room with no windows and return to the audition beneath the florescent lights. Amy Goldstein's eyes are wide with shock. Belief has been suspended.

I get the part.

I think of the sea. The wide, blue sea.

A Day at the White House

The gleaming W Hotel on 15th Street NW in the heart of Washington, D.C. bills itself as the closest hotel to the White House, which is why I choose to walk to my destination in my Puma sneakers on this unusually warm April morning in 2013. My heart is racing like it did when I ran a series of sprints on the basketball court in sixth and seventh grade. Strange how that memory visits me now.

With a leather satchel around my shoulder and a large purse on my arm, I make my way on foot on 15th Street for half of a long block and then turn left onto famous Pennsylvania Avenue. A deep sense of pride fills my heart as I spot the South Portico's bleached white columns, a storied symbol of America's most prominent residence.

This isn't my first time at the White House. I'd visited before when I was asked to meet with federal officials for on-and-off-the-record discussions regarding human trafficking and violence against women and children. This time around, I've been invited to participate in the White House Forum to Combat Human Trafficking, but I would be more than an attendee; in the late morning, I am scheduled to deliver a keynote address before a gathering of Obama Administration officials, Health and Human Services staff members, key Homeland Security personnel, several FBI officials, top representatives of various non-governmental organizations (NGOs), and a cluster of academics. In the afternoon session, I will participate in a forum regarding six different human trafficking initiatives that need to take place in the United States.

My White House liaison told me that for my first talk, I will have eighteen minutes—and not a minute more—to share a bit about my life story and the innovative work I am doing as the CEO and founder of More Too Life, a social justice, anti-sexual violence, and human trafficking organization.

As my feet carry me past the White House, I feel a surge of excitement and a tingly rush of nerves. For some reason, I don't think I deserve the honor of speaking at a White House event. I feel this way because of the horrors that happened to me not long after my sixth grade sprints across wooden basketball courts.

When I was fifteen years old, I was coerced into an underground human trafficking trade connected to the Mafia. This wasn't the only trafficking group that did this to me, but it was the first. For too long, I thought the world of sex trafficking was normal, but it is not.

Even after I escaped, I lived day in and day out with a strong sense of shame tugging at my heart. Years later, even though I was free, educated, and overflowing with knowledge about helping victims of rape and trafficking, and reaching men in prevention, I still lacked confidence and feared rejection by others. In public situations like this, the monster of my past would rear its head and tempt me to scurry like a tiny mouse clinging to the corner of the walls.

I slip into a coffeehouse across the street from the White House and wonder if anyone can tell how nervous I am as I grab a small Americano with honey and almond milk and a croissant.

I take a table. My thoughts race. I see images of my past— flashes of men licking me like wild, angry animals by a brook. Men foaming at the mouth with sick grins. Or of being sucker punched, right in the gut.

Stop, I scream in my head. *Look at how far you've come! You're invited to the White House! You have a chance to influence the influencers!*

But I question my existence, my leadership, and my voice. I know all too well that victims of repeated sexual crimes—we feel like we emit a stench to those around us—plagued with anxiety and PTSD that is often crippling. Will this Washington audience see me as a second-class citizen and a throwaway because of what I'd been through?

I do understand today's event is more significant than me; this is my chance to help millions of victims in this country and beyond our borders—girls, boys, women, and men. As I step back out onto the busy street, walking along Pennsylvania Avenue, I whisper a quick arrow prayer. I ask God to give me the right words to reach any closed minds and widen those already open. As one of my mentors prophesied, *I could become a stealth bomber of change. A secret weapon. Someone who would do good, someone they didn't see coming.*

As I near the White House entrance, a quote from cultural anthropologist Margaret Mead comes to mind: *Never doubt that a small group of thoughtful, committed citizens can change the world. Indeed, it is the only thing that ever has.*

After considering the thought, I remind myself that my role is to share my ideas—many are unique—on how to combat this scourge against humanity and inspire these political leaders to help victims of trafficking and prevent it from happening in the first place.

I also want to remind everyone that they are tasked with implementing President Barack Obama's call to end trafficking, which he voiced seven months earlier in September 2012. On that occasion, the President delivered his first full-length speech on the topic of human trafficking at the Clinton Global Initiative, saying this:

> *Today, I want to discuss an issue that ought to concern every person because it is a debasement of our common humanity. It ought to concern every community because it tears at our social fabric. It ought to concern every business because it distorts markets. It ought to concern every nation because it endangers public health and fuels violence and organized crime. I'm talking about the injustice, the outrage, of human trafficking, which must be called by its true name—modern slavery.*
>
> *Now, I do not use that word "slavery" lightly. It evokes obviously one of the most painful chapters in our nation's history. But around the world, there's no denying the awful reality.*

With the President's words ringing in my ears, I approach the White House entrance gate and its black-iron fence and guard booth. An African American sentry, dressed in black slacks, white shirt, and black tie and wearing a cap, sits behind a thick Plexiglas window with other security personnel.

"Can I help you?" he asks.

"I'm here for the White House Forum to Combat Human Trafficking."

"Name?"

"Parker Bello. Brook Parker Bello."

I reach into my purse and fumble for my wallet, which contains my passport and my Florida driver's license.

The guard behind the glass accepts my ID and fingers through a sheath of papers. While I wait, I adjust my black horn-rimmed glasses, which I always wear in a professional setting. I've learned that people—especially elected officials—make value judgments on how you look, the way you dress, and the way you talk. I have to measure up in all categories. It is all about being a voice for those who could not speak.

When the White House guard finds my name, he hands me a lanyard.

"You're all set, Ms. Bello. We have someone who will escort you to where you need to go."

I know I'm not walking into the White House but to an adjacent building known as the White House Conference Center. I am supposed to meet—

"Hey, Brook!"

I hear the voice of one of my mentors, Dr. Barbara Williams-Skinner, who has told me that I was *the stealth bomber of change.* For fifteen years, this public policy strategist and CEO of the Skinner Leadership Institute and co-leader of the National African American Clergy Network had taken me under her wing in more ways than one.[1] More than a trusted advisor, Barbara had been a tremendous resource for me as I grew as the founding CEO of More Too Life, which opened its doors eight years earlier.

Standing next to Dr. Skinner is Mara Vanderslice Kelly, a Senior Policy Advisor to the White House Domestic Policy Council. She helps lead the President's Advisory Council on Faith-Based and Neighborhood Partnerships to combat human

---

[1] Dr. Skinner and her late husband, Tom Skinner, also founded the Congressional Black Caucus Foundation Prayer Breakfast.

trafficking. Ms. Kelly invited me to deliver the keynote address, based on Dr. Williams-Skinner's recommendation.

Dr. Skinner outstretches her arms. "Welcome to the White House," she says, wrapping me in a hug. "Let me introduce you to Mara."

We shake hands. Mara and I have connected over the phone several times, and I like her. She looks young—in her mid-thirties—to be a Senior Advisor in the Obama White House, but I know she is an outspoken advocate for those caught in the maws of human trafficking.

"I'm so pleased you're joining us," Mara says. "We need to hear your perspective as a survivor and a leader in the fight against trafficking and its root causes. You're the perfect person."

I thank her as they guide me toward the White House Conference Center, part of the New Executive Office Building in the northwest corner of the White House grounds. Before the forum kicks off, there is a coffee reception. I'm nervous—all of the important people.

I look around at the conservatively dressed and highly educated audience I will be addressing. For this special White House event, I had shopped for a new floral-print blouse at Ross Dress for Less, where I purchased straight-legged black pants and a jacket. That's all I could afford.

As my eyes scan this buttoned-up crowd, I realize that they are the crème de la crème of Washington, having attended the nation's top universities and graduating with honors and advanced degrees. They are trying to make a difference as shapers of public policy in the United States and around the world.

They are poised, strategic. Me? I feel like a visionary whose mind didn't stop. A cloud of fog is lifting little by little, and my ability to prepare schematics, processes, math, and other analytics is becoming crystal clear. My childhood gift of experiencing what I called "knowings" is always easy if I am not emotionally connected.

For instance, I can see their backgrounds in their faces, which greatly differ from mine. At a time when they were visiting Ivy League campuses before the start of their senior year of high school, I was waiting at deluxe resorts, private homes, upscale hotels, and seedy motel rooms for the next "rape session." At a time when a loving parent was stuffing textbooks into their backpacks along with a nutritious lunch, I was totally on my own, wondering if my trafficked life would ever change.

Knowing I am among these elite political leaders, I struggle again, feeling like perhaps I don't belong here, but then I remembered the politicians, business owners, and prominent men who purchased me for thirty minutes, or sometimes all night, or even for two or three days. Because of the trauma I'm overcoming, I tell myself that I belong here.

Each time Barbara or Mary introduces me to someone new, however, I feel like that person is looking into my heart and can view all the pain and ugliness I experienced.

But I also hope they see me and why I am here.

Just after 9 a.m., we are invited into a small auditorium of roughly two hundred people.

On a low-rise stage a simple podium in lacquered brown wood stands in front of a red-white-and-blue American flag. A blue curtain opens halfway to show an enormous monitor to the right. On the display screen, against a deep blue backdrop, is the White House logo and the title **White House Forum to Combat Human Trafficking**, along with the date of April 13, 2013, and the hashtag **#EndTrafficking**.

The MC is Tina Tchen, an Asian-American attorney in her fifties. "Welcome to the White House," she begins. "I wear many hats. I'm the Executive Director of the White House Council on Women and Girls, and I'm also the Assistant to the President and Chief of Staff to the First Lady. We are thrilled to have you today, an important day here at the White House."

I like hearing her say that. For too long, the issue of human trafficking had been swept under the rug in terms of awareness and political influence. Few people are aware that human trafficking is the third-largest and fastest-growing crime industry globally,[2] haunting the dark corners of society. In its simplest terms, human trafficking is the exploitation of men, women, and children—especially young children—against their will. The forms of trafficking are commonly: forced labor, domestic servitude, and prostitution. There are many ways to oppress adults and innocent children, including the recruitment and use of child soldiers.

After Tina Tchen's opening remarks, we hear from a succession of Obama Administration officials that I've seen on television many times, including Senior Adviser Valerie Jarrett, Attorney General Eric Holder, and Secretary of Homeland Security Janet Napolitano.

I appreciate what Valerie Jarrett has to say. "It's such a pleasure being here, looking around the room, and seeing so many leaders and advocates who have helped shine the light on this devastating issue, one of the greatest wrongs the world has known," she begins. "When I was in New York the day before the President gave his remarks on human trafficking at the Clinton Global Initiative, Tina and I visited a center that helps survivors. We met a young woman named Emma from Indonesia who was brought to the United States at seventeen. She thought she was

---

[2] The largest international crime industries are illegal drugs and arms trafficking.

coming here to be a nanny. Instead, she ended up working eighteen-hour days, cooking, cleaning, and often getting beaten, but she escaped. Today, she's not only back on her feet, but she's thriving. She's an advocate against trafficking, and she has even testified before Congress.

"I will never forget the look on her face when she met the President. She's about this tall"—the diminutive Ms. Jarrett holds her arm out at shoulder height—"and she was looking up at the President and said, 'I can't believe you care about me.'

"It's because of young survivors like Emma that the President remains steadfastly committed to the ongoing goal of remedying this horrible ill on society. That's why we're all here today and why we're determined to find additional solutions and put those solutions into action."

When Ms. Jarrett finishes, there is polite applause, as there is for each speaker that follows. Not only are we hearing from people who have the ear of the President, like Attorney General Eric Holder, but inside the auditorium, I recognize several CEOs of some of the top NGOs, and nonprofit companies involved in the fight against human trafficking.

I see Gary Haugen, CEO and founder of the International Justice Mission, a global organization that protects the poor from violence throughout the developing world. I recognize Brian Gallagher, president and CEO of United Way Worldwide, and Stacey Stewart, the U.S. president of United Way, the nation's largest nonprofit organization.

Meanwhile, my anxiety increases as the time approaches to give my keynote talk. I swallow. My mouth is dry. I try not to remember that I'd thrown up in my hotel room from nerves the day before. *Breathe. Relax.*

I think about how I want to educate these government officials from a champion's perspective. You see, I don't like nor use the term "survivor" anymore because a survivor's mindset is engulfed with stories of rape, murder, pedophilia, addictions, shame, and despair. The idea I want to get across to this audience is that there is more to life than just surviving. Victims must overcome this type of violence to the brain and heart and *discover their identity.* Victim to survivor, survivor to thriver, and thriver to champion—this is the motto I've created and where my work flows from.

I will also tell them that I don't like the term "sex traffickers." I call these horrible people "rape traffickers" because that's what they are really selling clients: the chance to rape young girls or boys, and adults, against their will.

Many people still refer to these hideous individuals as pimps, but I don't like that term either because when people hear the word "pimp," they think of a gold-toothed dude with gaudy chains atop a hairy chest, decked out in fur and driving a black Cadillac Escalade, treating his "stable" like a benevolent or violent dictator. They think he pays the girls what he says he'll pay, but that's so far from the truth.

Or people have a pop-culture perception of a larger-than-life dude "big pimpin" in the 'hood or glamorous call girls like Julia Roberts in the film *Pretty Woman* or Nicole Kidman in *Moulin Rouge*—hookers with a heart of gold. Hollywood even awarded an Oscar for Best Original Song to the makers of the movie *Hustle & Flow* for the hip-hop song "It's Hard Out Here for a Pimp."

The reality is much closer to a different film from the 1990s— *Bastard Out of Carolina*—a dark and ugly hellhole of a movie starring Jena Malone as a poor, physically abused, and sexually molested girl. Take it from someone who's been there: human trafficking, also called forced prostitution, is not about having sexual encounters with rich and thoughtful do-gooders in five-star hotel room suites with lots of fluffy pillows, Swiss chocolate, and sips of wine. The old Hollywood version is a fairy tale—far, far from the truth. Trafficking is paid rape. It is unpaid labor. It is domestic bondage.

The reality is that she doesn't want to be there. She is never willing—no one I ever met during those dark times was willing. I know, because I never voluntarily agreed to be raped by a criminal buyer of children and young adults or be forced to clean homes and hotels. Neither do victims have an insatiable desire to have sex, like many movies portray. I did it because I was made to do it. I did it so I wouldn't die, and then I did it just to get high. That's exactly how it was for me. That is exactly how it is.

You see, I was a victim, invisible to the world and identifying with historical young Black slaves and children who were "sold down the river" in Louisville, Kentucky, back in the pre-Civil War days. Instead of picking cotton, planting rice and tobacco, and doing harsh labor on slave plantations in the Deep South, I was ordered to please clients by participating in acts so vile that they removed layers of dignity, self-worth, and self-esteem until I had nothing left to give emotionally.

And here's another thing that people didn't know: like all victims, I had to give everything to the trafficker, the abuser. If I didn't, I'd get beaten up—or worse. I was told where to go, what to do, how long to take, and how much money to get from the buyers during a transaction that was purely a commercial rape act.

To cope, I shut my eyes and pretended I was someplace else to make it through another sick fantasy, using my vivid imagination to be on the wide blue ocean, the moon, hike a tall mountain, or be with my family in some other dream. I'd dream of a starlit sky. If I happened to mentally exit the hotel room or home bedroom or wherever I was, I'd sometimes get slapped back into reality. Even so, I'm thankful for my imagination. It certainly kept me alive. The ocean stretching out to the horizon and my feet in the sand became so real that I felt I was really there—which made snapping back to my painful reality much harder to face.

Eventually, I made it out. This morning I will tell these government officials the story of how I finally escaped—or, at least, the cliff notes. During my eighteen minutes, I want this influential audience to hear from someone who overcame this form of cruelty and urge them to use the levers of government to enact change.

As I review in my mind how I can advocate for those still trapped—I whisper another prayer that God will move mountains with these elites.

And then I hear Dr. Williams-Skinner introducing me. This is a crucial moment. I know women, young men, and children are being groomed somewhere at this moment, and some are dying out there. We must help. Today, these people at the White House need to hear their story.

They need to hear mine.

The Bad Seed

"You're just like your father. All he does is think the world revolves around him."

I'm a kid. Our kitchen smells of hush puppies, johnnycakes, tamales, and Cajun gumbo. The savory musk of Soul food, the spice of Mexican, and Creole cuisine perpetually hovers in the air. Momma spots me. She glares at me as I watch my father crush his Kellogg's Corn Flakes in his bowl. He adds melted butter and sweetened coconut flakes. He grins and says, "Snowballs." I mimic him. He is my giant. I love my giant.

My bowl of cereal spills milk onto the table. I mop part of the mess into a puddle with the hem of my dress. "Brook!" my mother glares.

I am the scar. I am the bad seed.

Even though she is mad a me, I am in love with Momma.

She is stunning, frightening, and beautiful. A Black American with African, Eastern Europe, and a little Spanish blood in her background. Eyes dark as brown magic markers. When she smiles, which isn't very often lately, the room lights up.

I want to be like her.

She is often upset, which gets in the way of my fun. She doesn't seem to love me like I love her, or maybe I just don't know how to recognize her love. She calls me a dreamer because I chase ladybugs, make wishes, climb trees, and count stars when the nighttime skies are clear.

My dad will share with me much later that Momma had her dreams too, and that she was deeply hurt, neglected, and abandoned as a child. Later, her spirit of apathy and disdain for my existence will grow and dramatically affect my behavior. But right now, being so young, I accept that this is the way things are.

This is this.

I'll learn a lot about my parents in the years to come. I'll learn that I am originally from Los Angeles, and my parents—Norman and Jane Parker—divorced when I was four years old. I'll piece together my family background: my father grew up in the middle-class community of Jamaica in the New York City borough of Queens as a Black American with a West and North African heritage and an extensive Northern European background from Irish, German, British, Norwegian, and Portuguese/Spanish blood on his mother's side.

My father is proud of his family history. His aunt, Elizabeth Schomburg, was married to Arturo Schomburg, founder of the Schomburg Center for Research in Black Culture in New York City's Harlem.

Upon graduating from high school, Norman enlisted in the U.S. Air Force. He was stationed in the Los Angeles area when he met my mother, Jane Watson, who was attending USC on a full scholarship. My mother was stunning. Like Dad, she was a mixed Black American with various African countries, Eastern Europe, and a little Spanish blood in her background. Norman and Jane were twenty and barely nineteen, respectively, when they were introduced. My mother was a freshman in college and an activist in various groups on the Trojan campus.

I'll come to understand how they were attracted to each other, given they were both academically gifted and working on getting ahead. They both experienced tragedy at a young age. When my mother was in elementary school, she and her younger sister were living in different places because my maternal grandmother was in and out of the hospital. Then a strict aunt took my mother and her sister in and raised them. When my mother and her sister were fourteen and twelve, they got a knock on the door with news that their mother—my maternal grandmother—had died under mysterious circumstances.

My father was a similar age when my paternal grandfather was murdered, which had to be even more horrible. During my parents' courtship, they bonded over these calamitous events in their past.

After my mother lost her mom, she attended Manual Arts High School just south of downtown, which, at the time, was a predominantly white school. Jane, innovative and extremely bright, turned out to be an exceptional student who graduated near the top of her class and was awarded academic scholarships to USC and UCLA; quite a feat for a Black female student at the time, but nothing new to her extended family.

A great aunt, Vada Watson Somerville, was the first Black woman licensed to practice dentistry in California after graduating from the USC Dental School. Aunt Vada also devoted herself to civil rights activism. She was active in groups like the National Council of Negro Women, the NAACP, the Los Angeles County Human Relations Committee, and the Council of Public Affairs. She and her husband, John Somerville, built the Dunbar Hotel in downtown Los Angeles, relying entirely on Black contractors, laborers, and craftsmen. For years, the Dunbar was the only major hotel in Los Angeles that welcomed Blacks. Aunt Vada drank coffee and conversed with prominent Black celebrities like W.E.B. Du Bois, Paul Robeson, Duke Ellington, Louis Armstrong, and Josephine Baker.

Aunt Vada's legacy at USC was why my mother chose the cardinal-and-gold of USC over the blue-and-gold of UCLA. During Jane's sophomore year, Norman swept her off her feet, and they married at the end of the school year. They didn't waste any time starting a family with the arrival of a son they named Ricky.

I was born in Grand Forks, North Dakota, home of Grand Forks Air Force Base, because my father was stationed there. My father named me Brook, after a water brook, a river, or a stream. I love how rivers flow—free—all running down to the wide blue sea.

I arrived via Cesarean section. Momma had a way of reminding me of this fact.

The hem of my dress is getting heavier as I still try to mop up my spill. I know what Momma is about to say—though I'm not sure what she means yet. Through gritted teeth and pointing to her abdomen she says, "Brook, you see this scar? You caused this scar because you're the bad seed."

This is this.

I get along better with my father, my giant. He is tall with warm eyes and a voice like thunder. Then there's my big brother, Ricky. He is beside me gobbling down his breakfast in a bowl with milk.

My parents sometimes get mad at each other, and they argue. When my father loses his temper, he often hits Momma. He is also gone for long stretches because he is involved in some secret outfit that he never talks about.

I'll eventually come to recognize that even though my father was smart and streetwise, he could turn into an unemotional, aloof individual prone to flying off the handle at the slightest provocation. My mother will one day tell me that his clandestine work turned him into a different man. But Momma had her own emotional issues, creating a volatile cocktail of hurt within our home.

My mother will state she can only take so much abuse. After a final blowup, she'll pack up and move Ricky and me back to Los Angeles. We'll settle into an apartment at 426. S. Manhattan Place, not far from downtown. Divorce proceedings will begin.

Momma will take a job with the USPS Worldway Postal Center near the LAX airport and continue to work toward her college degree. She'll have a full-time job and she'll take night classes. I will be placed in the care of Sister Ethel, who will have black translucent skin with lines on her face that show her age and her struggles. She'll have a stoutly kind of beauty that commands attention. She'll be a part of the Nation of Islam, led by Elijah Muhammad, with adherents that included heavyweight boxing champion Muhammad Ali.

Sister Ethel will wear a flowing white robe and wrap her hair inside a white turban. She won't be a mean babysitter, just one who wants to be sure a full house of kids are alive at the end of each day. Sometimes she'll give us hard butterscotch candies and candy corn and let us watch *Batman*. She'll act as though the movie is for us, but I'll be able to tell that Sister Ethel loves *Batman* too.

She'll also chew tobacco and spit into a Chock Full o'Nuts coffee can, which will be gross, and then she'll make one of us kids dump the spit down the toilet and clean and wash the makeshift spittoon. I will hate the onerous chore—I'll want to puke.

I won't be fond of helping one of the girls in our daycare. Older than me, she'll wear her long, thick black hair straight. She'll be handicapped and confined to a wheelchair. When she'll have to go to the bathroom, Sister Ethel will make me and a couple of other kids lift her off her chair and onto the toilet. I'll like her, but she'll be so heavy that we'll be afraid that we might drop her.

Sister Ethel will make a big deal about dressing us in white. We will pray on our knees on mats in the attic. With our heads on the floor, we'll pray to someone named Allah. I'll have no idea, but I'll go along. I'll wonder who or what this God person is.

We'll pray twice a day in Sister Ethel's care. I'll get into mischief the rest of the time, which won't endear me to her, but we'll be fine. She'll let me be me. I just know it.

But all of that is to come. Right now, milk is spilling over the edge of the table. Momma is again pointing at her tummy. "The bad seed," she mutters angrily. She reaches for a towel.

To Momma, my every move is out of step with the rest of the world.

This is this.

I am six years old, and my father picks up Ricky and me to spend the weekend with him. He lives at an apartment complex with a pool. All I can think of is *fun*.

The following morning, my dad says, "Hey, wanna go with Daddy to the barbershop?" Hearing him ask like that is like listening to sweet music. I stop playing in the pool with a couple of girls and shout, "Yeah!" Friends say they will watch Ricky.

When we get into the car, I look at my father with admiration. He is very handsome and a huge flirt with the ladies around the pool. I always think he is just sweet.

We pull up to Connie's Barbershop, owned by my dad's friend. Once inside, I inhale the wonderful smells of shaving cream, aftershave lotions, and talcum powder.

"Hey, Norman! What's up, man? Oh, wow, is that little Brooky? Is that your girl?" says his favorite barber.

"Yes, it is. That's my little belle," my father say with pride in his voice.

"You are getting big, Brooky. Pretty as I don't know what," the barber declares. My cheeks heat up and I smile. Others chimed in, saying, *Yeah, she sure is pretty.* I am transported into a perfect world where I am a princess.

My dad doesn't go to the barbershop to get a haircut, however. His goal is to have a "taste," which was a gin and 7-Up that went down well with good conversation about politics, history, pop culture, and the latest books. When they talk of women, they speak in quieter voices if they think I'm listening. Of course I'm listening. I hear everything.

My Uncle Rupert is there. He is my dad's best friend, and we often visit him at his beautiful home. He served in Vietnam like my dad and is a professor of Computer Science at Pepperdine University. We love him like family, and his wife, Priscilla, always gently taps her finger on the tip of my nose and smiles into my face. I love her smiles.

A year later, I am seven. I am waiting on the porch. Dad promised to pick up Ricky and me, but he doesn't come. Hours pass. I become glummer by the minute. This happens a lot.

My big brother and I argue about whether my father will make it. I say, "He's coming, he's coming. I know it."

Ricky shakes his head. "No, he's not coming. He's a liar, just like Momma said."

My brother is right about that—he doesn't always come. But the times Daddy does show up and says he is sorry for not being there before, I believe him. To make up, he asks if I want to learn how to drive. Like any seven-year-old kid, I say *yes*.

Daddy pulls into an empty parking lot and lets me sit on his lap while explaining how the steering, blinkers, and mirrors work. Then he puts the car into gear and lets me take the wheel. We drive slowly around the parking lot as I "steer" the big car, laughing joyfully.

"Wooooooo!" I cry out. "I'm driving, I'm driving."

Looking up over my shoulder, bursting with joy, I see a shadow cross Daddy's face; sorrow and pain darkening his eyes. I know he wants to do more. I don't know what could be holding him back, but something tells me that this isn't easy for him.

He loves me, though. I don't know why he hits Momma, but it doesn't stop me from loving him, even though I see him only a couple of times a year. He's my Daddy.

He's my giant.

In my early elementary school I am an adventurous dreamer, a happy-go-lucky kid who loves my German Shepherd, King—for sure my buddy. Ricky and me take cardboard boxes and build forts out of them in the living room or ride our Hot Wheels on the sidewalks. Life is fun and challenging at the same time. I am not sure what I'll grow up to be, but I know somehow I'll be better off taking each day at a time.

Momma has a natural talent for magic tricks. Sometimes, when dressed in my pajamas, my mother says, "Check your pockets good."

And that's what I do, folding them out and showing her there is nothing in them. Then she has me put my pockets back in my pajamas.

"There's nothing in them, right?" she asks.

I press my hand against my pockets. "Nope. Nothing there."

Then she directs me to go into my closet and close the door.

"Okay, check your pockets," she says.

That's when I find a coin or something cool!

Mind blown.

I can't figure out how she did her magic tricks, but I see her sometimes practicing something scary—dark. She reads Tarot cards and palms, and she uses a Ouija board. Once, I saw her levitate objects.

"How did you do that, Mommy?" I ask.

When she doesn't tell me, I try a different tack. "Show me how you did this trick. Please, Mommy."

She looks me square in the eyes. "I can't."

"How come, Momma?"

"I'm a white witch, the good kind, and I never reveal our secrets. Someday you'll learn about the magic of the universe, but not today."

I want to understand what she means, but my mother has never been open with me. I am shocked by what she said and I think of the good witch in *The Wizard of Oz*. Maybe that's what she means.

Eventually, she will shed all that magic stuff and even toss her tarot cards and Ouija board in the trash. After that, Momma will never do magic again. She will find God in a little Baptist church.

Despite my mother's lack of praise, I grow up with an inner feeling that I am born for something special. I daydream of becoming an actress, a scientist, and a writer. Perhaps all three. I have no idea how I will ever achieve any of these things, however.

Maybe that's why I am a curious kid growing up, always asking Momma or any adult who will listen, "Why?" I know I drive my mother crazy, and I'm sure my teachers aren't far behind. But some teachers listen to me. One is named Mrs. Schneider, and she inspires me to greater heights during my third-grade year.

"Brook, you're a wonderful writer with such a beautiful imagination," she tells me after the last bell one day. "You're going to do great things one day, but you must focus, listen, and try to sit still. But I do love reading your poems."

Her voice is so kind and loving. I soak up Mrs. Schneider's encouragement and the emotional support I receive from other teachers and coaches. They fill my sails with just enough air for me to keep on trying.

As I grow older, I realize that I love playing sports. From the minute the last school bell rings, I play until it is dark and I have to go home to do my homework and eat dinner.

It helps that I run fast and have excellent hand-eye coordination. I start running track in second grade. I'm a sprinter. Relays and the 100-yard dash are my favorite races. But I also play baseball in the schoolyard. I love sprinting across the wooden basketball court—the sound of my feet pounding and squeaking when I turn. I'm a tomboy.

I like my math and science classes and even joined the Science Club. This is where I find order because outside the classroom, away from the playground or beyond the ball-field, my home life is a mess.

My mother has different boyfriends and two more husbands throughout my elementary years. I guess my mother hopes to change the men she marries because Husband No. 3, Brian, is abusive also. He and Momma argue often, and I am sometimes blamed for their quarreling. I can't understand how adults can blame their young children for their problems, but they do sometimes. Brian is the father of my baby brother, David, born when I am around eight years old. But that marriage blows up and ends within a few years.

Momma copes by getting drunk. She loves Manhattans—a cocktail mixed with American whiskey, Italian vermouth, and a dash of aromatic bitters. She teaches me how to make Manhattans after David is born. When my mother gets on a roll, she'll let me mix one for her. I think, *If I can make a perfect Manhattan, then Momma will like me.*

I see what each cocktail does to her—the slurred speech, the loss of coordination, and the bouts of frustration about men gone from her life. I'll later understand that she drinks because she was hurting. I'll try to help slow her drinking down by adding more ice and cutting back on the amount of whiskey and vermouth.

I also notice that we never have many pictures of the family around the house. I mean, pictures were taken and tossed into a shoebox, but she won't let my brother and me look at them because those photos cause so much pain for her. It seems like Momma never wants to look at the past. Her mind is set on getting through the day because life is chaotic, especially after she and Brian decide to move us out of the city to Lake Elsinore, a small municipality of 5,000 located sixty miles southeast of downtown Los Angeles. The high desert community is situated next to a large freshwater lake that draws boaters from the more populated suburbs of Los Angeles and Orange counties.

Moving out of a predominantly mixed area with mostly Black, Asian, and some Caucasians—we lived near Baldwin Hills at the time—to a nearly all-white community introduces me to a whole new world. My new blonde-haired, blue-eyed friends invite me to the beach an hour away in San Juan Capistrano and San Clemente, where I learn to boogie board and surf. I am not afraid to go in the water alone. I love the wide, blue sea.

In Lake Elsinore, we live in a rural neighborhood where homes are spread out, a world of difference from L.A.'s gritty streets. Our yellow two-story, four-bedroom house sits on an acre with twenty-four fruit trees and several rows of grapevines. The trees present us with a bountiful harvest of oranges, lemons, peaches, and plums in the summer. I am convinced that we were living in the country.

We have a big hill at the back of our house that is also a great place to explore with neighborhood kids or by myself. We love climbing one of our trees and picking delicious fruit or watching King chase gophers into their holes.

On Saturday mornings, I play on an all-boys youth baseball team—the only girl in the entire league. Like Tatum O'Neal in *The Bad News Bears*, I am a pitcher with a live arm and love striking out the boys. I can hit the ball, too. When I'm not pitching, I anchor the infield at shortstop.

After one morning game, I am about to enter the house, dressed in my baseball uniform, ball-cap, and carrying my mitt, when my stepfather storms out of the house, marching toward his car parked on the street.

"I'm sorry, I'm sorry," Brian mutters. He keeps his head down to avoid eye contact as he passes by me.

"Sorry for what?" I have no clue what my stepfather is talking about.

I watch him drive away in a huff. When I step into the house I find my mother sitting at the kitchen table, hunched over and crying inconsolably. After wiping away her tears and glancing in my direction, I get a good look at her. What I see horrified me so much that I almost fainted.

I can barely recognize her; the damage to her face is terrible. Both eyes are almost swollen shut, and her beautiful face is marked with substantial bloody bruises and purple splotches. My stomach twists in pain. I feel dizzy and foggy and want to throw up. As I try to keep myself together, I want to be supportive, but I also hope what happened isn't my fault.

Ricky paces the kitchen floor. "I'm going to kill him," my fifteen-year-old brother promises. "I'm going to take him out for what he did to Momma."

I am frightened by the scene. "Are you going to call the police?" I ask my Momma.

She looks away. Her beaten face, which no longer looks like her, is full of sorrow. She says, "What can the police do?"

David, my preschool-age brother, is crying and upset. I pick him up and do my best to console him, but I can't take my eyes off my hurting mother, wiping away tears. I am crying. We are all crying. How could he be so violent toward her? Why would he hit her so ferociously?

I watch my momma light up a cigarette, even though she had quit. She sits silently, in despair. I don't know what to do with her pain or what to say to improve things, but I hold on emotionally and stare at her. Her sorrow moves through my soul and becomes a part of me.

"Stop looking at me like that!" she yells.

So, I look away, sorry for Momma. She turns from me and takes another long drag on her cigarette.

"Yeah, you should have seen what he did," Ricky says, breaking the silence. "Dragging her by the hair down the stairs and to the gravel driveway, whomping on her. I tried to stop him, but he was too strong. But the next time . . . ."

With Brian out of the picture, Momma somehow muddles along. She works long hours as a social worker to keep food on the table and continued night school for her master's. I don't see her until bedtime.

Ricky and I fend for ourselves in the kitchen, where we get good at preparing simple meals like heating TV dinners and chicken pot pies in the oven or warming up canned chili or Campbell's Tomato Soup on the stove. We also make peanut butter sandwiches or fried Pillsbury biscuits and top them with butter and jelly for dessert. On weekends, we get some delicious home cookin' from Momma.

Fortunately, our paternal grandfather, Grandpa Arnold, is around. He owns a small house a few miles from us, so we see him a lot. Grandpa Arnold's main job is working for a chain of liquor stores owned by Japanese Americans, but he has a side business picking up eggs from local farms with chicken coops in their back yards and reselling the eggs to families and small grocery stores. He drives a gold Chevy station wagon on his route.

Grandpa Arnold drives to Los Angeles to see his wife, Mabel, who has suffered a traumatic brain injury when she got hit by a car, leaving bits of her brain on the pavement.

Grandma Mabel had been a brilliant nurse, but she is now prone to bouts of mental illness and unpredictability after the accident. Sometimes, if you walk past her, she is apt to kick you or trip you. I am afraid of her because I never know what she will do to me. If there's one thing kids hate, it is unpredictability. When her mean streak comes out, everyone knows Grandma Mabel is not of her right mind, which is why Granddaddy choses to spend most of his time in Lake Elsinore.

Another reason my grandfather likes being close to us is because he had met a woman named Olivia and is carrying on with her. They don't bother to hide their relationship. Granddaddy and Olivia come over to our house a lot, and Olivia's son, Mike, usually joins them. In his late twenties, he is a Black man who stands well over six feet tall and probably weighs 180 pounds.

The three of them have ingratiated themselves into my family. They are around so much that my brothers and I called Olivia's son "Uncle Mike." He is family—the way he tosses the football back and forth with us or when he asks me to play catch. If I want to practice pitching, he always volunteers to be my catcher.

I look up to Uncle Mike.

Our house is always full because we have lots of relatives driving out from L.A. to escape the hustle and bustle of city life and enjoy the wide-open spaces of Lake Elsinore, framed by foothills of sagebrush with a blue diamond lake in the valley. There are times when there aren't enough beds to go around, so Momma converts part of the garage, which has a side room with a bathroom, into another bedroom.

Walls are built, and drywall is added to construct my new bedroom underneath the house's main floor since our home is situated on hilly property. To enter my bedroom, I have to lift a trap door from the family room with a black railing in front of it so no one would walk on it. Whenever I want to go to my bedroom, I gingerly make my way down a steep set of wooden stairs, holding a flashlight; the light switch is at the bottom of the stairs.

I make sure King, my German Shepherd, sleeps with me, but I have to sneak him into my bedroom because Momma doesn't think dogs belong inside the house. I don't want to sleep down there. I hate it because I am afraid—so much so that there are times I'll cry hysterically and make a ruckus. Momma doesn't care, however. She calls me an emotional drama queen. *The bad seed.*

Sometimes before bedtime I stand looking down the steps of the opened trap door to the dark room below—the rough wooden stairs fade to black—the hidden light switch—a room with no windows—and I wish Momma would let me sleep outside beneath the tree in the yard. I'd build a fort with blankets and chairs, and King and me would count the stars until we fell asleep.

I don't get used to going down there. Every time after I brush my teeth I stop and look down. My toes grip the edge of top stair before I take the first step down.

"Shut up," a voice hisses.

—*there are things that happen to each of us that change everything*—

A large hand is clamped over my mouth. Another grips my throat. My eyes pop open. Pitch black—the room with no windows. I want to scream. A whispered hiss: "Shut up." It is Uncle Mike.

—*everything we thought we knew about life*—

I freeze. I feel a profound and horrific pain between my legs, like a knife blade.

—*the death of a loved one, for example—or the first time you fall in love*—

Horror fills my soul, and I begin to scream and cry into his thick, stifling hand.

—*a tragic car accident, or an act of God*—

Tears sting my eyes and sear hot lines down the sides of my face.

—*a moment you know that nothing will ever be the same*—

The sharp, stabbing pain is nearly unbearable. One hand is wrapped around my throat, pressing me into the bed, while the other covers my mouth.

—*there are beautiful and terrible things that transform our reality*—

I fade away—can't breathe. The hand over my mouth and nose slightly eases pressure, barely. When air reaches my lungs, I squirm and gag under his weight, in full panic.

—but this—this causes the glittering stars to die—this stains the blue sea to black—this erases all that came before—this will be a ghost within me, always with me—

He is cruel, relentless. I continue to resist despite his overwhelming strength. Feelings of death take over. Every second that passes I lose myself—I starve for oxygen. Like a dry leaf that blows away, I am gone. I pass out.

What was he doing?

Why was he doing this?

What?

I knew boys were different, but I know nothing about what is happening to me. My mother hasn't told me anything about the birds and the bees. I don't even know I have a hole near to where I go to the bathroom, but I feel like it is on fire as he pushes into me.

I gain consciousness, I can't see anything in the dark, but I can smell his musky body. He mercilessly lurches into me for another five minutes—or forever—then a final grunt.

Something profound is hijacked, stolen, taken, and cut away from me. I am not sure what, but I know my carefree life will never be the same.

"Why?" my cry is a whisper.

"Don't say anything to anybody," he says. The sound of his clothing ruffles. He buttons his pants. There is an edge in his voice I've never heard before, "If you say anything, it'll ruin your momma, and you're going to ruin the house. It's not going to go well for you. Everyone will think you're crazy. It was your fault."

How was it my fault? I haven't done anything. I don't want Momma to get in trouble or give her a reason to throw me away.

He starts to walk up the stairs and through the trap door to the main part of the house. When he closes the trap door behind him, the sound of silence fills my room. My heart beat against in my chest like thunder. I go into the bathroom, kneel, and cry. I am in pain and don't understand what my body is going through. I've lost track of time. I fall asleep on the floor, shivering by the toilet.

When I wake, I hope beyond hope that what happened in the middle of the night is a bad dream. The overwhelming pain between my legs and in my heart and mind tells me otherwise. I pull myself up and walk over to my bed, where I see several blotches of dried blood and milky stuff on the sheets.

I think about my protector, King, outside. He doesn't know a thing, but I can only imagine what he would have done if he'd been in my bedroom during the attack.

I have to go to the bathroom again, but walking is difficult. Back in the bathroom, I pee. I cry because of the pain.

I stare into the mirror at my reflection. For the first time, I hate myself. That was it.

But what did I do wrong?

Why it is my fault?

How come I don't understand what my body is doing?

Why was there all that blood?

Why did it feel like I was gone?

Why, why, why . . .

I take a shower, but I don't feel clean no matter how hard I scrub. I want to tell Momma and big brother, but how can I? I am the bad seed already, and as Uncle Mike said, it is *my* fault.

I make my way upstairs. I see Momma flipping over slices of bacon in a cast-iron skillet in the kitchen. She barely looks my way.

I like the smell of bacon frying in the morning, which brought joy to the house, but at that moment, I know this incredible smell will mean something different in the future—a reminder of when a child's innocent joy was robbed from me. At that moment, I believe that ending my life might be my only way out.

—the glittering stars will die—the blue sea will stain to black.

"I'm not feeling so good," I say to Momma. "I'm going back to bed."

"What's wrong?" she asks, tending to the bacon.

I don't answer. I can't answer.

When she comes to check on me later that morning, I keep the covers pulled over me and pretend to sleep.

In the coming years, I will pretend that a lot of things didn't happen to me.

Wishing I Was an Elephant

So much is different after the rape.

The sky I loved to stare into is no longer quite as blue. I think the pain I see in Momma's eyes feels like I feel. Before the rape, I loved Michael like an uncle. He always made us laugh and played sports with my brothers and me.

I read *The American Yawp Reader*.[3] A former slave, Harriett Jacobs, describes her experience with sexual assault from her enslaver at the start of the Civil War.[4] "The secrets of slavery are

---

[3] *The American Yawp Reader* is a collaboratively built, open American history textbook.

[4] Harriet Jacobs was born into slavery in North Carolina. After escaping to New York, she eventually wrote a narrative of her enslavement under the pseudonym of Linda Brent.

concealed like those of the Inquisition," she writes. "My master was, to my knowledge, the father of eleven slaves. But did the mothers dare to tell who was the father of their children? Did the other slaves dare to allude to it, except in whispers among themselves? No, indeed! They knew too well the terrible consequences."

Harriet Jacobs is writing about white slave owners, and I kind of understand the wickedness and pure evil. But the person who raped me is Uncle Michael, and he is Black. I thought he loved me.

I hate what he did to me. I hate it and don't understand why it happened. Now I see my mother differently. She was abused. I saw it happen.

I have trouble coping with how my life has changed. Even my favorite foods don't taste the same. A Naugle's cheeseburger with cheddar cheese and extra pickles always puts a smile on my face, but after the rape, my ideal fast-food meal has left me wanting. Fries dipped in ranch dressing also brings a moment of good cheer, but salty tears aren't far behind. When Momma got beat up, she always recommended comfort foods as a cure, but not even my favorite meal of spaghetti and meatballs is working for me.

I have nightmares. I run from men who look like monsters from out of caves and dark worlds—it feels real. Still asleep and dreaming, I somehow run up the stairs and through my bedroom trap door toward my mom and stepfather's bedroom. I slam against the wall to their room. My mom comes out and wakes me. Shivering, I tell her I had a bad dream and that I'm scared. My stepfather appears and tells me to go back to my room— down the steep stairs. I go down. I keep my bedroom trapdoor open. I sneak my dog King in and I fall asleep next to him.

These nightmares recur for years to come.

Everything has changed. Before the rape, I didn't know what my body was for yet—or a boy's. But after I was violated, my eyes are opened. I now see the world in a whole new way. Even though I am eleven years old, I feel ancient, like someone who suddenly has a starring role in a monster movie. Feeling dirty and distant from my friends, I cringe when boys or men walk by. I no longer look up to the male teachers at school, and I hate the boys in my class.

Whenever Mr. Gavin, my homeroom fifth-grade teacher, smiles at me, I look away. Many of my friends had been boys—other athletes and science geeks—but now I view them through a new prism: *they can't be trusted.*

Questions rumble through my mind:

What am I supposed to do now?

Where is my daddy? My giant?

Will anyone protect me?

I read once that animals could sense when their young were in danger, especially elephants. Since Momma didn't pick up on how I've changed, all I can think is: *I sure wish I was an elephant.*

When the shock and disbelief began to dissipate, poignant feelings of guilt, shame, humiliation, and embarrassment led to a wide range of mood swings. For the first time, I hate my life.

At school, while dissecting a frog during a science experiment, I walk out of class and slam the door for no good reason other than I can't deal with what happened to me. When my mother finds out, she grounds me. "You're just like your father—crazy," she tells me.

Then there is the physical hurt. The constant pain between my legs reminds me that what happened is real. The itching and burning sensation when I pee will not go away.

I think about where my father might be more often. I long to see him, speak to him, but no one knows where he is. We haven't seen or heard from him in several years—it is as if he has disappeared from the face of the earth. I am angry at my mother for not knowing his whereabouts, but I can't tell her *why* I am irritated because she will ask questions. Bad things will happen if I tell her what Uncle Mike did. Trapped. I am trapped.

My tenuous situation isn't helped when I start my first period about six months later. The sight of a pinkish discharge in my underwear prompts me to scream in the bathroom. I have no idea what is happening.

Momma hears me shriek and knocks on the bathroom door.

"What's going on? Can I come in?"

I can't refuse her.

"I won't stop bleeding, Momma."

My mother makes a face like I am overdramatic.

"Looks like you got your first period. I'll be right back."

Momma leaves and returns, holding a three-inch tube.

"What's that?"

"A tampon. It's what you use when you have your period. Here's how you put it in."

So much is happening too fast. As she mimics what I am to do, I start crying.

"This is normal," my mother says. "Happens every month like clockwork, so you better get used to it. Go ahead."

I try to put it in but freeze and cry.

"Momma, I don't know what to do."

Losing patience, my mother takes the applicator, grabs some Vaseline, rubs a little on it, and puts it in for me—prompting another scream because it hurts!

"You hush now. The pain will go away. I'll get a smaller size tomorrow."

And this is this.

I am angry at my body. I am angry at my vagina for being there, and I am sure my vagina is angry at the world.

I used to think and dream about the impossible before I was raped, but I can't remember those carefree days.

If I do imagine something good happening in my life, ugly creatures will jump in the way, or thoughts will shout at me about how ugly I am.

My friends are not the most compliant kind. They smoke and ditch class to go to the 7-Eleven to buy microwave burritos with gobs of hot sauce in each bite. I am caught between playing the sports I love and hanging out with new friends who seem tough, strong, and unafraid. Like Josh, a surfer dude who is smart but doesn't like school. He has dreams of becoming a surf bum and traveling the world in search of the perfect wave. There is Diana, an Italian girl with a wise-guy mouth like a bartender at a truck stop. She is funny and makes me laugh enough to forget my own life.

I don't share my life with anyone.

I operate from a mindset instilled by my mother, who always says, "Whatever happens in this house stays in this house." We know better than to cross that line. We are all scared to defy a rule that originated during slave times when my ancestors got used to being hush-hush out of necessity. At least, that is the reason my grandfather gave me. This is why I never felt like I could talk about Momma getting beat up, the drugs my stepfather sold, or the rape of my body. Which means I can't get better.

Nothing is drawing me close to home. Ricky, my older brother, is in the middle of his high school years and branching out with new friends and new interests. He has stopped asking me to play basketball and says he is too busy to show me some new moves on the court. A lot of his free time is taken up with girlfriends.

I hold it all inside and begin to dream that one day I will leave all this behind and go far away. Then I hear about kids who ran away from home and hitchhiked and traveled. When Josh talks about hitting the road to surf at places he'd seen pictured in *Surfer* magazine, he makes it sound so easy and awesome. The thought of being out on my own consumes me.

But I have a lot to learn about the outside world.

I am driving around with Grandpa Arnold, running errands with him. We are at a stoplight when he says, "See her, Brooky? She's a prostitute, probably hooked on drugs or something. Your family is educated, and we've had our challenges. But drugs and that kind of life are something you should stay away from. You got that?"

"Yes, Granddaddy."

I am not exactly sure what he is talking about, but I feel terrible for the raggedy-looking woman wearing a revealing mini dress and wonder how she could do what happened to me. But I also wonder what has happened to my mother to make her not love me. Maybe the lady standing on a street corner doesn't have a momma or a daddy who loved her either.

I cope by fantasizing about living one day in a beautiful home on a hill by the beach with two fluffy dogs, where I can gaze upon the world as a great actress, scientist, and philanthropist. Those are my dreams. But now, I am not so sure if my dreams are possible.

I still enter the world of imagination, though. Not about my future but more about how I picture my life will turn out. I see myself sailing on a big boat with Momma and hugging my brothers. As the bow cuts through the warm water near the shoreline, we feast on plates of food as one happy family. I probably formed this picture because there are tons of boats on Lake Elsinore, but frightening voices and bad images often crash my thoughts.

A girl at school tells me I am gay because she thinks I'm not interested in boys. "You're just like me," she says.

I don't believe her. But she keeps being friendly, telling me we are more alike than I know. And then, in a private moment, she leans over and kisses me full on the lips.

Her kiss seems so kind and soft.

Maybe that's why I didn't like it when he raped me.

But I still know I only like boys, so I am confused. I recall that during the rape, Uncle Mike told me that all girls liked what he was doing to me.

Huh? I hated it, so I think, *Well, maybe I'm different.*

Being different isn't what I wanted, but losing my virginity to a rapist are the cards I have been dealt. I have no idea if anything good will come next.

When I hear my mother's friends say to me, "Brook, you have an old soul," I feel like I understand what they are saying for the first time. If having an old soul means I feel things no child should have to, then my soul is old . . . so old that maybe things will never change.

Is that why I have always feel so sorry when I look into the eyes of others, smiling or not, and see sorrow or worry? Because I will have to face it? I used to feel so much joy about each day, but not anymore.

So how is life going to turn out for me?

I don't know, and I worry over it.

When I turn thirteen—making me an official teenager, a scary thought—my mother doesn't even have a birthday party for me. Preoccupied with her own life, she is struggling, too. Maybe that explains why she constantly rags on me. My response is to slam doors and retreat to my bedroom, where I'll lie on my bed and wonder what I've done to make my momma so rigid in her affection for me.

At school, my grades are slipping a little, and while I play on the volleyball and basketball teams and run track, I still feel like I am pretending and not getting anywhere. Eventually, I start ditching school once a week with like-minded brokenhearted kids who dream of going someplace far from home. It's all I think about.

Before the school year is over, Momma takes my brother and me to the San Diego Kool Jazz Festival in the big stadium where the Chargers played. The headliners are famous Black artists like Natalie Cole, B.B. King, Marvin Gaye, and tons of popular jazz bands.

Between acts, Momma and Ricky leave to get hot dogs and Cokes, but when they come back, they are acting weird—like they have seen a ghost.

"What's going on?" I ask my older brother.

"Dad's back there," he says, jerking his head toward the back of our seating section.

What? My father is here?

The news excites me. I haven't seen my father since I was seven, so it has been more than a few years. I am as giddy as a schoolgirl hearing the final school bell before Christmas vacation.

"Momma, can I go see him?"

My mother squashes that idea. "No, you stay here."

Fortunately, I don't have to climb over her to exit our row. As soon as I finish my hot dog, I get up to find him.

He is easy to spot. My father, Norman Parker, my giant, is sitting only ten rows behind us in our section. I am thrilled to see him. Sitting with my father is his third wife, Sheila—the mother of a half-brother and a half-sister considerably younger than me.[5] My father immediately makes room for my arrival, and we enjoy a song or two together before I to back to Momma. When I say goodbye, I ask him for his phone number.

"Can I call you sometime?" I ask.

He seems to hesitate. Then my father looks at his wife for guidance on how to respond. A small smile comes to her lips, meaning she approves.

"I'd like that," he replies.

Ricky is graduating from high school in a few weeks and is thinking about going into the military. With him out of the house and me running away, what would my little brother, David, do when we have gone? I hate the turmoil that consumes our home.

Momma senses that a change of scenery would do me some good. When summer vacation starts, she signs me up for a month-long program headed up by the California Conservation Corps, whose motto is: "Hard work, miserable conditions, and more!"

The next thing I know, I am living in a tent in the nearby mountains, hacking at the brush with a pickaxe and clearing away limbs to make way for fire trails. While I like breaking a sweat and being outdoors, I don't enjoy learning that I am part of a work camp for troubled kids.

---

[5] I also had another half-sister from my father's second wife.

So that's what Momma thinks I am? Just another problem kid? That's what I feel after she flies to Hawaii on vacation, taking my big brother with her.[6] I do receive one postcard from my mother while I am confined to a cabin for three days because of a serious case of bronchitis. During my time in the mountains, my dad comes to visit me, which feels incredibly special since I am feeling a bit neglected— and I yearn for the attention and love of a father.

Following Momma's return from Hawaii, I call him whenever things got tough at home. I love hearing his voice and began daydreaming about living with my dad someday.

One time, I feel emboldened to ask my father if I can come live with him.

"Sure, baby girl. We can make room for you if your mother says yes."

Norman and his family live in an apartment near Leimert Park, Baldwin Hills and Crenshaw, close to where Momma grew up. I bunk with my half-brother, but after a few weeks, my father has trouble paying the rent—so much trouble that we have to move three or four times over the next six months because we keep getting evicted.

After one eviction notice, my stepmother has one last opportunity to get our clothes and belongings before the locks are changed. She fills the back of a truck with our furniture and boxes of clothes but left a cardboard box full of my trophies and ribbons back in the apartment.

When I ask my stepmother why she left my box of mementos behind, she replies, "I didn't think about it. They only gave me a small window, so I just got some of our stuff and left."

Then my younger half-brother turns five years old. He gets a nice birthday party with a cake, candles, and several presents.

---

[6] My younger half-brother, David, stayed with his father.

How come my father has never been there for any of my birthdays? I refuse to come out of my room, which sets off my father.

He comes into my room with fury on his face. "Why, you ungrateful bitch!" he screams. Then he backhands me in the face, sending me to the ground.

This will not be the last time he physically abuses me. After too many smackdowns and too many eviction notices, I decide to return to my family in Lake Elsinore.

My mother greets me with a smirk. "I told you it wasn't going to work out. I told you—"

"I got it, Mom."

And then she has some news for me.

"Don't get too settled. We're moving to Las Vegas."

While I hate saying goodbye to my friends, I figure it might be good for her.

As we were packing the car I call King, "Come on King, we're moving!"

My mother turns to me and says, "King isn't going."

I don't hear her; this can't be a fact. "King, come on buddy."

Again, "He can't go." Momma tells me that there aren't any apartments that can take a big dog like him. "I've arranged the neighbors to take care of him."

I begin to scream, cry, "No! Momma No! why, what?" I grab King and hold him. She then yells and tells me to get into the car. My little brother is already inside.

I am in shock—as though the ground was taken from beneath my sneakers, and the sky turned to black. My whole body grabs my friend. I hold him tight, looking into his deep brown eyes. She snatches me away and thrusts me toward the car door, "Stop being so dramatic, he will be okay." My body is quaking as I sit in the car. Momma starts the engine. King is staring at me. All I could do is scream, plead, and beg.

From the rear seat, as she begins to drive away, I watch my protector, King, run and run chasing after us until he can't run anymore. I scream and cry as he gets smaller and smaller.

While I hate saying goodbye to my friends, leaving my dog and friend, King, to live outside in the neighbor's yard is even more devastating. Momma said there aren't any apartments that can take a big dog like that.

From the rear seat, I watch my protector King run and run after the car until he can't run anymore.

I scream and cry as he gets smaller and smaller.

I don't know much about Las Vegas except that it is a big gambling place in the desert with a lot of shows. I enroll in a nearby high school and make some friends in my freshman class. Momma gets a job as a social worker and moonlights at the Imperial Palace. With a décor heavy on carved dragons and giant wind chime chandeliers, the Imperial Palace is the only Asian-themed resort on the Strip and has a budget reputation.[7]

As a change girl, Momma strolls through rows of slot machines wearing a sparkly outfit and grasping a tray held up by a neck strap. The tray is filled with heavy rolls of silver dollars, quarters, dimes, and nickels, so Momma often complains of a sore back after exchanging coin rolls for paper money from the gamblers. Because she works two jobs, our paths rarely cross.

I have plenty of free time when the school day is over, which is why I join an after-school "study group" organized by my science teacher, Mr. Singh. In his late thirties, he is tall and speaks with an accent. He loves telling us his story of coming from India to attend a university in the States and then deciding to stay. Mr. Singh is unmarried, although he makes it known that he has a girlfriend. My science teacher is the first person I have ever met from India, which I think is cool.

---

[7] The Imperial Palace was across Las Vegas Boulevard from Caesars Palace. Today, it's known as the Linq.

Several times a week, Mr. Singh organizes field trips for anyone who wants to join him. It might mean driving forty-five minutes to Mount Charleston for a backcountry hike, where Mr. Singh will point out various species of trees or vegetation. Or he'll take us to one of the big Strip hotels and describe the type of architecture or point out the intricate lighting. Sometimes his girlfriend joins us. She is African American, which raises my admiration for Mr. Singh.

Other times our after-school group will hang out in his classroom to do homework. Having Mr. Singh around is like having a tutor.

One evening, Mr. Singh hears that I will be walking home since I didn't ride my bike that day.

"Would you like a ride?" he asks in front of everyone.

There doesn't seem to be any harm in accepting his offer. I know that Mr. Singh has given plenty of my friends a ride. He is friendly by nature, the sort who will go out of his way to help his students.

When our study session is over, I hop into his car. Exiting the parking lot Mr. Singh asks, "Would you like to see my place? It's on the way."

"Sure," I reply. I have always been an adventurous kid, and I have nothing better to do.

He leads me to his apartment, which is nicely decorated and filled with shelves of books. Thought-provoking pieces of Indian and African art hang on the walls. I figure his girlfriend's presence has inspired the African art. As Mr. Singh explained the meaning behind a few paintings, I am fascinated by everything I see. I feel like I am part of an art appreciation class and enjoy having an adult take an avid interest in me.

After showing me around, Mr. Singh offered me a lemonade, which I accept. He is sociable and I sit on the couch and listen to this teacher talk about how special his girlfriend is. He really seems in love with her.

Maybe a few weeks go by when Mr. Singh asks me if I need a ride home again after one of our study sessions. "You hungry?" he asks. "I have some good Indian food leftovers."

Like any teenager, I am always hungry. "I've never had Indian food," I respond, which is true.

"Then there's a first time for everything," he says with a gleam in his eye.

It is five o'clock when we arrive at Mr. Singh's nicely furnished apartment. I toss my backpack to the side and watch him heat leftovers from a Tupperware. I notice chunks of chicken and potatoes swimming in a reddish sauce.

"What is it?" I ask.

"Saoji chicken curry. Indian curries aren't complete without using spices like turmeric and cumin, which are beneficial for digestion and have anti-inflammatory properties. The Saoji curry comes from the Nagpur region and is considered a specialty throughout India."

Once again, I feel like I am receiving a lesson. This time it is cultural.

"Would you like a glass of wine?"

I am flattered by the request, though I haven't tried alcohol up to this point. I appreciate how Mr. Singh isn't treating me like a school kid but more like an adult—even a peer.

I nod as I watch him open a bottle of red wine and partially fill two stemmed glasses. I take only one sip as Mr. Singh stirs the chicken curry in a saucepan.

Mr. Singh ladles small helpings on a pair of plates and carries them over to a coffee table in front of his couch. We settle in, clinking glasses again as I dig into the leftovers.

"This is spicy!" I exclaim after my first bite. I don't mind spicy food, but the seasoning is different than what I am used to. We continue to converse and take sips of wine—the wine easing the explosions happening with my taste buds.

"Let me give you a little more," he says.

Instead of refilling my glass, Mr. Singh sets my glass down on the coffee table and scoots closer to me.

"You're a very beautiful young girl," he says. And then he touches my face, leans in, and kisses me. Everything happens so quickly—

—as he pushes me back. Suddenly, I am on my back as he lifts my skirt and forcefully tugs on my panties. I freeze. I am terrified.

Was this really happening again?

I go into a flashback as my world disappears.

I am raped a second time.

When the horrible experience is over and Mr. Singh was zipping up, I run into the bathroom, shedding tears.

I look in the mirror. Once again, I can't believe something awful like this has happened to me. But it has.

When I come out of the bathroom, Mr. Singh is still on the couch, watching the local news on his TV as though nothing out of the ordinary has happened five minutes earlier.

"You are a beautiful and amazing person," he says. "So special."

I am still in shock. "I'm going home," I mumble.

"Then let me give you a ride."

I don't reply. As I gather my backpack, Mr. Singh stands nearby, as if he is hovering.

"Don't tell anyone," he says. "Nothing happened here. Nothing."

Yeah, right . . . .

"If people find out," he continues, "you'll get labeled as a troubled kid because they won't believe you. You'll get taken away from your mother and end up in foster care. That will happen if you say something."

I have no idea if he is telling me the truth. He probably is, but what do I know? I haven't even had my Sweet Sixteen birthday yet, not that I ever will.

I slip the backpack strap over my shoulder and step out of his apartment without saying goodbye.

Mr. Singh didn't know it at the time, but he and Uncle Mike have set me up for exploitation of the highest order.

Summer Break

I don't go straight home from Mr. Singh's apartment. My body is messed up, and my head is reeling from the brutal rape.

I walk to a nearby park and spot several kids from my school. They are drinking and laughing—not the type of kids I would ever hang out with. But I have always admired their sense of fearlessness, a trait that I am searching for on my own.

"Want some?" One of the guys holds out a fifth of vodka.

I have never tasted hard liquor before, but that doesn't stop me from taking a huge swig. After wiping my mouth with the inside of my shoulder, I am about to take another gulp when my friend grabs the bottle.

"Hey, take it easy," he says.

It's good that he stops me in my tracks because I am feeling woozy. I'm not drunk, I don't think, but I'm not in complete control of my faculties either. I decide to start walking home. With each step, though, thoughts of suicide race through my mind.

You're the bad seed, a mistake. I try to imagine going to a better place—I wish for a better Creator who doesn't let things like this happen. *If you end it now, it will be much better for everyone.*

As soon as I step through the apartment front door, my mother lights into me. "Where the hell have you been?" she demands.

"Nowhere, Momma."

"Yeah, right. You expect me to believe you? Look at you. Are you high on something, Brook? What's wrong with you?"

"Everything," I reply angrily, insinuating with my eyes that it's her fault.

I can't believe I am talking back to Momma that way. Neither can she.

Momma slaps me, then wrestles me to the ground. "Say 'I'm crazy!' Say it now!" she demands, repeating herself several times.

Defeated, I give in. "Okay, I'm crazy." I hang my head in shame.

Momma doesn't let up. "You disgust me. You're just like your father! I don't know what to do with you. You're out of control."

I shuffle to my room, flop onto my bed, and think of all the things I can do better. I want my crummy life to change, but I don't know how to make it happen. If only my big brother, my father, or my grandfather—the only men who love me—were around. They'd help me. They'd protect me. They'd at least try.

I hear Momma pick up the phone and dial a number.

"Hello, Brenda?" I hear her say.

Brenda, a close friend of my mother, is also a social worker.[8] I listen as Momma describes the ugly situation between us. She leaves the impression that I am an out-of-control teen who comes and goes as I please—up to no good—maybe drinking or doing drugs, she doesn't know, but the fact is, I'm not well.

I hear more back-and-forth conversation until my mother says goodbye and sets the phone on its cradle. She barges into my bedroom. "You're going to a group home," she announces. "They have a program for messed-up kids like you. Maybe they can talk some sense into that thick brain of yours, because I sure can't. Start packing."

Within the hour, her friend Brenda arrives at the front door of our apartment. I plead with my mother to change her mind, but she is firm: I have to go.

Brenda attempts to diffuse the swirling emotions. "Let's not make this any harder than it needs to be," she says as she leads me to her car.

Arriving at the the group home for teens, she helps me check in. Though the facility doesn't have any bars across the windows, I feel like a convict—trapped.

After four days of group therapy sessions with other troubled teens, I am allowed to leave, which is a relief. I don't tell any of my counselors or anyone else what has happened. I can't. I don't know how. When the therapists ask me how my relationship is at home with Momma, I say that it's great. I don't think they believe me, but they don't pry. Instead, they make it clear that I have to stick to house rules since I am a minor. I can't just run away. *Or can I?*

---

[8] My mother and Brenda shared something else in common: they were each working on their master's degree in social work. Even though Momma was smart and educated, she didn't speak to me about school or future goals. I wouldn't understand why until much later.

When I call and ask Momma for a ride from the group home, she pulls off the scab. "I don't know if I should let you live in my house," she declares.

Though her words wound me again, she comes for me.

On the ride home, I settle on this disturbing thought: the hell that I have been through is all my fault.

There isn't much to do during summer vacation, so Momma makes sure I get a part-time job at a fast-food restaurant. She says I should earn pocket money and stay busy. When I am not working my shifts, I hang out with my girl jocks; rich school friends with big backyard pools. The best thing to do outside in Las Vegas' 115-degree broiling heat is swim in refreshingly cool water.

My closest friend outside of my fellow athletes and actors in theatre is Denise, a Black girl in my class. Like me, she was also neglected and emotionally abused by her mother, a single parent. I like chilling with Alex, a gay white kid with a single-parent mother. Alex is a great dancer—and isn't on the make. We are almost as close as Denise and I.

Denise's mom has to work as much as my mother to make ends meet, so she isn't around that much either. Because Momma and I are barely on speaking terms, I stay away from home and sleep over at Denise's apartment. Technically, I'm not a runaway since I periodically go home and stay for a few days, do laundry and pick up new clothes. If Momma happens to be home, she makes snide remarks, but I get the feeling she is calmer when I'm not around. Since that makes her happy, I stay away as much as possible.

Like other teenagers, Denise and I are always looking for something to do. Going out dancing at a Vegas nightclub sounds mysterious, even a bit dangerous. But we need fake IDs. Alex shows us how to change the year of our birth on our IDs by placing new black type on top of the old date and then laminating the IDs again. Alex fixes both of us up.

I look young for my age—so there's no way I can pass for twenty-one, but I hope to look old enough to be eighteen. Eighteen-year-olds are allowed inside and are given wrist bands. The wrist bands show you're underage and cannot be served alcohol. The ID works: our entrance ticket to the hottest nightclub in Vegas on Harmon Avenue near the Strip: *Jubilation*. Throbbing beats pound the walls—infectious and electronic dance music (EDM)—constant motion—dance and expression——a kind of paradise for Denise, Alex and I.

Things really start heating up after 11 p.m. DJs crank up the tempo of their heavy-beat music.

We become a part of the room. We will return here to dance and laugh together many times.

One night, Denise, Alex, and I are on the dance floor, catching our breath after a hot number. A cocktail waitress with barely anything covering her breasts taps Alex on the shoulder.

"Sabrina wants to buy you a drink," she shouts over the din of high-decibel music, nodding over her left shoulder.

We turn toward the massive bar behind us, where a woman in her late twenties lifts a glass tumbler in our direction. Dressed smartly in a navy skirt suit and cream-colored chiffon blouse with neatly trimmed black hair, she looks like a professional woman—except for her blood red stilettos strapped around her feet and ankles.

Sounds good to us; we are thirsty. We walk in the direction of the bar to grab a soda when the perky cocktail waitress returns carrying a tray above her head. She swings the tray to waist level and hands us what looks to be three orange juices. If she notices the absence of green bands around our wrists, she doesn't say anything.

"Thank you," I say, taking a sip.

I immediately pucker my lips. This isn't plain ol' OJ. *There is enough vodka in the drink to drop a mule,* I think.

"Having fun?"

I look up. The dark-haired woman from the bar stands before me, a broad smile on her face. She is olive-skinned, perhaps Italian.

"Sure . . . are you Sabrina?" I ask. "The cocktail waitress said you bought . . ."

She nods and shouts over the pounding music, "Think nothing of it. I like to see kids have some fun. They don't make it easy in here when you're under twenty-one, especially when you're under eighteen."

Busted. She knows we are underage, but she doesn't seem to care.

Sabrina locks eyes with me. "You know, you're gorgeous. A charmingly beautiful girl. But you probably hear people say that all the time . . ."

"Well, sometimes," I stammer. "Sometimes. . ." I don't know how to answer.

Thoughts of suicide haunt me. I am at a breaking point. No one knows. I hide it everyday—every moment. And this dark model-like woman with red stilettos thinks I'm beautiful, charming. I feel a sudden rush of self-confidence—and gratitude maybe. It feels good to be complimented. But the feeling is brief.

My self-consciousness returns, not really understanding where she is coming from— and I feel like every partier in this popular nightclub have turned in my direction. I play it off, as if her compliments aren't a big deal.

There is an awkward pause. Sabrina senses the moment and asks, "Would you all like to take a break and sit for a moment?"

We've been dancing nonstop for a good hour, so we follow her to an empty table, where more OJs spiked with vodka are set in front of us. Sabrina takes control of the conversation, asking a bunch of *get to know you* questions. Questions like: where are we from? What are our goals? What do we see ourselves doing ten years from now? The attention from someone older feels good, but I wonder why she's asking. Why would she care?

Alex and I break off and dance together a couple of more times. Each time we return to the table, Sabrina is waiting with a cheerful smile. Sometime after midnight, she has an idea: "Hey, you guys want to get some breakfast?"

Like any fast-growing teens who haven't eaten anything in the last few hours—we are all starving. "I'd love something to eat," Denise says.

Sabrina offers to drive us to one of the casinos on the Strip that advertises cheap 24-hour steak and eggs breakfast deals to lure gamblers inside. We pile into a glistening burgundy Cadillac Seville that looks showroom new.

Wow, nice car, I think.

"You sit shotgun," she directs me. Denise and Alex hop into the burgundy leather back seats.

From my perch, I take in the millions of shimmering, pulsating lights that are the Las Vegas' calling card. I look up and notice a sunroof.

"Can we open it?"

"Of course." Sabrina reaches up and pushes a button. Just the sound of the sunroof opening is cool. Denise leans forward and thrusts her hands through the sunroof to touch the sky. I joined her, as did Alex. The warm breeze felt nice on my fingers. Sabrina turns up the music on a rock station as we swing onto the

Strip, where the blinking lights and colorful neon signage makes Las Vegas the brightest city in the world. As Sabrina navigates past the big-name casinos flooded with tourists and gamblers— the MGM Grand, Caesars Palace, the Flamingo, and the Sands—I feel more important by the minute. Driving along Las Vegas Boulevard, I see the stars above blur—and millions of lights along the Strip are stars—I am one of them. My troubles seem to be far away.

We pull into one of the smaller casino resorts known for their after midnight breakfast. I order steak and scrambled eggs, hash browns and toast. The hearty but light atmosphere promotes terrific conversations. I notice how Sabrina treat us like we are the most influential people in the world. She is quick to ask what we think about the food, the people around us, or what it is like living in Las Vegas.

I am impressed with her, but I can't understand how such a put-together woman is so generous with her time.

She picks up the tab with a smile.

After our plates are bussed away and the conversation dies down, Sabrina tosses out another idea. "Hey, the evening's still young. Does anyone want to listen to some music at my place?"

Who wants the perfect evening to end? Certainly not three teenagers having fun in the adult world.

It is 1:30 a.m. when we arrive at Sabrina's condo not far from the Strip. Her pad is as new and shiny as her Seville, seven floors up with a postcard view of nearby casinos and the sparkling stars set high in the desert night sky.

"Make yourself at home." Sabrina fetches several bottles of cola and beer and sets out a bowl of pretzels for us to munch on. She approaches her stereo and thumbs through a two-foot-tall stack of albums. When she finds the one she wants, she sets the vinyl record onto the turntable. With a press of a button, the tonearm raises and settles onto the record. A complex jazz tune floods the room.

"Who's on the trumpet?" I ask.

"Miles Davis. That's one of his most famous songs, 'Bye Bye Blackbird.'"

"My dad and mother love him," I say.

I look around her stylish condo that appears to have a decorator's touch reflecting the owner's tastes. I find a spot on her living room couch and notice an array of fashion magazines fanned out on her coffee table: *Vogue, Elle*, and *Vanity Fair*. Sabrina looks as coiffed, dipped, and tucked as the glamorous supermodels gracing the glossy covers.

Sabrina sits down next to me, her intent eyes meeting mine.

"Let me massage your back." The wailful sounds from Miles' trumpet fills the air. "I can feel you're tense," she says. "Just relax."

I turn my back to her and allow her skilled fingers to knead the knotted muscles at the base of my neck, down through the region between my shoulder blades, and tapering off around their lower tips.

I close my eyes. "Thank you," I say.

While her fingers work my muscles, my friends gather on her balcony, beers in hand and lose themselves in conversation.

"Have you ever traveled anywhere?" she asks.

"Not really."

I wistfully tell her that I dream of walking past the dress shops along the Champs Élysées in Paris or gondola rides in Venice, Safari in Africa. Sabrina says she's been to those magical places many times.

"Travel can be very liberating and opens your mind to new things," she says. "I know that travel has made me a better person and has given me experiences that I could have never encountered if I had stayed here in the desert. You deserve the same chance in life, and I hope that happens to you someday."

Sabrina stops rubbing my back. "I can do a much better job if you're lying on your stomach," she says.

I'm nervous. *I hope she knows I'm not gay.* I am not sure if she is coming on to me or just being nice, like a big sister. Inside, my thoughts are exploding with confusion about what she wants. I don't know how to react.

Sabrina stands up and motions to the bedroom with her head. She seems harmless and soft-spoken. Somehow, I feel like she understands me. I let go of some of my caution and go with her. Inside, she directs me to sit on the edge of a bed.

She resumes massaging my shoulders. The conversation is kind. I am getting sleepy, so I lay down. I feel like she is paying attention to me in a way no one ever has before. When she asks me about my mother, I suddenly became teary-eyed as I explain how bad things have been at home. "My mother's always on my case, and she doesn't know what happened to me."

I stop. I am not ready to say anything more—and I can't believe I've almost told a total stranger something so hard and personal. Only King and I know about my struggles.

Sabrina doesn't press me to find out what I am referring to. "I went through the same things with my mother at your age. It wasn't easy. I understand. Not all mothers know how to care for their daughters, especially if they didn't have a mother around, or a father, for that matter. It's been said that mothers have a hard time letting go of their sons and getting along with their daughters."

"I don't know if my mother loves me," I mumble. "I just wish she would listen to me."

Sabrina's fingers press from my shoulders to the middle of my back. "I know you're not old enough to be in dance clubs," she says.

"You do?"

"Really. So how old are you? I think you could pass for thirteen, but you're definitely not eighteen."

"I'm fifteen."

"So much of life ahead of you," she says wistfully, as if she is thinking about what her life was like at that age. "Listen, I don't have any answers to the meaning of our existence. All we have is today. I've heard it said that hardships often prepare us for an extraordinary destiny. I believe you're destined for greatness."

Sabrina's words are like billowy gusts of wind filling my sails. The wide, blue sea stretching out.

I close my eyes and feel peace. A peace I've not felt since I was a little kid. Since before—before it all happened. Maybe that trap door can open and let me out.

I visit Sabrina's apartment a dozen times or more during the summer, usually with Denise and one or two of my guy friends and occasionally alone. Sometime Sabrina picks me up at home or a friend's house, and then we will go out for a bite to eat. Sometimes we play tourist and eat at a casino buffet or steak house. Other times, a hip diner or an ethnic restaurant. Whenever I reach into my purse to pay, Sabrina touches my arm. "I got this, Brook," she says. "You need to save your money."

It's fall. I am perched on Sabrina's couch, sipping a soda pop she has given me, feeling like I have a friend.

Sabrina gently steers the conversation toward my sexuality. I am not about to breathe a word about the two times I'd been raped. Then I'm compelled to communicate to her that I like boys.

Sabrina's response startles me. "I think you like me," she says. "Trust me. I know these things. You can like boys, do things with boys, but I think you like me too."

I don't know how to respond. "Really? I don't think so. I mean, I'm sorry. I do like you, but not like that, we're friends."

"I'm sure you do like me." Her boldness unnerves me.

Sabrina rises out of her chair and sits next to me on her sofa. She draws me close and wraps an arm around my shoulders.

"You just shush, honey. You don't worry about a thing. I won't hurt you."

I don't want to be hurt, and I don't think she will hurt me, but this is getting strange.

"Let's have some fun, this will help you heal from all that pain you carry," she says.

She opens an end table drawer, where I spy a small brown bottle like the ones I've seen in my grandfather's medical cabinet. Sabrina removes the lid. Inside are white pills. She takes one out, chops it into two with her teeth, and places one of the halves back in the bottle.

"It's a pharmaceutical," she says, holding out her hand with a half-pill on her palm. "It's something doctors give you to relax. It'll make you feel better. Don't worry. Sometimes we all need a little help to let the healing waters flow."

I believe her. I think she is offering me something like a pain reliever or aspirin, but stronger, something that will take the pain away.

I watch as she places the half-pill between her teeth. Then she leans in to kiss me. I don't want to push her away because I don't want to seem inexperienced. I don't want to insult—I don't want to lose a friend. *Maybe this is how it's done.*

Still, I resist, but it happens so fast. She kisses the pill into my mouth. I swallow, and before I can recover from the shock, she kisses me again. Sabrina's tenderness leaves me perplexed. It isn't just her kissing me without permission—it is the attention she gives that feels like something else.

Is this what it feels like to be loved by someone?[9]

Her attention is more important to me than not being gay. Sabrina takes my hand and stands me up. She leads me to the bedroom. I trail behind her wondering if I should make a dash for the door and never look back. I am conflicted.

She sits me down on her bed, slowly easing me back.

"Relax, this will be fun," she says softly.

Sabrina makes sure my head is on a soft pillow. The room is spinning a little, but it isn't so bad—the drug she gave me delivers the most amazing feeling— a sensation I have never felt before. I don't feel any pain—physical or emotional. The pill rushes through my bloodstream.

"I'll be right back." Sabrina pulls a comforter over me. The sheets are soft.

My thoughts race. Oddly enough, I think, *I have never been in a bed this huge and comfortable. Maybe at my aunt's house? No, my aunt's is a twin bed—nothing like this. This one is soft and has fluffy pillows that smell like flowers.* My hands press down into the heavenly cushion. It feels like pushing through clouds. Everything I touch delights. The pill. The pill.

---

[9] It's important to note here that Sabrina was slowly grooming me, a predator, what a convicted trafficker like a Ghislaine could have been asked to do for convicted a sex offender like Jeffrey Epstein. At the time, I had no idea this was happening. As groomers suspect, I was focused on the attention and what I thought was kindness. In reality, it was evil personified. A child can't consent to this sexual abuse, which meant I couldn't consent, and Sabrina knew that. They all do.

I want to lay here and fall asleep as if inside a passing cloud, but Sabrina returns quickly slides into bed beside me. She touches my face, twirls my hair, and then kisses me again.

Her hands begin exploring my body.

"It's okay, Brooky," she soothes.

How does she know my nickname? She eases her hands onto my chest. I freeze.

"You're so beautiful, so young, so firm, and so strong," she says. "I can show you how to protect yourself and take care of your body, just like a model."

I want to speak, but the room is floating. Her touch—her words—her friendship.

If this is what it takes for someone to focus on me—care about me—love me, I will let myself go.

I don't hurt.

The desert sun is just peaking above Sunrise Mountain on a weekend morning when Sabrina drops me off at home. My clumsy arrival stirs my mother from bed, which is not good. I have been out all night, hanging out at Sabrina's place.

Momma is somewhat resigned to me hanging out with Denise and that's all she thinks I'm doing. I think she tries to understand why I am acting this way, but she doesn't say anything. She informs me that I will be watching my little brother while she goes off to work. I fall asleep on the sofa and awake to find my little brother watching TV. I feed him some canned chili with cheese and crackers and a glass of Kool-Aid. We go outside and throw the baseball around a little.

Denise calls and asks me how my evening went. She has been at Sabrina's apartment, too.

"Isn't she nice?" I gush. "Sabrina told me that I was a special person destined to do big things in life. She said she would be there for me and cheering me every step of the way."

"That's funny. She said nice things to me but not that nice while you were in the bathroom," my school friend replies.

"Well, she is a positive person," I say.

After hanging up, I return to the sofa, thinking about Sabrina and how she makes me feel like I matter. Sabrina treats me with respect. Instead of seeing my mom's face of disapproval or noticing my father's lack of presence, Sabrina looks at me with love in her eyes. Besides my grandpa and my brothers, she is the first person—a grown woman who makes me feel like I am the center of attention and an individual with depth.

Sabrina makes me feel like I can go places in life, be a famous actress or scientist and travel the world helping people. If someone like Sabrina is in my corner, anything is possible. She has given me attention and love at a time when I wanted to die. And now I have a budding friendship with a sophisticated adult woman over twice my age.[10]

Soon, I'll be sixteen.

---

[10] I didn't know that Sabrina was a "bottom girl" for one of the most notorious underground sex trafficking and illegal prostitution rings in Las Vegas. This particular ring was connected to an escort service. In the sex trafficking world, the "bottom girl" is seen as someone special to the pimp and receives extra privileges. She's proven her worth by bringing in the most money or by handling details for the pimp: booking hotel rooms, transporting girls to clubs or private homes, or bailing them out of jail. Bottom girls sit atop the hierarchy of working prostitutes and are trusted with recruiting young girls to sell their bodies.

Knots and Ties

Every week, or so it seems, Sabrina invites Denise and me to places like Caesars Palace or the MGM Grand, where we pass through the exquisite restaurants and buffets and talk for hours about our moms, about school, and about life. While I still receive the lion's share of attention from Sabrina, I notice she is similarly engaging my best friend Denise with smiles and attentiveness.

Sabrina also asks us to accompany her to extravagant parties held inside magnificent homes, hotel resort suites that we would otherwise never step into with adults—beautifully appointed places where Denise and I are, by far, the youngest persons around. She begins to dress me and order me around here and there. I figure she's simply trying to protect me—keep me safe.

I accompany Sabrina to a championship boxing match at the MGM Grand Garden. Before the big fight, Sabrina introduces me to several people, including someone called Mr. Marino, a successful man in his forties sporting a solid blue suit and slicked-back hair.

"How ya doin'?" he asks as he pumps my hand in greeting. His accent has an authentic New Jersey tough-guy sound.

"Fine," I say.

Mr. Marino is cordial. He scans me top to toe. His eyes seem to wrap around me like a rope. He quickly excuses himself and disappears into the elite scrum of fight fans surrounding the boxing ring.

As soon as he was out of earshot, Sabrina whispers, "He's my boss."

Her comment stops me cold. All this time, Sabrina has never mentioned that she had a job or what she did for a living, I thought she was her own boss. I thought she worked at an office somewhere or just had money. That's how she made it seem.

"So, what do you do?"

"I run an escort service."

"What's that?" I ask.

"A lot of businessmen come to Vegas for meetings and conventions. They like to have an attractive professional woman or young lady like you on their arms when they go to cocktail parties, out to dinner, or take in a show, so they ask us to arrange an escort. Or it could be older gentlemen looking for company, someone they can talk to over a nice dinner, so they don't have to eat alone. It could also be a young woman who's in town for a wedding, and she wants to have a male escort to show her friends that she's not an old maid. We're kind of a club for lonely hearts. We even have a softball team."

The following day, I sit next to Sabrina at a city park baseball diamond while we take in a co-ed softball game. The escort service has put together a team of cute, young women wearing tight red-and-black-stripped tops and flaming red sweatpants, while the guys wear T-shirts with the escort service's logo and light sweatpants. They are all employees, she tells me.

Between innings, Sabrina's face lights up.

"Hey, we need someone to cover the phones a couple of days a week at our main office. It's good part-time work, cash under the table. Think you would be interested?"

"Sure, I can help you out," I heard myself saying knowing that it will please her. I'm scared inside, but what could be worse than what I've already been through.

I arrive at a respectable-looking commercial building a couple of blocks off the Strip. The escort company office on the fourth floor has a professional sign on the door and a nice view. The furnishings are in fine shape, and the office person seems friendly. Everything looks legitimate.

I am shown to a cubicle and given a few instructions. A document of what I am supposed to say is taped to the wall. When I receive a call, I am to get names, telephone number, the name of the hotel or business they are calling from, and the date and time they need the escort.

"Follow the script," she says. "No matter what the caller says."

A typical phone call starts like this:

Hi, my name is Phil. I'm in town for a convention and would like to have an escort for an important dinner meeting.

Or this:

Hey, I just flew in for a bachelor party and need an escort later tonight.

The phone calls are weird and monotonous, but Sabrina promises to pay me more than what I would get for flipping burgers or working retail in the mall. *Maybe I could help Momma*, I think.

Less than a week later, Sabrina drops by the office and invites me out for dinner. We drive over to her place and she surprises me with a new outfit that she has picked out: a beautiful silk suit —blouse, skirt, and jacket. Then she has me step into a pair of her black stilettos. I think of her blood red stilettos from the night I met her. I see them in the corner of her closet. As she leans down, helping me to slide a shoe on, she says, "I love we have the same size." She wraps the leather strap around my ankle and tightens it.

Sabrina has been teaching me how to walk in stilettos and other high heels, something I am not very good at. She sits me down in front of a mirror and does my make-up and hair, talking the entire time about what lip color and eye shadow to wear. When she finishes, she presents me with a bottle of expensive perfume.

"You look beautiful, Brooky. Like a princess," she grins. "Dressed for success."

On this occasion, she takes me to Palace Court at Caesar's, where the maître d' welcomes her by her first name as we enter this high-end restaurant known for its stained-glass dome, fine-dining ambiance, and exquisite food. After we are seated, she presses a $50 bill into the palm of the maître d' as a tangible thank-you for escorting us to a nice table.

Insane, I think. *How does she make so much money?*

Sabrina immediately orders a glass of wine and a cranberry-pineapple juice for me in a cocktail glass. The white linen tablecloth is perfect.

"How's the job going?"

"Fine."

"Flirting with any of the callers?" she teases.

"No, gross! Why would I do that?"

"Why not?"

Then Sabrina turns reflective. "Do you wanna make more money than you are now, fulfill your dreams?" she asks. "You have to start saving for college, you know. I don't think your mom will be able to pay for all of it, if anything."

"How would I do that?"

"I can train you to be one of our escorts, it's totally legal. You'd be great at this. You're attractive and have plenty of poise.

I know you're not eighteen, but no one has to know that. Besides, our fake IDS are better."

This rubs me the wrong way. I think, *keeping some business guy company and making small talk? I don't know. I could get hurt.*

"What about if a guy asks you to, you know, do more?" I inquire. I have heard a few things about escorts in the last couple of weeks that aren't so good.

Sabrina sets down her glass of wine. She leans in, "Listen. If you don't want to do something, you never have to, no matter what it is. We protect our team. That's the way we operate. Besides, I don't want anyone touching you but me. But some of our girls are willing to do a little more than hang on to a guy's arm while he's in Vegas, go shopping, travel. If they feel that way, that's their business, right? But let me worry about that. I can tell you this: a little more gets a lot more," Sabrina rubbed the tips of her fingers like a seasoned maître d' expecting a fat tip at a Vegas show.

Chills run down my spine. I see all sorts of things that could go wrong. I am not interested in doing *a little more*, whatever that means. Sabrina scoots closer to me inside the booth and starts caressing my left cheek with tender strokes.

"Hear me on this," she says, holding me with her eyes. "I'm always going to take care of you because we're in this together. Just follow my lead. You're the love of my life, my best friend. Let me show you how you don't have to do anything you don't want to. Then you can decide. Okay, baby girl?"

I know Sabrina has my best interests at heart.

"Okay," I hear myself say.

Whenever I hang out at Sabrina's apartment, she always wants to kiss or fool around. I don't resist for two reasons: I don't want to disappoint her, and I feel like she cares about me. I also enjoy the freedom from anxiety and sadness I receive when I am with Sabrina.

One time, I ask what that half pill is in the little brown bottle—the pill she always takes and sometimes gives to me.

"They're called quaaludes, but on their street, they're known as '714s.'" She takes a handful out of the bottle and shows me how each one is stamped *714* by the manufacturer.[11]

"They're safe," she declares.

The 714s make me feel relaxed. The pill takes down my defenses.

The feeling of calm with Sabrina leads me to believe I'm not in danger, but having not been exposed to anything like this before, I am confused about my sexuality and her.[12]   Sabrina senses my confusion, my conflict and makes sure we have more and more one-on-one time.

Sometimes, after the act—an act I don't fully understand, she shows me pictures that she has taken with her fancy camera—places she's visited around the world and the important people she's met. Not that I recognize anyone or know the places, but traveling is a dream of mine. I tell Sabrina. I share my desire to be an actress.

"Then you should do some modeling," she says. "There's a lot of travel involved when you're good, and your dream to be an actress goes hand in hand. You could be on the front cover of *Elle* someday. I know some people. Let me take a few photographs of you sometime because you have the look magazines want. Maybe I can open a few doors."

---

[11] I would later learn that quaaludes were a powerful sedative and hypnotic medication formally known as methaqualone.

[12] Groomers knew exactly how to manipulate the minds of young people, especially those who were struggling like me.

I stand on the balcony with the iconic Strip in the background. I am fully clothed. The sun is high. The sky is brilliant blue. We move inside. Sabrina appraises me and nods, "How about a little more skin, baby. Get loose—more pouting." I don't see the harm —she has promised she will not share the shots of me topless with anyone else—those are just for her. As Sabrina clicks away, she tells me that these photos are *art*— no different from the nude masterpieces in Paris' Louvre Museum.

The pills. The photos. The care. Affection. Emotion. Rape. Defense.

All strings. Knots.

We walk to a penthouse suite that overlooks the Strip. We are wearing breezy evening dresses that she has purchased for us. I feel cared for. I watch Sabrina walk. I love her confident stride. My legs move but not like hers. She watches me. I have a different stride. She says it's innocent and elegant. "You remind me of me at your age. Now, I fake my way to appear innocent when I'm not." Her statement stuns me. We keep moving.

Inside, several dozen people are milling about, mostly men with drinks in their hands and eating caviar, cheeses, olives. Sabrina turns on like clockwork, her whole body smiles, the music is loud—so loud that I can hardly think. But my thought process are muted due to the half-dose of 714 she pressed me to take on the way to the casino hotel.

I make sure I am never more than a couple of feet away from Sabrina, my promised defender, as she introduces me to people and several guys. This is a party given by the escort service. All the men, well dressed in coats and slacks or stylish designer clothing, are considerably older than me. They are primarily white—some Asian.

Sabrina takes a look at me. She pulls me aside. "You look like you need a hug." Instead of embracing me, she leans in and kisses me full on the lips—a lingering, sensual kiss between a teenager and an older woman.

And then things get weird. I notice a well-dressed businessman in his late thirties or early forties come behind Sabrina and grab her by the waist while she continues to kiss me. Out of the corner of my eye, the guy unzips his pants and takes out his member. One hand continues to caress her while he masturbates with the other.

My body freezes. Sabrina says, "Relax. I won't let anyone touch you."

She kisses me again. The man grunts and lightly moans—and I try appearing calm though the sounds. The trap door opens. Uncle Mike is here. Tears well. Sabrina has promised not to let anyone touch me or hurt me. I focus on her. I wrap my arms around her and knot them behind her back. She is protecting me. She is defending me.

"You handled that well," she says later. "You flinched, but he didn't notice, so that's good. I'm proud of you."

I don't know whether I should feel pleased or grossed out by the experience. Then again, I am not entirely sure what was happening, but I figured everything would work out since I was with Sabrina.

This is her thing. I am safe.

"Because you did so well, I'm going to take you on your own shopping trip," Sabrina says.

The next day, we spend a leisurely afternoon at the mall, where she purchases a couple of blouses, shoes, pants, and a pair of jeans for me, paying with a few $100 bills.

Sabrina invites Denise and me to a party in nearby Henderson, one of the wealthiest zip codes in Southern Nevada.

"Some people want to meet you," she tells me.

What is she telling these people about me? I wonder. But I don't want to ask.

The Spanish-tiled mansion, surrounded by cultivated grounds, is fairly dark when we enter. Well-dressed people are gathered talking and drinking, sure of their social status. Several men, I notice, follow Denise and me with their eyes.

We are served wine and noshed on small bites of food passed out by young women from the escort service, some looking my age. The delicious edibles are chased by a half 714 pill (Sabrina insists). By now, it is no surprise. I am convinced Sabrina is a drug addict. Not long ago I discovered a needle under the carpet in her bathroom. She must have been shooting up something— probably heroin, which I've heard about at school.

"A couple of men would like to see you do a show," Sabrina says.

I know precisely what Sabrina means. Denise and I are to strip off our shirts and dance—act like we are turned on.

"I said you would do it as long as they wouldn't touch you. Can you do that for me, baby girl?"

Neither Denise or I want to disappoint our benefactor. We nod.

"Good. Then follow me."

Sabrina leads us down a darkened hallway with closed doors left and right. She knows the correct one to enter. Inside there is just enough light to see two men in silk suits. Their tousled brown hair, dark olive skin, and long, pointed noses look like wise guys, like in gangster movies. 13

Loud dance music pounds as introductions are made. I hear the same accent as Sabrina's boss—New Jersey.

---

13 I realized later that they were likely associated with the Mafia.

"Okay, girls, you know what to do," Sabrina commands.

Denise and I look at each other and make a show of unbuttoning our shirts. We take them off slowly, one button at a time—then our pants, leaving only our undergarments on. That's when I hear the familiar panting and muffled groans from the two men, jacking off in the semi-darkness. I focus on the music. I focus on the pill. I stay close to my friend Denise. I keep Sabrina in the corner of my eye.

I ignore the trap door opening on the floor.

There are a half-dozen other weird encounters like this.

Sabrina takes me out for an expensive Asian dinner with a wealthy white couple, well-known in Vegas. They want to check me out because the couple liked to bring a young girl into their home to do weird stuff. "Not to have sex with them," Sabrina assures me. "Don't worry, it will be more like acting, like playing a role."

When the entrees are brought out, the conservative man in an expensive suit has a question for me as he digs into his Peking Duck.

"So, where do you think you'll go to college?" he asks.

"I'm not sure yet," I say.

"Well, let me tell you about college," the man says taking the opportunity to brag about his Harvard education—all a part of the game.

As I slowly eat, I notice that he and his wife look like the perfect yuppie couple. They even let it slip that they have children my age.

After an uncomfortable dessert of mochi, the man asks if we were interested in having a "nightcap" back at their home.

Sabrina looks in my direction and tilts her head. *You passed.*

On the drive to this couple's mansion, Sabrina's demeanor changes. Before entering the extravagant residence, she says, "Don't take anything personal. Be cool." She is serious. I realize for the first time that what we are doing is *business*.

In their bedroom I am told to watch them hit each other hard with rubber phalluses and then watch him use it on her. He begs me to join them. I pass. They make me shout at them and tell them how horrible they are for being so mean to each other. Out of nervousness, part of me wants to laugh, but the other part is so scared that my stomach twists into knots.

When the bizarre evening is over, I start to question the world, the masks people wear, their inner thoughts and secrets, and their private acts. My fears grow, as well as the sense of bondage I am feeling. And there doesn't seem to be any way to stop the noose from tightening around me.

At times, Sabrina senses my fear. She says it wouldn't last much longer, that I have to play it cool—or she can get hurt, go to jail, or lose her job because I am underage.

"And don't think you'll get off scot-free," she says. "You could be locked up in juvenile hall."

A week later, Sabrina and I enter one of Las Vegas's glitziest casinos sometime around midnight. The last time we were here, in one of the big gambler's suites, one of the men tried to herd me into a bedroom.

"No, not her," Sabrina told the man.

The man immediately released his grip on my arm. That's why I trust Sabrina. I know she is looking out for me.

We find ourselves in a bedroom inside another oversized suite. Beyond the door, people are partying. Mounds of cocaine—laughter—loud music.

"Let's sit down," she says, leading me to a sofa. Reaching into her purse she produces her personal drug paraphernalia. She spreads white powder from a small vial in a straight line.

"This *blow* isn't for you," she states. She snorts the powder into her nose, leans back, and breathes in.

I have heard about cocaine from my friends, but this is the first time I've seen it used. Her actions fit a pattern: she is an addict.

"Time to get down to business," she declares with sudden and unforeseen intensity.

She leads me to another elaborate room inside the suite. There is just enough light for me to make out seven maybe eight white men, and also Mafioso-looking characters and a couple of Black guys, gangsters maybe. I'm not sure. They are huddled around a pair of card tables next to a couple small beds. They don't seem friendly. They, too, are snorting cocaine from two trays of white powder. A couple of lighters, and glass pipes are there as well.

I look at Sabrina. She grips my hand, but I see something uncomfortable in her eyes.

"Just relax, we will be gone soon. Everything's fine," she comforts. "They're basing. Be cool, I promise. This is the last time."

We sit down at one of the tables, where I watch a heavyset guy pour a few white rocks from a baggie into the bowl of a glass pipe. Then he flips on a gold initialed lighter and lights a wire with cotton dipped in something.[14] The pipe slowly fills with smoke. Then the overweight man inhales the vapors.

---

[14] It was Bacardi 151 rum.

The drug-taking continues for probably another 30 minutes. I am not offered any blow, thankfully. It is like these guys know better than to ask me to partake, perhaps because I look so young.

Sabrina is at the other table, joining in and getting high. There are shouts of euphoria as each hit kicks in. The guys encourage each other to take one more snort. They are serious addicts in suits.

Every now and then, guys stand up and walk around the room. There's a few of the Las Vegas night lights glistening in the distance. I want to stretch my legs, too, right out the door or fly through this window and find the ocean and never look back—

—when I feel a pair of monstrous hands wrap around my neck. In a flash, I am slammed onto a bed, slapped in the face. Air leaves my lungs. Fear chokes my ability to think. When the man turns me around on my back, I look up to see the heavyset man pressing me—his eyes wild—red—angry.

"You want it, bitch!" he yells as he holds me down. Some of the guys look shocked, as though they want to stop him. But they don't interfere—as if the man is their boss.

Some don't care or even notice—they are too high. It is as if I have disappeared as this monster squishes me beneath his fat body.

I cannot defend the attack. This thing is too big. I fight and cry with its thick claws on my mouth like a tightening muzzle. I can no longer breathe. I resist—my lean, small, track-star body almost about to break from the massive weight. But as I struggle and cry, it grins as if my physical and emotional responses excite this thing even more. As each interminable second passes, I stare at the stucco on the ceiling. I disappear. I fly out of the window to the sea—the wide blue sea. For a minute I'm gone, almost touching the ocean, until, I wretch. I can taste my own vomit.

I pass out.

Where is Sabrina, my defender? Why isn't she protecting me?

I have a flash of King running after the car as we leave from Lake Elsinore to Las Vegas. He runs and runs as I scream at Momma for not letting us bring him with us. She says we can't take him, but he will be fine with the neighbors. King runs out of breath—watches like a statue from the center of the road as we turn a corner. I'll never see King again.

I wake. I begin to cry. I scream so loudly until I am heard. The monster looks upset as I again try to free myself from beneath it.

My fearful, traumatized eyes find Sabrina in the back corner. She is high—crazed and hyper. When our eyes meet, I'm in shock. As she starts laughing as if this was the plan all along. How could I let this happen? It's all my fault.

For the first time, I truly see Sabrina. She has done her job. I was her job.

I can't recall how I got home. This time I arrive with the sun. Momma and my little brother, Stanton, aren't home as I fall into bed. Momma has already left for work, and Stanton is off to summer school.

When I wake, I call Denise and tell her what has happened. My friend cries for me. Tells me she's sorry. Shares that she hates Sabrina. She then shares an awful story of how she was raped by her uncle.

It hurts to hear.

Our eyes have been opened. We have been exploited by cowardly monsters—people who find pleasure in physically, mentally, and emotionally hurting and violating children and teens.[15]

After my phone call, Denise and I had to see each other, so we met up at a taco shop. She wanted me to eat to take away the pain, so we ordered combination plates of Mexican food with gobs of cheese, hot salsa, and sour cream. We were angry and distraught at the position we found ourselves in: unseen in a parallel world next to our own and unloved by the world we thought we knew. We are all alone.

"We need to get out of Vegas and start fresh," Denise said.

"You mean run away, as in really running away?" I queried. "Where would we go?"

Denise shrugged her shoulders. "Los Angeles? You grew up there pretty much, California?"

That was true.

"So, how would we get there?" Even though I am sixteen, I didn't have a car, let alone a driver's license. Neither did Denise.

"Stick our thumbs out."

"Hitchhike? Isn't that dangerous?"

"We'll stick together. I hear there are lots of nice truckers who pick up hitchhikers."

We talk of running away—from our families, our education, Sabrina. I tell Denise that I am late in my cycle. A sense of doom fills my gut. If I am pregnant by the monster, my life, as I know it, what is left of it, will be ruined. I could share this development only with: Denise. Her voice is frightened, "You have to get tested."

---

[15] I didn't know it then, but the terror I experienced, the anguish I endured, and the pain I was subjected to was human trafficking by force, fraud, and coercion. Everything began the moment Sabrina exchanged anything of value for me—drugs, money, or anything at all.

I purchase an over-the-counter pregnancy test. My hands tremble as I wait.

When I see the result, I sit and place my head in my hands.

I am pregnant.

That 300-pound monster in the hotel suite—means there is a monster in me. Disgust. Horror. Anger. Rage. Insanity.

I'm afraid.

I don't see a way out, but I can get an abortion. Sabrina always says getting one is the automatic next step if I ever got pregnant.

Sabrina. The other monster.

I remember the name of the clinic she uses. I call and asked how much the procedure costs. The $285 amount will empty my piggy bank. The escort service still owes me money from answering phones, but something tells me I will never see that money. I wasn't paid anything for what I did for Sabrina.

Filled with shame, I hardened my heart—I focused on this all-consuming thought: *You can do this.*

My dancing buddy, Alex, drops me off at the clinic, where a nurse hands me a clipboard with a standard form to fill out. No questions are asked about whether I was raped, violated by a family member, or how I found myself with something in me. When I am told someone would have to pick me up after the procedure, I give them Alex's phone number. I say he's my brother.

When I finish filling out the form, I take a chair in the waiting room. My heart beats fast. After my name is called, I am led to an examination room where my blood pressure and vitals are checked, and a urine sample is taken for a pregnancy test. The result confirms my at-home test: I am, indeed, pregnant.

"You want to proceed, right?" the nurse asks.

With pursed lips, I nod. I am guided to another room, where I see an operating table covered with a white sheet and surrounded by several weird-looking machines, illuminated by a single bright light.

I feel like I am part of an out-of-body experience as I lie back and a nurse inserts an IV into the crook of my right arm. After local medication kicks in, I am drowsy while the doctor performs the procedure. It is a strange feeling, painful in more ways than I imagined.

After a certain amount of time in a recovery room, a nurse says they can't reach Alex.

"Is there someone else we can call?" the nurse asks. "We can't let you go unless someone picks you up."

My only option is my mother, which means I would have to face her. I dictate our home phone number.

Forty-five minutes later, the nurse returns to the recovery, where I am still groggy from the anesthesia. "We reached your mother. Looks like she's waiting for you at the end of the parking lot, but she has to come in." she says.

I look outside and see my mom's car in the distance. I knew she wouldn't come in. The nurse says, "You've been given drugs for the pain, you are not walking straight or speaking clearly. She must come in." I plead with her in tears that my mom will not come in, "Please don't make it hard for me." The nurse looks not-so-kind and says, "Whatever," and walks me to a side exit. *She thinks I'm just another young stupid girl who got pregnant and had an abortion.*

When the nurse opens the door, my mother is still sitting behind the wheel of our car with the engine running. Emotions engulf me, and I start sobbing.

The indifferent nurse ignores me and doesn't assist me all the way to the car. She lets me stumble out the door, shaking her head as I gingerly walk past other cars through the parking lot, toward the vehicle. Wiping away tears with each step, I open the door and slump into the bench seat in the front.

I am dizzy from the medications. When my weakened body slides a little to the left, my head accidentally bumps on Momma's shoulder.

She pushed me away from her, sneering, "You're disgusting." I am stunned. Embarrassed. Broken.

But she is right. She's always been right. I am disgusted with myself, too. The bad seed.

All I can do was straighten up and look away from her at the passing traffic.

"You had an abortion, didn't you?" my mother states, matter-of-factly.

I don't answer straight away. "I'm fine, Momma. I'll be okay, eventually," I lie.

The ride to our apartment is tense. When I get home, I make a beeline to the bedroom I share with my baby brother and flop on my bed. I stare at the ceiling and consider what to do next.

All I know is that I hurt.

Momma's newest *friend* stops by that night carrying a paper bag filled with a six-pack of beer and a bottle of Jack Daniels. Momma quit drinking a while back and has been doing well, but her resolve disappears with this new guy egging her on, and she slips up.

Luke, the new friend, is white. Momma rarely hangs out with white men, that I know of. Luke and I don't gel at all, and soon get into it. He gives me a hard time about getting pregnant and calls me a *silly nigger* in a whisper.

I can't believe he used the N-word on me. My mother happens to be in the kitchen, so I run to her. "Momma, can you believe what he said?"

"What?"

"Luke called me a *silly nigger.*"

Momma is shocked—but defensive. "No, he didn't."

I know she didn't hear him, so I roll my eyes at Luke. He follows me to the kitchen. He doesn't cop to the truth. Instead, he grins as if to say, *See? Your mother doesn't even believe you.*

The confrontation spirals out of control with lots of screaming and finger-pointing.

When I can't take it any longer, I shout, "I'm leaving!"

"Good! Then go," Luke shouts back.

Momma doesn't try to stop me. She mumbles something about how out of control I am.

I go to my bedroom and find my backpack for school. I stuff a book, some toiletries, and packs of gum inside. I don't pack any clothes. *I can figure that out later,* I think.

I make my way to Denise's apartment. She is glad to see me. We both know it is time for us to strike out on our own and head west to California.

"Let's do it," she says.

"Yeah, let's do this," I agree.

I try to sleep on her couch, but I wake up every hour or so feeling queasy about running away. I resolve there is no turning back.

Her mom works the graveyard shift, so we know we have to leave early before 7:30am. Not long after the sun comes up, we walk in the morning heat to the outskirts of Las Vegas.

The desert heat. Baking asphalt. The taste of dust along the roadside.

We eventually find ourselves moving along on the shoulder of southbound Interstate 15 with our thumbs discreetly in and out so we won't get caught hitchhiking on the freeway. I don't have any money in my backpack or purse; I spent it all on terminating the pregnancy. Denise has a few quarters and dimes. Just two teenagers on our own with no money, no place to stay, and no fundamental job skills.

What could go wrong?

The City of Angels

The sizzling dry heat—and the noisy racket from passing traffic—our thumbs point the way we want to go on Interstate 15 to Los Angeles. After thirty minutes of hitchhiking, we are wondering if we'll ever get a ride.

Then, a Ford pickup truck with a big ol' country-looking dude behind the wheel swerves off the freeway in a cloud of dust.

"What do you think?" Denise's asks uneasily.

I don't have a good feeling either. "Let's check him out. But if it doesn't look safe, we won't take the ride."

We hustle toward the pickup when another vehicle pulls in behind us. From watching old movies, this looks like a vintage car—a sparkling light green Buick from the 1950s with a distinctive front grille and whitewall tires. I am shocked that this prim-and-proper-looking couple would stop to pick up a couple of teenage hitchhikers. They look like they belong to another time —the era of the Fifties film, *Peyton Place*.

The gentleman driving the Buick wears a plaid shirt and square-shaped glasses; next to him is a matronly-looking woman dressed in a turquoise blouse with pearl-like buttons, and curly brown hair that might have been in rollers all morning. She steps out of the vehicle.

"Can we offer you girls a ride?" she asks politely.

Denise and I look at each other and immediately nod.

"Yes, ma'am," I say. We start walking toward the classic car.

Simultaneously, the angry-looking redneck in the Ford truck speeds off, his wide tires kicking up small stones and a plume of dirt into the air.

"He's not happy," Denise says.

"No, he's not. But we didn't want to go with him anyway."

We plop down in the back seat of the Buick, upholstered in beige leather and in mint condition. The older couple, probably in their sixties, immediately engage us.

"How are you?" says the friendly lady.

"Okay," we reply in unison.

"Where you all off to?" she asks.

"Los Angeles," Denise replies.

"Yeah, California's nice," the man says.

He pulls back onto the interstate. "We're glad to give you a ride, but we're only going as far as Barstow. Hope that's okay."

"Sure, it'll work. Beats walking there," Denise replies, trying to lighten the air. I have traveled the I-15 enough to be aware that Barstow, located in the middle of the Mojave Desert, is nearly halfway to Los Angeles.

The couple isn't in a hurry to get there as we tool along at 55 mph on the freeway, cars and trucks passing us at will. I don't mind. I need time to think about what's to come. *What are we going to do when we get to Los Angeles?*

The couple speak in a homespun manner out of rhythm to the way I've experienced people converse—they seemed divine, almost—articulate—kind—empathetic.[16] When the matronly lady turns and declares to me with the utmost sincerity, "You need to be safe out there," the hair on the back of my neck stands up. A coil of curly brown hair blows gently at her cheek. Her eyes as blue as the desert sky.

I stare at her. I want to cry.

We pull into the outskirts of Barstow as the sun sets. The older gentleman steers the bulky Buick into a truck stop with an old diner restaurant.

We thank them profusely as we exit the Buick. When the older lady and I lock eyes, she smiles.

"Do take care, dear ones," she says.

As they drive off, I wave goodbye.

Maybe I should go back home.

I suddenly flash to standing in front of a Catholic church with my stepfather. I was nine years old. As we stood outside, I stared up at the high steeple—the bright cross glinting in the morning light. The air was crisp and cool. A cluster of birds whirled across the rooftops. At that moment, I felt God was real—and He was with me.

That same feeling of peace returns. It is a good feeling. Maybe I am not so alone after all.

Denise snaps me out of my daydream.

"What do we do now?"

We are famished and haven't eaten since the morning. We only have a dollar or two between us. I scan the horizon for ideas

---

[16] I still feel to this day that we were picked up by angels that day.

when I spot a couple dozen big rigs parked beyond the gas pumps.

"Maybe we can find some loose change," I say, pointing to the trucks.

Most of the empty trucks, to our surprise, aren't locked up. We find several dollars in quarters, dimes, and nickels underneath the seats, enough money to buy us a meal.

We sit down in a booth with a brown Formica tabletop and scan the menu. With five dollars or so to work with, ordering will be tricky.

I look around at the cast of characters scattered throughout the diner. Most are truckers and blue-collar types filling their bellies before hitting the road again. I don't belong here. A sudden chill of fear—my menu begins to shake in my grip. I set it on the table.

Our waitress, an older white woman with a sandy brown wig, approaches.

"Good evening, girls. What y'all want?" Her pencil is poised above a writing pad.

"We'll take a large order of fries," I say.

"To drink?"

"Water will be fine."

I don't think we are the first runaways this waitress has served; she brings a half-dozen packages of saltine crackers with our glasses of water. When the french fries come, we dollop gobs of ketchup on the fried taters *and* the crackers. We have enough money left over to give the nice waitress a 30-cent tip. It isn't much, but it's all we have.

Now we have to figure out where to sleep. We don't want to hitchhike at night. So, we walk around the restaurant and find an engine room that happens to be unlocked.

We shoehorn ourselves into the noisy engine room. There is just enough space for us to lie on the floor and use our backpacks as pillows. Fortunately, the hot water heater creates some warmth. We get some much-needed rest, until Denise wakes, soaked to the bone at daybreak.

"Damn it! Look at me! And my briefcase! It's wet!"

"There must have been some kind of leak at the base of the water heater," I offer.

She stands and holds up her burgundy leather on the outside— kind of a half-backpack, half-briefcase.

"What do you have in that thing?" I grin.

She opens it to show me. Fortunately, none of the moisture has seeped through because nearly half of the case/pack is filled with tampons.

"I'm on my cycle," she says. "You don't want to be short of these."

We share a light laugh.

We dry ourselves off and make our way back to the road.

It takes two more rides to get to the city. Both drivers scare the crap out of us. Denise and I keep making sideways glances at each other as if saying, *I hope we make it there alive.*

We somehow arrive at Hollywood and Sunset Boulevard—a pair of teen runaways wandering among the homeless and streetwalkers. Regarding the latter, I think about what Grandpa said: "You don't want to end up as a prostitute on a street corner."

Not me, I think as I eye a scantily dressed woman across the street. *I will make something of myself.[17]*

We stroll up and down Sunset Boulevard with no game plan on what to do, taking life by the hour. We are starving with only gum and a handful of apple-flavored candies to suck on.

---

[17] I have to say, though, that the women who worked the streets were friendly to us, even giving Denise cigarettes when she asked to bum one. I didn't smoke because I still viewed myself as an athlete, but Denise was letting herself go.

A women approaches us. From the look of her, she must be a prostitute.

"Y'all look hungry," she says.

I'm sure we do. I feel listless—tired—foggy.

"Let me get you something to eat," she offers.

The lady, dressed in a tight stretch skirt, leads us to a nearby street vendor. She buys one hot dog for us to split, adding that she didn't keep her money, so that is all she can spare.

We don't care. We are grateful. The hot dog looks like the most exquisite meal ever. As we slather ketchup on the kosher dog and take our first yummy bites, she leans in to give us some advice: "Y'all don't need to be here. You're gonna get into trouble if you stick around. Get outta here and go on home."

A lock of blonde hair dangles at her cheek. I suddenly see the older woman in the classic car turning in her seat—her eyes are blue—kind, "Be careful."

My stomach growls. The dog is gone. The memory of that matronly woman fades. We thank the woman for the hot dog and the advice. I know she means well, but returning to Las Vegas isn't an option. We have burned our ships in the harbor, and there is no going back.

Where are we going to sleep?

We have no idea.

We connect with a mix of Greek and Middle Eastern types who say we can crash at their pad. We walk into a good-sized ground-floor flat on Sunset, where male and female Eastern Europeans hang around, along with a few homeless-looking guys. Some acknowledge our presence. I get the feeling that the front door is more of a revolving door.

We get a bit of food, and Denise and I are able to take a shower, which feels divine. One of the kind women gives me a clean shirt to wear. For sleeping, we can lay down our heads in a corner crowded with others, or we can go up to the flat roof of the two-story building overlooking busy Sunset Boulevard. We choose the roof, figuring we would be safer there.

The sound of cars rushing along the strip makes me think of ocean waves crashing along a shoreline. I close my eyes and try to imagine gulls, shells, sand between my toes, and the wide blue sea—nothing out there but sky.

We are just getting comfortable when Denise and I learn there is a price to be paid for staying there.

Two swarthy guys appear at the roof door.

"You think you're going to stay here for free?" one says.

We stand and back away.

They close distance, lay hold of us, and push us down.

I am sexually assaulted against my will—suffering yet another indignity. Denise is forced to give the guy a hand job.

This time, I cry. Anger. Fury.

When the violence is over—and the men leave, Denise takes out the only smoke she has, and with shaky hands, lights up. We talk about leaving. Denise's eyes darken as she studies me. I feel the tears burning along my cheeks. Reaching for me, I scoot into her embrace. She holds me. Rocks me gently. My friend—like a mom or a big sister—I had never been rocked to sleep like that before. I never knew the comfort.

We stay on the roof top. Our fee is paid.

In the coming days, Denise will hold and rock me. It will be the only way I can fall asleep.

The next day, I am frozen, but I manage to get to my feet and walk. We aimlessly stroll west on Sunset Boulevard, talking about food and how awesome it would be to eat a thick hamburger with a side of fries—our stomachs growling like moon dogs. We don't talk about the men—the rooftop. We pretend it didn't happen.

A newer Mercedes slows down next to us. A couple in the car look in our direction. Then the gray sedan speeds up, pulls ahead, and turns into a parking lot.

The couple, in their late twenties, get out of the car and walk in our direction. They are Black. The guy's thin frame and short curly hair reminds me of the photo of Michael Jackson from his *Off the Wall* album. As for the woman accompanying him, she gives off an earnest, do-gooder vibe.

They both sport broad smiles as they approach and make eye contact with us. The woman, carrying a designer handbag, stops us while the guy hangs back.

"My big brother and I saw you walking out here, and we wanted to check up on you. How are you doing? Are you okay?" she asks.

I'm suddenly moved that strangers thought to take time to see if we were in trouble. A black cloud in my periphery—the men on the rooftop. My thoughts tick to the vintage car woman and the kind lady that bought us a hot dog—*City of Angels.*

"We're fine," I reply.

"Are you hungry?"

"Yes."

I immediately regret saying *yes* so quickly; giving away how we are living on the streets—our desperation. But maybe they can't tell. We've been runaways for less than forty-eight hours.

The woman's face brightens. "Hey, my brother and I are part of an outreach that helps kids like you. I'm Tabitha, and this is

Darnell. Whaddya say we get you something to eat and talk about it? There's a nice restaurant here on Sunset that's not too fancy called Ben Frank's. You can order anything you want."

Denise and I are too weak to consider whether this is a good idea or not. "Sure, that would be great," Denise replies. "But we don't have a car."

"You don't need one. We'll give you a ride."

Denise looks at me as if to say, *You think this is okay?* But at the moment, the altruistic couple is the only thing we have going.

How bad can it be? I think. After all, they are brother and sister— I have a big brother too.

"Sure, that would be nice of you," I hear myself saying.

When we arrive at Ben Frank's, the first thing that strikes me is how the midcentury A-frame building slants upward to the front and the back of the restaurant.[18] Open twenty-four hours, Ben Frank's is the kind of place that serves breakfast around the clock. After being seated in a booth, I order scrambled eggs and hash browns with a side order of pancakes. Denise follows my lead: we both need calories—and lots of them.

Denise digs in like it is her last meal, and I try to eat slowly and keep watch, but all seems as safe as it can be for now. The food is heavenly. Tabitha does most of the talking. She asks friendly questions about where we are from, what our families are like, and how we've found ourselves in Los Angeles.

I answer in generalities . . . *We're from Las Vegas . . . my mom's a social worker . . . my father's out of the picture* . . . but I wonder if I can trust her. I quickly decide not to mention my involvement with Sabrina and the escort company, or my childhood. But I feel like I had to give Tabitha something because

---

[18] I didn't know it at the time, but Ben Frank's was a favorite hangout for rock artists like the Rolling Stones, Buffalo Springfield, and Fleetwood Mac back in the day because its proximity to recording studios and its 24-hour comfort food menu.

she is paying for this wonderful meal. "There are problems at home," I say. "Momma won't listen to me, but that's nothing new. No big deal."

My story receives understanding nods from both individuals. "I'm sorry to hear that," Tabitha says.

Denise piggybacks on my statement. "Since our mothers are too busy to see us, we left. We figure Los Angeles is a good place to start all over. Brooky wants to be an actress one day."

"It's tough on the streets," Tabitha says. "You can die out there. We've seen it happen, and there are stories in the newspaper all the time."

"We're being careful," Denise says.

"Where have you been staying?"

"A place," I interject. "Some of the people give me the creeps, but it's okay."

Darnell smiles and asks if I know where my dad is or any other family.

"My dad's somewhere in L.A. I'm not sure how to find him. He moves around a lot."

"Maybe I can help you find him," Darnell offers.

My spirits lift.

"Tell you what." Tabitha's voice is filled with empathy. "Why don't you come to our place, and we can talk about the next steps you can take. We can make some phone calls on your behalf and get you some help."

There doesn't seem to be any harm in that.

City of Angels.

As we pile into their car, stomachs full, a place to sleep for the night, and the possibility of finding my father, I can't believe our good luck, finding this cool brother-and-sister team. Maybe Tabitha and Darnell know somebody who can give us a job and help us find a place to live.

Things are falling into place.

Tabitha and Darnell take us to an apartment near Sunset Boulevard on the top floor of a four-story building. The place isn't fancy like Sabrina's. But it is homey enough for a ministry outreach place for kids on the street. They say something about this being an extra place they keep to help kids like us.

From the moment we stepped inside the apartment, sometime around eight o'clock, Tabitha and Darnell give off a weird vibe, but I can't put my finger on why they look different. Maybe it is the serious looks on their faces.

I am knocked against a wall and then to the carpeted floor. Darnell uses his knees to pin my arms. Satisfied that I am defenseless, he slaps me full in the face. My cheek burns. Tears rush.

"You belong here now. You belong to me!" he yells.

Confused and suddenly afraid, I look at Denise, eyes wide, mouth agape.

His hand cracks across my face again. And again.

"What? What?" I cry.

He strikes me again and again. Hard slaps to the body now. He punches into my full stomach. I lose my breath. He grips my throat. His red, fiery eyes burning into mine, "You're going to do what I say! You are mine! Mine!"

Blows to my back and shoulders as I squirm to free my arms. I hear myself screaming. I am losing strength. My resolve to resist is evaporating.

Denise is shouting, "Stop it!" over and over. Tabitha has her by the throat.

I can no longer see what is happening. Then Darnell yanks me to my feet, his right hand grips my left arm like a vise. He pushes me into a chair, growling, "You're my property now, and that means you're gonna do what we tell you to do."

Denise is taken to another room. I cower over, my arms over my abdomen.

"Time to party," Darnell announces as he reaches for a small leather pouch and a baggie filled with a beige substance.

"What's that?"

"Heroin."

Darnell dangles the baggie in front of me. "We can do this the easy way or the hard way. Your choice."

The only drugs I'd ever taken were the 714s a few times with Sabrina. I have no idea what this will do to me. I am scared. Sabrina appears in my head. People buy people because of Sabrina.

"I want to go home," I cry.

"You don't have a home, remember," Darnell hisses as he fumbles with the drugs.

Stay calm, I think. *Play along. Maybe I'll be okay. Maybe. . .*

"Lean back," he directed.

I hesitate. He strikes me again. Stunned, I quickly do what I am told. He brusquely stuffs a pinch of powder into my left nostril, and another in my right.

"Snort it, bitch!" he hisses—his eyes in mine—a hand raised to strike.

I obey, my eyes trained on his open palm like a hideous wing hanging overhead. The hit sets off sickness and euphoria at the same time—and intense fear about what the drug is doing to me. Everything blurs as Darnell stuffs my nose with heroin three or four times over the next hour or two. Each hit ushers in feelings of disorientation, clouding my senses.

I throw up on the floor. I don't know what is up or what is down. I grip my distressed stomach, keel over. I moan. The room is spinning.

I am half-passed out when Darnell drags me into the bathroom, "Get in the tub, strip down and don't get out until I tell you!" he yells. "I need to check you out."

I am lying on the floor of the tub. I cannot reason. I know I must escape. I start to drift off, to imagine life before—fishing with Pops, playing with my dog King—until—until the trap door opens again and I am jolted back into the room.

Darnell stands in the doorway. "Come on! Give me your clothes. Underwear too."

I meekly comply, but the entire time, I am thinking, *I just met these people a few hours ago. How did I get here? I'm the bad seed. Momma was right.*

Darnell barks his next command. "Shut up. Stay there until I come back for you."

A ring of dirt stains the empty tub. I sit down, draw my knees to my chest, and sob. *Where is Denise?* I can't hear anything in the bathroom.

Every fifteen minutes or so, Darnell or Tabitha checks in on me. Tabitha is comforts, "Just do what we tell you to do, and it will all work out."

Darnell is tougher. Each time I ask if I can get out, he slams the bathroom door and turns out the light.

I should never have left Las Vegas. I begin to cry. I will give anything to be back in the safety of my home, as difficult as my relationship is with my mother, I love her. I miss my little brother Stanton and my big brother Ricky, who is away and I miss school.

For a long time, I am left alone in the dark. Then Darnell enters. Light stabs painfully into my eyes. He holds a straight razor in his hand—the type of razor I'd seen barbers use when I accompanied my father to the barbershop on Saturday mornings.

Darnell yanks me out of the bathtub and hustles me through the apartment. I resist as best I can, but he is wiry strong. Each whimper, each cry is met with his fingernails digging deeper into my upper arm.

The sliding glass door to a balcony is open. Darnell roughly shoves me through and leans my naked body up against the balcony railing—his left hand around my throat—the other brandishing the straight-edge razor. He pushes my head back so far that I fear he will push me over the edge to the street far below.

He pushes me farther until my head is pointed toward the distant sidewalk. I shriek and beg for my life.

"Please, no. Please, no," I cry through blinding tears.

"You ready to do what I say?" Darnell presses the razor blade against the skin of my throat, applying pressure.

"Do what? What?"

"Whatever we tell you to do. And if you don't, I'll let you drop and watch you hit the sidewalk. The cops won't do anything. You're a lowlife runaway. I'll tell them you were high and jumped off."

"Yes!" I cry. "Whatever you say." There is no way out.

"Oh, you're trying buck back, bitch? Okay, I'll give you that, but you better watch your tone wit' me, you hear?"

Darnell pulls me back onto the balcony, hoists me over his shoulder, and carries me fireman-style back to the bathroom.

Tabitha comes in. "Clean up, sweetheart," she says, turning on the shower. "I'll get you some clothes."

And then a slight smile comes to her face. "Then we'll take a little drive and see how you do."

I am not sure what she means. I don't want to ask.

Darnell pops his head in. "Oh, and one more thing. You have a new name."

"What is it?"

"Peaches."

The clock on the Mercedes dashboard reads 3 o'clock in the morning.

We are headed westbound on Interstate 10, passing the Wilshire district toward Santa Monica. I smooth the hem of my summer dress and look at the heeled sandals on my feet. Tabitha has given me a small purse filled with condoms and mints.

I marvel at how there are still plenty of cars on the freeway in the middle of the night. A dark thought enters: *If these drivers only knew the predicament Denise and I are in right now.*

My friend sits in the back seat with me as Darnell drives and Tabitha rides shotgun.

"Let's go over this again," Tabitha says. "If you get asked, you're eighteen years old and graduated from high school. You're working to save money for school. You don't know me or Darnell if you get stopped by the cops or anyone else. If you do good, we won't be hard on you. But if you don't do what you're told, you'll never go home."

I recoil from the threat as Tabitha continues her instructions.

"To stay safe—and I'm not playing with you—never use your real name, forget it, you have a new name now. Never reveal your real age. Always use a condom. Definitely no blow jobs without a rubber. Remember, you don't handle any of the money. We do that for now. But sometimes they'll pay you. If that happens, you must give all the money to us. If you don't, we have ways of finding out. If we learn that you're skimming, you'll regret the day you were born. Do you understand me?"

I nod, fearfully.

"Another thing: don't dilly-dally with my clients," she continues. "Don't forget—twenty minutes max. Time is money. Act like it's your first time, but no kissing. Clean up when you're done. Don't forget to smile. Any questions?"

"Where are we going?" I asks.

"You'll find out."

We take the exit ramp to the 405 Southbound. Soon, we pass the Century Boulevard exit taking travelers to the LAX airport.

What would I give to get on a plane and fly far, far away. I stare off through the window at a jetliner rising in the ink-black sky and imagine I am on it, going somewhere, anywhere. I could almost feel the vibration of flying. Wings spreading out. . .

Just south of the airport, Darnell steers the Mercedes onto Imperial Highway, a four-lane road that parallels the southernmost runway. Several nearby hotels like the Hilton and others are busy at this time of night.

We park off to the side. Tabitha gets out and walks to a corner of a self-parking lot, away from the valet and near the street. I see people milling about. Some are guys, others are women wearing provocative clothing. Every now and then, a car pulls in, and a window rolls down. A couple of men approach the car, but sometimes a girl would lean on the window and talk to the driver.

Whatever is happening, it all seem very organized. I watch the scene unfold in total disbelief. It is like I am in a movie.

A nice car—a burgundy Lincoln Continental—drives into the parking lot. When Tabitha approaches, the driver rolls down the window. They engage in a discussion for a minute, then the man pulls out a wallet and hands her some cash.

Tabitha thrusts her hands inside her coat pockets as she makes the way back to our car. The Lincoln pulls into a parking space about fifty yards away.

Tabitha hops into the front passenger suit and turns to me. "Your first date for us," she says. "Remember what we said."

My mind is racing. *How could this be a date?*[19]

"So, what am I supposed to do?" I don't know how this works.

"Walk to his car over there and get in the back seat. He doesn't want to get a room, so take care of him in the car."

My heart rate spikes as I gather myself for the walk to the car. Tears form in my eyes. With each step, I try to imagine that I am not really there. But this is happening, like I am a part of a horror movie.

When I arrive, the man has moved to the back seat. I get inside and see a tall white guy, fit, and in his mid-thirties. He looks like an actor I've seen before in a movie or TV show.

"You're really pretty," he says. "You know what to do, right?"

I'm silent. I stare at the wedding ring on his finger and wonder what his family is like. Does he have small children? Is his wife at home waiting or wondering where he is?

Marriage? What a joke, I think. *Why do men do this?*

Then I think about Momma. Is she looking for me? Is Stanton wondering where his big sister is? Tears fill my eyes, but he doesn't notice. Why would he? I have to let him do what he paid for, and that's what he does in a matter of minutes.

At a time when teenage girls get in trouble for fooling around with their boyfriends at the movies, I lose any faith in the goodness of men while in the rear seat of a Lincoln Continental in the early morning hours in the City of Angels near the airport. What I experience is a different side of the same underground world of trafficking that started with Sabrina's escort service in Las Vegas.

---

[19] Certain types of traffickers don't call clients "tricks" or "johns" in the grooming process. They call them "dates" to make it sound nicer than it is—and easier for victims to swallow.

From what has transpired in the last ten hours, I know that I will never be me. I'll never be okay. Brooky is gone, and Parker is not in the car.

Somebody named Peaches is all this john sees.

No Way Out

You belong here now. You belong to me.

Darnell's words rattle around my brain as we backtrack from Imperial Highway to the apartment near Sunset Boulevard. The way my teenage mind is processing things, the verb *belong* means he and his sister and partner-in-crime, Tabitha, can do anything they want with me. I have to do what they say—or suffer another frightful beating—or a slit throat and horrible death.

Over the next few weeks, Darnell and Tabitha reinforce this new paradigm. They make sure I understand who is boss by controlling every aspect of my life—from the minute I wake up until they let me go to sleep after getting assaulted by their last client—they make sure I am high from forced drug use, so I will stay calm and obey—and I am theirs in their bedroom to do whatever they want; and they do whatever they want to my body.

For Darnell, this means doing various acts—"Good practice," he says—or whatever his sick mind can think of. For Tabitha, it is the same, but a softer, sinister expression of pure evil.

I start to realize that she isn't his sister. *How stupid can I be?* I am so angry at myself. I am too naïve to understand that my controllers have adopted a passive-aggressive approach: Darnell, I find out also likes men, and will rape me with the same hostility that some tricks do. Tabitha will balance that by whispering not to worry, that it will be over soon, that I can go home—all this while I am partially unconscious from the drugs she gives me.

I will find out later that over half of the male traffickers and pimps like men. This underground group of men—and women—also do things that I'm too frightened to repeat. But those on the "down-low" are clear about secrecy.

Eventually, I am mixed up about what I am supposed to feel—about my body, about my sense of existence—*how can I ever trust anyone again?*

Within weeks my captors move me, along with a couple of other young women, into a four-bedroom house in a quiet residential neighborhood situated somewhere in West L.A.[20] Living all together in a rancher on a quiet street is an attempt to build a family-like bond between Darnell and Tabitha and the *stable* of young girls they are selling. The reality is that I am living in a brothel.

Each day, I have to please men who have no moral qualms about paying my captors to supply them with young women and underage girls like myself. They buy us for one reason: to get off

---

[20] I can't remember where this home was located, but it was west and south of Hollywood, maybe in the Culver City area because of its proximity to LAX and Beverly Hills, areas of high demand for prostitution. Denise was placed with a different trafficker.

with some bizarre high that blinds them of our victimization. I also learn more and more about the couples for whom normal relations between a man and a woman isn't enough: they need a third party in their beds, just like the conservative-looking couple in Las Vegas.

The days tend to blur and run into each other from the same monotonous schedule. I usually sleep until the crack of noon—or sometimes as late as two o'clock in the afternoon—because I rarely get back to the house before 3 or 4 a.m. We are allowed to sleep in because Darlene and Tabitha want us well-rested.

After waking up, breakfast is cold cereal and scrambled eggs and toast if we want to go to the trouble of preparing a hot meal. Then there are chores around the house—cleaning the kitchen, vacuuming the floors, scrubbing the bathrooms, straightening up the bedrooms, and changing sheets. The latter is important because we never know when Darnell will arrive with a guy looking for a quickie. These encounters happen in the afternoon while we are still there, because once it gets dark, it is time to hit the road. That's when our real day starts—like we are clocking in.

We are apt to be driven anywhere—apartment blocks, people's homes, high-end hotels, mansions, or gala events—to make them money or do drugs. Some of the parties in Beverly Hills are hosted by famous singers I've heard on the car radio. The celebrities are *friendly* and treat us well, knowing we are *on-call* for their guests and not knowing some of us are underage. They are also high as kites from snorting line after line of cocaine.

One time, I find myself at one of these fancy parties when Tabitha tells me to walk down a long hallway and take the second door to my left. When I open the door, it is pitch black inside, but I feel that I am not alone.

"Close the door," I hear a young male voice say.

I step inside, unable to see anything and getting creeped out by the minute. Then I feel various hands groping me all over.

I flashback to when the 300-pound man attacked me in Las Vegas. I run out of the room, not caring about the consequences. This time luck is on my side. Everyone is so high and busy that I slip out of the room without anyone noticing.

Here's what I learn quickly about this: it is all about the money, the drugs, and the dark and seedy side of addiction and greed. The faces of johns and couples no longer look human to me. But I can see who they really are, and it is frightening. *There has to be more to life than this. Don't they know that?*

At the age of seventeen, I am a full-blown cocaine addict. Drugs are how Darnell and Tabitha get me to do their sexual bidding: taking them is how I get through another day. But becoming an addict isn't my only problem. I am in a perpetual state of freak-out. Now I don't care what happens to me.

After starting me off with heroin, they introduce me to cocaine —the drug of choice at the time. Blow is a stimulant that floods the brain with feel-good messages. No more "714s" chased with strong Long Island iced teas for me, except when I need to come down before my chest explodes.

Drugs are always available, if I do what I am supposed to do. Either Darnell provides them, or the clients. I quickly catch on that the men buying sex almost always want me to be stoned, blitzed, or wired like them. Darnell says if they ask you to take something or have a drink, you have to agree. You can't say, "Sorry, I don't do that."

I have guys hand me one of their "snuff bullets," a small, plastic cylinder device that delivers a line of cocaine to the user.

Press a black knob, and all the cocaine—known as a "bump"—comes rushing up your nose.

I develop an addiction to blow and start freebasing in a very short time. When I start living in Tabitha and Darnell's rental, I still view myself as an athlete. I devote part of my day to staying in shape by doing sit-ups, push-ups, and planks. But drugs sap my energy, and exercise becomes an afterthought.

There is nothing I can do to change the downward trajectory I am on. It is like I am swirling around a drain, unable to pull myself out of the vortex. Then I have a seizure during one of my highs. Losing control of my limbs wigs me out, but it doesn't stop me freebasing a couple of hours later. I *need* to get high in the worst way.

This is how I live now. It is the way out.

I spend a lot of time in hotels, especially well-appointed suites in upscale brands like Hyatt, Marriott, and Ritz-Carlton—popular with businessmen who travel to Los Angeles for meetings or to attend a convention.

I have to dress the part if I am being dropped off at a four-star or five-star hotel: the fancier the property, the more likely there will be bellhops stationed at the entrance or the elevators to keep the riffraff out.

Many palms have to be greased. From the parking valet to the doorman, from the bellhop to the concierge, everyone has to be paid off. They are part of the network because they are the ones who have called Darnell's phone number or passed along his contact information after they are approached by a businessman, a celebrity, or a bachelor asking to arrange some *company* for them.

Darnell gets the call and drops me off at the hotel. I waltz through the lobby like I belonged there, dressed in a shimmery cocktail dress and heels. I keep up the act as I approach the bank of elevators. I think of Sabrina's blood red stilettos. Her smooth-as-silk stride across a hotel lobby—touching hands as she goes. Now, it's me.

Sometimes elevator access is restricted to hotel guests with a key card. A bellhop will be stationed next to the elevators, but all it takes is an exchange of knowing nods for me to continue to a specific floor and a specific room. I say the room number, he puts a key in the wall or swipe a key card, and the elevator whisks me to the appointment.

I arrive at the right floor, I steel myself as I approach the room number I've been given. I never know who is on the other side when I knock—or how they will treat me after I repeat my standard ice-breaking line: "Hi, I'm Lisa. I understand that you're a little bored tonight." I use different names.

No matter how the client responds or conducts himself, I have to be cordial and professional as I was trained to be. I can't cop an attitude, act disinterested, or present myself as if I am in a hurry. I have to act normal—like I *want* to be there, which is so far from the truth.

Sometimes they ask me personal questions, like where I am from or what I see myself doing someday. This is what I am coached to say: "Tonight, I'm here to focus on you. You're the center of my universe right now."

If they persist, I say, "You're the only thing that matters because right now, this is my first time."

First time?

I am always amazed how many men believe me. It is all about creating a fantasy world.

Two-thirds of the men have wedding rings on and don't think twice about committing adultery. A few sport untanned indentions on their ring fingers that give away their marital status. And then there are the bachelors—the other third of the clientele—are either filled with lust, addicted to porn, or bored being alone and want to do something about it.

Whether they are married or not, these people are either cold, mean, or weird-nice to me.

The buyers who treat me coldly—and with contempt—act like they are disgusted with themselves for what they are doing. These buyers want to get right down to the nitty-gritty and be done with it. It is like they didn't want to be there and are fighting through feelings of guilt and self-loathing. Nor are they interested in making small talk; for them, most encounters take ten or fifteen minutes.

Others are different—like the sick guys who are extra perverted. They are ticked from the moment I walk into the hotel room, like it is me who spoiled their evening instead of the other way around. They are quick to call me all sorts of names—the mildest being *bitch*. The verbal abuse goes downhill from there:

You cheap slut. You're nothing but a lowlife, you're nothing.

My self-esteem vanishes. And why wouldn't it? They are adults, and I am still a minor. They are in the power position, and I am not. To make it through one more encounter, one more buyer of commercial rape, I disappear and my mind vaults to school, to attend prom, or walk at graduation. I think about traveling to the great cities in the world. And since I love movies, I also live in them during the day, which helps me hold on somehow.

Whenever anyone speaks to me in a dehumanizing manner, I know I am in for it. Many attempt to choke me. Not in a way that will kill me, but they like wrapping their two hands around my neck and squeezing a bit, just to see how I will react. I never take it well since being unable to breathe is not an enjoyable experience. I fear for my life in those moments and know there are girls in S&M rings who don't make it back.[21]

Then there are the buyers who break into broad smiles when they answer the door, like I am a long-lost relative or the most gorgeous person they ever laid eyes on. They act like they are the nicest people on the planet.

"Oh, you're so beautiful and precious," they say. "Thank you for coming tonight."

As if I had a choice in the matter.

They are the ones who offer me a glass of wine or something to eat from the tray of food they have delivered to the room. But our interaction is forced and superficial, especially given the wide age gap between us. I mean, what does a successful businessman in his forties have in common with a high school senior?

But I am not even old enough to be called a woman. I am still a girl! Ever since I went through puberty, I look younger than my real age. I'm sure I shocked more than a few men with how young I appear, which was fourteen or fifteen.

Sometimes curiosity gets the best of them, and they ask, "How old are you?"

"I'm eighteen," I reply, which always prompts an exhale of relief.

By now, I almost was.

I know what they are thinking. *Good. She's a legal adult and not jailbait—even if she doesn't want to be here who's going to know?*

"Eighteen," the weird-nice types repeat. "You have your whole life ahead of you."

---

[21] S&M refers to the combination of sadism (inflicting pain) and masochism (receiving pain) to derive pleasure and sexual gratification.

So predictable and such balderdash, which is why I am convinced that the "weird-nice" types are psychopaths, capable of turning on me instantly.

"Slap me, slap me," they say while they are trying to orgasm. Others tell me to dig my nails into their backs as they work themselves toward a sick climax. I can always tell those are the ones who aren't married because a married man wouldn't want to return home and have to explain why there is a row of indented nail marks dug into his back.

Then some men buy me for a night or longer—like one or two days. They procure me so I will be available around the clock in a penthouse suite overlooking the Wilshire District or a manicured estate in Brentwood and Bel Air.

Whenever I walk through the front door of one of these mansions, these affluent men are so full of themselves that they really think I love being there. They believe their 12,000-square foot homes and superbly landscaped properties take my breath away. No. I hate the situation I've found myself in and what I do.

Darnell takes me to an estate. I know that we are expected to dress in a certain way, walk in a certain way, and act a certain way—all girly and elegant, always pretending I am not a victim, until I believe it. Speaking from experience, Darnell informs me that these particular guys will be flirtatious and touchy-feely but also need to believe I am refined.

On this occasion, I arrive at a fancy home in Beverly Hills—a kidney-shaped pool in the back yard and a pool house bigger than a typical home. I am introduced to a pair of Italian-looking guys smelling of garlic and parmesan cheese. They carry themselves like wise-guys in *The Godfather* movies.

I put on my skimpy bikini—looking fit and pretending I am having fun taking dips in the pool and warming up in the jacuzzi. Friends and revelers arrive. There is enough food and drugs for everyone throughout the day and into the evening. Every three or four hours, like clockwork, I receive a knowing nod from one of the dudes, which is my signal to meet him in the pool house. After our wet suits hit the floor, I have to pleasure him. I am theirs for the day or the weekend—they could do whatever they want. That's what they pay for.

Being put in these situations starts to seem normal. Sometimes, I even think these violators can be nice. Then there are the times when my thinking goes along these lines: *I chose all of this, and it was my fault. No one has any responsibility for my pain but me.*

I know it is not true. I know it.

No matter who I am with, my *dates*—as Darnell makes me call them—there are business transactions between my handlers and the clients at the end of the day. That means a fee is involved for me showing up. The cash is usually left under a book or something on a table or nightstand, or sometimes in a gift bag, which I scoop up discreetly.

If I meet my quota by midnight, then everybody is happy, and I can have the rest of the night off. But if business is slow, Darnell and Tabitha are apt to keep me up until three or four o'clock in the morning—so I can meet *their* quota.

I have things a bit better than the older ones in their early and mid-twenties, who usually look five to ten years older because of the drugs they've taken for so long and all the sexual and physical abuse they've endured.[22]

Whenever I am done with a trick, either Darnell or Tabitha will be waiting in a car outside, reading a magazine or listening to the radio. They've trained me to hand over any cash I have within

---

[22] I didn't know this at the time, but they didn't get as much as me because clients paid a premium for a "fresh face," which helped me reach my quota sooner.

minutes of arriving at their vehicle, especially the tips they know we all get.

On one occasion, they found out that I didn't tell them about a cash tip I received. After getting knocked around pretty good by Darnell, I vow that will never happen again.

Darnell rules by fear and intimidation, and he and Tabitha often threaten me. I made a huge mistake telling them everything about my family and my mother at Ben Frank's the first night— what she did, where she worked, what part of Las Vegas she lived in, and even her phone number. They use that information to say that if I choose to run away, they know how to find my mother *and* my little brother—and they'll be in danger.

Darnell says to me: "If you run, I'll cut up your face and kill you, and I'll hurt whoever you care about."

I believe him, which is why I am not tempted to escape. It doesn't take them long—say a month—before they feel confident I won't run away. But that doesn't stop the two of them from playing with my emotions. Darnell says one time, "Sorry we had to hurt you. Once there's enough money, everyone's going to be able to do their own thing."

I know now, that was an absolute lie.[23]

Sometimes Tabitha will take us out shopping and buy us some clothes. Or she'll drive us to Santa Monica and the beach for a day of sunning and relaxation so we will look healthy.

I am resigned to the fact that Tabitha and Darnell have their hooks in me. Since I don't see a way out, I live day to day and get high most of my waking hours, rarely thinking about my future.

After a few months or less under Darnell and Tabitha's oppressive control, I am near the LAX airport, one of many

---

[23] A common misperception is that those caught up in sex trafficking get paid well—or at least get paid something. This is far from the truth.

young women of the night attending a big party at some house. I am standing on the sidewalk out front, talking with one of my roommates, when several L.A. Police Department black-and-whites rolled up.

Raid!

Partiers, pimps, and trafficked women scatter like mice as a dozen cops begin arresting people and then asking questions. Some get away—like Darnell and Tabitha.

I don't know what to do since this is my first police raid. A cop makes eye contact and points toward me.

"Hand's up!" he yells, reaching for his handcuffs.

My arms are pinned behind my back, and a pair of silver handcuffs are slapped on my wrists. I am led to a police van parked down the street.

As soon as the van fills up with arrested folks, we are driven downtown to Central Jail. When I am processed, I don't have an ID on me—and by ID, I mean the fake ID Darnell has given me.

"What's your name?" says the cop behind the wire cage.

Peaches. "Lisa Johnson," I reply.

The cop takes the fake name in stride. "Age?"

"Eighteen." I am seventeen, still underage—and I know if I say I am seventeen, I'll be taken to juvenile hall and will have to enter a juvie program—remain locked up. By saying I am eighteen, I have a feeling I might be able to skip by and get away.

The cop isn't buying. "You sure you're eighteen? You don't look it."

I nod and keeping a poker face.

"Okay," he says, stamping my paperwork. "We'll figure it out later. For now, we have to take you in for loitering."

"I don't know why I was arrested. I wasn't doing anything."

"Where do you live?"

"I'm homeless."

"How come?"

"Things weren't good at home." I'm not about to volunteer a lot of information.

"What happened to your ID?"

"I don't know. I must have lost it."

I don't have a purse or anything personal on me—just a few bucks in my pocket. That's the way they made us roll.

The LAPD decides to let me stew inside a holding cell while they figure out what to do with me. But Central Jail is full, so I am placed in a van with other arrestees and driven to a nearby maximum-security prison.

I am ordered to take a shower. Even though I'm scared out of my mind, I know I'm safe for the moment when I'm tossed into a prison jumpsuit. Being locked up is scary, but I'm still alive. It is a shocking experience, especially since the correctional officers said the floor above us held hard-core murderers. Feeling numb, I am led to a larger cell-like room filled with a couple of dozen female inmates. A female correctional officer shows me an empty cot.

There isn't much to do except get some sleep, which is more stressful than restful. The following morning, I am still dozing when I receive a tap on my shoulder.

"Wake up, sleeping beauty," a fellow prisoner says.

She is standing next to my cot. She turns her head toward a correctional officer calling my name at the entrance. I am sleepy and groggy and can't remember what name I gave the cops.

Then I realize, *Oh, that's me.* I raise my hand.

"You're getting released," the female correctional officer says.

Before I leave I am told that I am being released on my own recognizance but that I have to return on a specific day to see a judge.

"Here's your court date," the lady cop says, handing me a piece of paper with the name *Lisa Johnson* written in one of the blank lines.

On a shabby downtown street, I step out of the maximum-security facility, bordered by razor wire.

A thought comes to me: *Darnell and Tabitha have no idea where I am. Why should I go back? I can escape right now!*

There is only one place I can go—home, meaning Las Vegas. I have friends there who will help me get my life together.

But how will I get there? I am not about to hitchhike, and I don't have enough money in my pocket to buy a bus ticket.

I know just the person to call—a guy I'd met named Johnny. Fortunately, I remember his number, which he has given to me verbally on a few occasions. I have a good memory for numbers, and his is really easy. Johnny has always said if I ever needed anything, call him. Using a phone at a gas station I dial him.

Good fortune smiles on me when an acquaintance picks up. I remembered a couple of phone numbers whispered to me, and Johnny had been the sorrowful kind of buyer—always curious about my age. When he has asked me if I was in trouble in the past, he seemed to read through my denials.

This time around, I don't have to lie. While cradling the phone, I describe the situation I've found myself in and where I am.

"I'll be right there," he says.

Johnny lets me crash at his pad that night—and asks for nothing in return.

When I wake up in the morning, I explain how I am free and have to return to Las Vegas and start all over again. "That's how I feel—like I have a second chance in life, even though I don't believe it, I know, I have to run," I say "It's a do-over."

"Good for you," he replies. "Guys like Darnell are cowards. They won't look for you, especially with a warrant and your real age. He'll just turn to someone else. But I can't believe you're telling me this. I'm sorry, Lisa, or whatever your name is. I'm truly sorry."

Johnny drives me to the Greyhound depot downtown and pays for my bus fare to Vegas.

We say goodbye. There are still bizarre moments of good in the midst of chaos.

As the sleek Greyhound bus motors across the Mojave Desert, I believe that I am moving toward a new beginning. Even though I hate the police because they have treated me like dirt in the past, this time is different. Their handcuffs saved my life.

I know I can find something better to do to support myself in Las Vegas. Maybe becoming a hairstylist will be my ticket to a better life.

My hands shake. A deep body ache—a restless itch—I want to be high. I need to be high.

I shift in my bus seat and breathe deeply, in and out. I try to take in the desert scenery. I feel socially awkward. I am afraid of my own shadow—afraid everyone hates me. I close my eyes and try to let the growling sounds of the bus engine rock me to sleep. *Where is Denise? Where is my sweet Denise?*

We cross the state line and spire-like skyscrapers on the Strip can be seen forty miles away.

I'm returning as empty handed as when I ran.

I'm returning with a weight I cannot bear.

Freedom Is an Inside Job

I don't go back and ask my mother if I can live with her. I don't think she will want me right now, or ever. Our relationship is strained from my anger and realization that she can't show her love toward me after the hell I put her through. It's a wrap because both sides don't know how. I called Momma when I was in L.A. once (when I had access to a pay phone for less than 2 minutes), shortly after Darnell and Tabitha abducted me. I thought she might cry or say she was worried, but that didn't happen. As soon as she heard my voice, she raised hers, loudly saying, "You ran away! You're a runaway!"

"Momma, it's not like that—"

"You're going to get into trouble! The police are looking for you!"

My heart sank as she continued to yell. Maybe that's how she showed her fear and emotions, but I knew I had to deal with what I was facing and do my best to try and survive. I blanked and hung up. It was barely a minute-long phone call.

Not long after returning to Nevada[24], I drop by Momma's house, feeling awkward, uncomfortable, paranoid, depressed, and stressed-filled. We both know I am not the same, but she doesn't know why. She is still my mom. Part of me wants to live with her and my little brother. I love my family, but I know it isn't possible, not right now.

I don't want to be a homeless teenager. I only have a few bucks in my pocket— and a coke habit I am determined to white knuckle through.

_____

[24] I started calling this Las Vegas "Nevada" because I didn't like saying "Las Vegas," which made me think of loss or being lost.

I sofa-surf with a few old school friends while I get my bearings. I go up to Mount Charleston Lodge, where I hike and enjoy a sugary coffee with milk sometimes (the lodge gives free refills). Going to the mountains or an airport to watch planes take off and imagine flying around the world to places I've never been to is my way of dreaming, hoping, and surviving.

Sitting outside the lodge under a canopy of blue skies, I bask in the wind blowing through the trees. Mount Charleston is a place to dream or pretend that everything has always been well. That Mom and Dad are proud of me and would be there when I walk across the stage to graduate from college, watch me get married, and have a family of my own. But I haven't had a prom or a Sweet Sixteen birthday party. I don't even know if I am a girl, a boy, or just a thing.

There are lots of things different about me. I cry a lot. I think I'm going crazy. I blame myself for everything that's happened to me. The shame I feel for existing, is overwhelming. I have to fight against flashbacks of the rapist, the buyers, the violence, the drugs—the horrible thoughts of monsters lurking in my nightmares: Uncle Mike, Sabrina, Darnell, and Tabitha.

I have been pressed and pushed by many of the men I met—and couples. No matter where I go, I can spot the freaks, the weirdoes, and the sex addicts—and even those in the Vegas nightclub scene, where I still go to dance, to forget. It is only a matter of a minute before I give in to temptation.

Besides the partying, one of the best parts about clubbing is meeting people—networking. At one club, a wealthy car dealer strikes up a conversation with me. When I was a trafficked kid by the escort service, he was a buyer. He was also a drug user and a *swinger*—someone into group sex with people he barely knew, married or unmarried. Threesomes and foursomes were his drug. Always one man and all women.

He seems genuinely interested in my story of Sabrina and the human trafficking by the escort service, hidden to the public but right in the open. I don't tell him about Los Angeles; I don't want to frighten him. I just tell him I am beginning my life. When I finished, he offers to help—but with a few strings attached.

"You can stay at my place," he says with *that* look. I know that look. A sicko with a smile, pretending to be a savior.

I arch an eyebrow. "Really . . . ."

"I'm an easygoing guy," he says. "Nothing that would shock you, right? Whatever I'd ask you to do would be your choice. It won't be that often, and you'll be safe."

Freedom is an inside job. I have escaped abductors, but my soul has been assassinated, and the bondage is very real in my mind; it is a part of whom I have become.

Some kids grow up learning through good observation, but not everyone is that lucky. These are the cards I that I have been dealt, or so it seems. His belittling coercion is all that I have, so I take his offer. Pretending that I am in control, the standards have been lowered to hell.

The truth is that I am hungry and I need a place to stay.

I learn that once you're exposed to something as a victim—or anything good or bad—it's easy to fall back or forward into that lifestyle. At this point in my life, no one is to be trusted.

When I am pressed to go with a friend of the car dealer to New York City and be part of an underground escort service I know I don't want to travel down that road again, so I try and return to normal life, determined to change and go legit as best I can.

The casinos are always hiring. I go to the restaurant workers' union hall and get a voucher for a job at one of the big casinos on the Strip. I soon set my eyes on waitressing, where the real money is. After showing my supervisors my mettle and can-do attitude for a couple of months, I am allowed to start training with the wait staff. My supervisors tell me that I have the right look for the "front of the house," which raises my confidence.

I like the work and interaction with people as well as doing something physical, like balancing a tray of entrées on the long walks from the kitchen to the linen-covered tables. Pocketing hefty tips sometimes give me a cushion, but too much of my earnings go straight to clubbing and shopping. I am trying to erase the past with new clothes and a new look.

Whenever I have time to take stock about where I am going in life, I can't stop revisiting my idea about becoming a cosmetologist—doing hair and makeup, and using my creativity —while I figure out how to become an actress or writer one day.

I check out a local cosmetology school and learn what I need to enroll: a high school diploma and enough money to cover the tuition. What a reminder of how much I have missed; my straight-A report cards, my work on the drama theatre club, my trophies and ribbons from basketball, track, and volleyball, and homecoming, prom, and graduation.

I recall how I was a pitcher/shortstop back in California and the first girl to play in an all-boys Little League team with my picture on the front page of a local newspaper in Lake Elsinore. That is entirely another life, a time when I used to love school and sports.

To move forward means passing a GED, an equivalent to a high school diploma.

I sign up to take the GED test at a Community College, which will measure my understanding of English comprehension and reading, math, social studies, and science. It is a hot spring day, and even though I take the test indoors in an air-conditioned room, I sweat buckets during the test. I don't normally perspire like this, but I have missed nearly all my senior year of high school and never liked testing. Even though I am frightened that I will fail and I feel like my mind isn't as clear anymore, I decide to just go for it.

A couple of weeks later I visit to the community college to get the results. The woman at the window has a sly smile as she hands me a piece of paper.

"You scored very well, way above most," she says. "You're really smart. You should go to college."

Her kind words cause my eyes to water. I grin at the paper in my hand. I study it. I see the scores. I stare.

This huge achievement encourages me to keep trying. I call my mother and tell her how well I did. She says she is proud of me. I know that must be hard for her to say. I am shocked and I burst into tears.

I am inspired to figure out if there is more to life than the horrors I've been through.

More to life.

I like that phrase.

I enroll at a local cosmetology school and qualify for a federal Pell Grant to help pay for my tuition, which cost over $15,000.

I am a natural when it comes to cutting and styling hair on men and women. At least, that's what my teachers tell me often. I can handle my coursework, like learning the difference between hair coloring techniques like balayage and ombré. My biggest issue is discreetly snorting a line of cocaine in the school bathroom during breaks.

One time, coming back to the classroom after doing coke, I see a poster on a hallway wall.   A new hair and cosmetic product company known as Aveda is looking for models.

"You should check them out. You'd be perfect," One of the aspiring hairstylists in my class says, stopping to read the poster.

"You think so?" I ask. "But couldn't this modeling call be a front for weirdos?"

"You might be right," says my friend. "Anything can happen in Vegas, but I still think you should check them out. I don't think the school would let them put up their poster if this wasn't on the level. If they ask you to take off your clothes or do something shady, then you'll know."

I scribble down the phone number to make an appointment.

When I arrive at Aveda's makeshift offices in an industrial park south of the Strip, I exhale. Not only is the Eurocentric staff friendly and very cool, but I am impressed when I am led into an office and introduced to Horst Rechelbacher, the company's founder. He look to be in his forties and speaks with an accent.

"Welcome to Aveda," he says, pumping my hand. "Please take a seat."

He studies my face.

"You're gorgeous," he says. "You have a very striking look. Would you mind if I took a Polaroid?" he asks.

I see nothing wrong with that. "Sure," I reply.

After taking a couple of Polaroid shots, I tell Mr. Rechelbacher that I am a cosmetology student—it feels good to say. This is one of the first times I think I can authentically straighten my shoulders.

Mr. Rechelbacher says he is from Austria and had started as a barber when he was fourteen, before becoming an apprentice hairstylist in Rome. He eventually moved to the United States and was inspired to launch the company after a trip to India introduced him to Ayurveda, a system of medicine that relied on a natural and holistic approach to healing. Aveda's skin-care products, he explains, were made without toxic chemicals. The company name means *knowledge of nature* in Hindi.

"We believe there's a huge market for natural hair and skin products and cosmetics in the United States, and we're looking for models who have that strong natural look," Mr. Rechelbacher says. "You have a unique bone structure. We're having a photoshoot tomorrow with several models. Can you join us?"

I don't see any harm in that. The following afternoon, I show up at one of the top hotels, where Aveda has leased part of the swimming pool for the shoot. Everything is spectacular, from the models to the photographers and staff. There is delicious food, healthy beverages, music by a DJ, and tons of beautiful-smelling products and essential oils to try out.

I am asked to sign a release. Before I can sign, I am quickly rushed off to meet with a makeup person.

After makeup, Horst is glad to see me, but he wants my mascara to be different. He tells the makeup person that he wants it removed from my bottom lashes and slanted to the side, not straight up on my top lashes.

I feel Horst wants the best for me. It is rare that I meet a man who makes me feel special without wanting to touch me. I often see men like him as father figures; at least, they seem like they would be good dads.

They already have my measurements and they put me in several bathing suits until they find the right one. Horst says he will personally shoot me. I am so nervous during the first few clicks of the camera that I am tearing up. Horst sees what is happening and pulls me aside. "Are you okay? This is going to be great, and you look amazing through the lens. Let me show you."

He takes a few Polaroids and shares a few images. I am amazed as I have not seen myself like that. It is as if I am someone else. When we resume shooting, he says "You're powerful. You're stunning. Yes, good. You're unshakeable. You're gorgeous."

That does it. His encouragement helps me get through the shoot. After a break for lunch, he thanks me for my time and says, "We'll stay in touch with you."

Several weeks later, I am called back to his office, where an array of color and black-and-white photos are strewn across a table. Mr. Rechelbacher holds up one of the photos.

"Outstanding," he says with energy. "Has anyone ever told you that you should become an actress? You could do this for a living."

"No," I reply, although acting has been my dream for a long time.

"We would like to use your likeness in our company advertising, so I had my team prepare a contract. I hope you will find that acceptable."

I sign the contract without reading any fine print.

Horst then asks me to return for another shoot. This time around, he proposes an idea: "I'd like to cut your hair, with your permission. What would you say if I give you a mod hair vibe, something much shorter that would show off those impressive bones and beautiful skin you have," he suggests.

I am flattered and immediately say yes.

Horst sits me down in his stylist's chair and lops off seven inches of my crinkly brown hair, which has been curly for as long as I can remember. Then he works his scissors and clippers with surgical precision until he has massed the hair on the top of my head into a form that looked like a crown that the Queen of Sheba would wear. This high-top look has an impressive angle, rising a good three inches from the top of my forehead and sloping toward the back of my neck.

Horst then takes a straight-edge razor to my sideburns, raising them to match the height of the top of my ears. He clips my eyebrows and colors my hair pitch black. This will define my look for many years to come.

HAIR, MAKEUP AND PHOTOGRAPHY BY *HORST & FRIENDS INTERNATIONAL*

HAIR BY HORST
MAKEUP BY HORST
PHOTOGRAPHY BY HORST

HORST & FRIENDS
INTERNATIONAL

Horst Rechelbacher had an artist's eye in styling hair and photography. These photos were taken in color, but Aveda had prints made in both color and black and white. I've heard that one of the color ones hangs at the Aveda Institute in Minneapolis with a special painting design overlayed by Horst.

"You look fabulous," he says as I gaze at a handheld mirror. "Look at you. The runway awaits you. Maybe the red carpet too. That's the look of a star!"

I am blown away at what this man's hands are capable of. My friends gush their approval of my new hairstyle. Now when I go clubbing, the bouncer treats me deferentially, like I am a celebrity

—but I'm afraid, awkward in my own skin still, and clubbing is losing its luster.

Aveda's graphic design team goes to work incorporating images of me into their product line and promotional efforts. It takes a while for things to ramp up, but my face will become the focus of a major Aveda ad campaign in magazine print ads for *Elle* and *Vanity Fair*—and on Aveda packaging.[25]

Whenever I see boxes of Aveda products with my stark crewcut photo printed on them, my spirits soar. I really believe I am destined for something greater.

The only black clouds on the horizon are my broken heart, my anxiety, depression and very confused mind, and the coke habit that I am still fighting.

I make it a few weeks being clean—then I do coke again and get so high I'm up for five days. I even smoke pieces of plastic, thinking they are little white rocks instead of everyday household plastic. I freebase a lot and can't kick the habit. I can't get myself together in the morning after waiting tables and clubbing with friends till four or five o'clock in the morning.

I start having seizures again. I lose control prompted by soul-searching about what I am doing to my body. Flashbacks and thoughts of suicide hit me daily. I think I am lost. There are times when I vow to never, ever take drugs again, but my resolve crumbles in the face of others around me who offer me hits with ease. I have to change my circle of friends to healthier, non-addicted friends. I know I have to change my life, but how?

And then there is the matter of my sexuality, which is just as unpredictable. I am uncertain if I am attracted to girls or the

---

[25] I would see my picture everywhere on Aveda packaging for years and in magazines. I was never paid for being an Aveda model nor did I sign a release, yet it gave me more in how it lifted my spirits . . .

trauma. I have always liked boys until I was raped, coerced, and trafficked by Sabrina. I was purchased by couples when the partner or boyfriend wanted to watch me with their woman—as some sort of turn-on for him. Being exploited where voyeurism took place, along with how men abused me at an early age have caused me to develop a shaky identity and question whether I am gay, straight, or bisexual. I am totally lost.

I party at straight clubs and gay clubs in Vegas and don't lack attention when I saunter into either type of nightclub wearing a stunning outfit. I can feel more than a few heads spin in my direction whenever I make my entrance.

It is a mask I wear.

I still worry that I am an ugly nobody.

Drugs help give me a false sense of confidence, and clubs are where I socialize and do blow. I meet a woman from a wealthy European family, Charlene. She is a successful entrepreneur in Las Vegas, youthful looking but probably fifteen to twenty years older than I.

We embark on an affair. She tells me that I am person she is supposed to be with the rest of her life. I learn later that I am caught up in a love triangle. Charlene's girlfriend, Marie, hears about me. She is pissed. Marie is connected to the Mafia or some other crime gang—and psycho enough to put a hit out on me in a city where life is cheap. The Las Vegas newspapers are filled with stories of dead bodies turning up in the desert.

One evening, I am out on the dance floor with Charlene, having a good time in one of our favorite gay nightclubs. I am shaking my hips and moving my arms when out of nowhere, an Italian-looking man the size of a sumo wrestler comes out of the shadows and rushes me.

I don't see the fist that strikes me square on the mouth and face —the impact of his knuckles knocking out half of my front tooth and cracking another. A blast of pain overwhelms me as blood and other fluids gush onto the dance floor. I have never been punched with such violence before.

Shook to the core, I fall to the floor, where I writhe in pain and scream for help, creating a scene. I am rushed to the emergency room and patched up. A gay guy-friend connects me with an emergency dentist, who gives me a temporary crown.

Charlene calls me as I recuperate. She says she feels that I am not gay, adding that the more she has gotten to know me, the more she realizes I just need to be loved and that I am probably willing to do anything to receive that love. Stunned by her insight, I know she is right. Then she offers some advice: "If you don't leave Las Vegas, it's not gonna go well for you."

I listen and agree with her—the punch from the wise-guy is a warning shot. If I continue a relationship with Charlene, I could very well wind up in the desert, my lifeless body dumped into a shallow grave.

We decide to stop seeing each other while I figure out what to do next. I go underground. I still haven't completed cosmetology school, but I am very close to finishing and taking my state boards. I speak with Horst Rechelbacher, who has shown a genuine interest in me and someone I feel I can trust. There is nothing sexual between us; Horst is happily married with two children. He is kind to me.

"It's time for you to strike out on your own," he says. "You're blessed with a distinctive and beautiful face, and you're a special person. I would take my Nevada state boards, work a short time, and then move to Los Angeles. Then you can take your California boards and work in a salon and see what happens. Maybe you'll get discovered by Hollywood. I can give you our tear sheets and stills from our photoshoots. I'd also be willing to make a few phone calls for you."

Filled with conviction that it is time to leave Nevada, I thank Horst for his time.

The thought of doing hair and becoming an actress takes hold as I tread water in Nevada. I am working in a salon when another stylist introduces me to an older guy named David. He is friendly and asks me out for lunch at a Chinese restaurant.

I say yes, even though David has to be in his mid-to-late sixties with snowy white hair. Though I'm younger, we have one thing in common: we're both lonely. I've heard that sometimes older men and younger adult women find love. Age is just a number sometimes.

I enjoy David's company as we share spring rolls and servings of Kung Pao chicken and sweet and sour pork. I agree to more restaurant meals together since I know he is picking up the tab, but even more, he was interesting to talk to.

Widowed and without a wide network of friends, David is a sweet guy who has done well in the business world. He is the first person to talk to me about how to make money through investments. I am fascinated and seem to connect to his inner knowledge. David explains how compound interest works, what stocks are all about, and the importance of investing in blue-chip companies. "I bought into the Coca Cola Company, Pepsi, and Heinz years ago and have done very well by them," he says. "I let my money work for me."

I figure he is worth millions of dollars, especially after inviting me to his big, Mediterranean-style home—but I don't care about that. I am happy being around someone that kind. He is a beautiful man who *doesn't* want me for my body. Age has caught up with him in the bedroom. He could no longer perform because of ED troubles, so he doesn't try.

Our May-December relationship is simple: mostly we talk, listen, hold hands, go to the movies, and cook in his beautiful kitchen. Everything is quite normal in my mind. David likes to be held and cuddled, a desire that beats in the heart of any human. He also likes to watch me bathe, and so he sits beside the tub, and we talk. It feels peaceful.

Whenever we go out on the town, I know he will be escorting me into Las Vegas's nicest restaurants and top shows on the Strip. With an age difference of nearly fifty years, I imagine that the sight of a ruddy-looking Irish senior and a lighter-skinned Black person in her college years probably has the maître d' scratching his head. Maybe he figures he is seating a grandfather with a granddaughter who is a product of interracial marriage.

"Let them think what they want," he says after we settle into a leather booth at a fine-dining establishment. We both can tell that people around us are staring in our direction. While David never holds my hand or tries to kiss me in public, I know others feel awkward in our presence. I feel awkward sometimes, too— especially after he begins talking about marriage—but is it impossible?

Naturally, I am hesitant, but I don't want to say no—and I'm not sure what to do. *How could this work? What would married life be like? What would others say? Does he need me to take care of him only and not work on my dreams of becoming an actor or writer?*

David is helping me with tuition for cosmetology school and believe that if I plan out my future, I can do well at anything I try.

"You're smart, Brook. Just don't rush it. You'll get there."

But I know in my heart marriage won't work, given the broad age gap—and I'm too messed up—panic attacks—the trauma. What's more, I don't want to be stuck in Vegas. I plan to follow through on my plans to move to Los Angeles once I pass my cosmetology state certification exam.

I think about it; living a life with a kind person who only wanted what I did—to be loved. I am not sure how I feel, but I know I have to move forward. I am searching, reaching, and running from a troubled past and I need to find out who I am.

"I'm too young for you, in more ways than my age, and I don't know who I am yet," I tell him. "I'm not ready to be married, at least not yet. I need to see what it feels like to be free."

David gives me the saddest face. "So, what does that mean for us?" he asks.

I explain my desire and need to move to Los Angeles and he doesn't seem to want to move forward if it's not marriage. "Maybe I'll come back one day, but I have to do this," I say. "I don't want to lose you as a friend, but I won't make it if I don't go."

David has heard me cry day and night, has seen me shiver and go through panic attacks, but doesn't know everything that has happened to me. There is another issue at play. I have ducked and dodged and stayed away from Charlene, but now it is time to go. I want to be safe—not the kind of safe that others promise, but the kind where I am no longer afraid of my thoughts, my feelings, and my life in general.

"Then let me help you," he offers.

"No, I couldn't," I stammer. "I'm a big girl now."

"That is bravado talking", he says. "You don't have enough saved or transporation. Getting around L.A. won't be easy."

"I want to do this for you," David interjects. "Listen, I have plenty of money. It would give me great pleasure to give you a head start in life."

David pats my hand in the restaurant. "The first thing you need is a car. Why don't you say we go visit a dealership tomorrow?"

My heart skips a beat. Really? I couldn't believe this was happening, but it was.

David isn't interested in buying me a used car.

His smile beams as he leads me into the Jim Marsh Jeep dealership on Centennial Parkway. "Do any of these models look good to you?" His hand sweeps a showroom filled with various Jeep Cherokees, Wagoneers, and Wranglers, all shiny and new.

We take a test drive in a white Jeep Wrangler Laredo with brown and beige pinstripes that meet the "cool standard" for me. When we pull back into the dealer lot, David has one question for me: "Do you like it?"

I am afraid to say yes—but not too afraid. "Very much," I say.

"Then congratulations," he says, handing me the keys.

He generously offers to help me get into an apartment in L.A.

I find an unfurnished one-bedroom apartment in Studio City off Cahuenga Boulevard. When I sit down with the property manager, she asks for my credit history.

This presented a problem since I don't have any credit. I do have David backing me, but the property manager wants a lot more than just a first/last month's rent and a hefty security deposit.

"What about if I pay for the first six months in one lump sum, and then I begin paying rent again on the fourth month?" I ask. "Could I sign a lease then?"

The property manager, who has probably heard every story in the book, relents. "As soon as you give me a cashier's check, I'll let you sign the lease."

I call David and tell him what is happening. After he explains that he's sending a cashier's check, he tells me to open a new bank account so he can wire me the money. When I mention that the apartment comes unfurnished, he adds $10,000 to the transfer.

I tell David to come out and visit me anytime—that I am grateful for his gifts, for his kindness, and for him—for taking care of me. I realize suddenly that I am as lonely as him. David says he believes in me and would have been the right guy if he was the right age.

After hanging up, I drive to LAX to watch planes take off. It is breathtaking watching these beautiful airplanes lift into the blue sky over the blue Pacific. Questions fill my mind. *What will happen next? Can I survive?*

When I drive past Imperial Highway, I want to vomit when I see a young girl walking on the sidewalk. An innocent, young girl. No defenders. No King. No giants. No David. Just a little girl in a dress that barely covers her body—alone.

I grip the wheel—I squeeze my eyes shut and see myself and Denise—wandering—wondering—looking for a place to sleep.

A woman passes with red stilettos.

This must change. I want the voices to stop, the ones in my head that say:

No, you're not . . .

No, you won't . . .

No, you can't . . .

You never will matter to anyone.

I feel like the scum of the earth.

I keep moving.

I drive back to my new apartment. I resolve to do two things: find a job—and quit doing drugs.

Breathing Forward

I pull in air. I push air out. My chest rises. My chest falls. *Why am I suffocating?*

This is all too much. I am emotional. I am stressed. I count to ten—I am crying at number seven. I can't breathe. My thoughts are scattered. I am scared. But if I an just see the forest for the trees, as my father used to remind me, I can take each day and build from there.

The past does not leave me. Where is Denise? If I step out my door will Darnell and Tabitha be waiting outside with the car running. Darnell with a straight razor in his fist. "You are mine. I own you."

I think of suicide. I think of drugs. I think of escape.

But I have escaped. At least, part of me.

A new beginning. A brand-new start.

I must try. I will overcome.

I have never had my own place before. Settling into my Studio City apartment feels great. I lay down in the middle of my living room and hug myself. I laugh.

I have fun shopping for a sofa, a new bed, and a dresser—something I've never done before. Waving my finger like a magic wand, the new furniture arrives by truck. I buy a nice watercolor painting of flowers for my living room wall. I blow kisses to David. As soon as Pacific Bell installs my new phone, I call him and share my excitement—my eagerness—my joy.

As I take stock of where I am, I don't want to live a double life; being healthy and looking my best but still dealing with a broken heart, a pained mind, and a drug problem. I decide to do something about the latter by finding a nearby Alcoholic Anonymous chapter even though I am not an alcoholic. I discover that I prefer the AA meetings over Narcotics Anonymous (NA), and the folks who attend the Hollywood meetings seem interesting. I immediately embrace AA's twelve-step program to recovery.

Imbued with confidence from those who'd kicked some serious abuse habits, I try "white-knuckling" it—stop taking coke completely. Although there are times when I slip up, I eventually stop taking drugs. They call it a *spiritual experience* at AA.

I meet new and stimulating people, including actor and comedian Keenen Ivory Wayans, the host of *In Living Color*, a sketch comedy series on the Fox Network. When we go out to eat, we enjoy each other's company. He takes me to the set of *In Living Color*, where I meet actor Jim Carrey and a young dancer named Jennifer Lopez.[26] But Keenen is seeing someone else already. I don't want to interfere, so I ask if we could remain friends.[27]

I get a waitressing job at Hamburger Hamlet in nearby Sherman Oaks, a restaurant opened by actors Harry and Marilyn Lewis. Their comfort food menu is legendary: lobster bisque, crispy hash browns filled with sour cream, fried zucchini circles,

---

[26] Jennifer Lopez got her big break when she auditioned for *In Living Color* and was chosen to be one of the "Fly Girls" dancers. She performed on *In Living Color* for two years and then left to become a backup singer for Janet Jackson. Eventually, she segued into acting and singing and became a huge success.

[27] Keenen became a confidant for a while. When so many guys were trying to sleep with me—including famous producers and directors—I asked him advice on how to handle those situations. He told me to always say, "I'm in love with someone else." It was good advice.

and juicy hamburgers with blue cheese, horseradish, A1 steak sauce, red onions, and garlic fries. Since I am starting at the bottom, I am given the early morning breakfast shift.

Celebrities arrive in droves. Each time someone like Silvester Stallone, Cher, or Madonna waltz through the front door, a buzz goes through the restaurant—but everyone keeps their cool. There is an unwritten rule in force: *Don't bother them.* That rule is followed most of the time.

I approach a corner booth with a single customer: an older, good-looking guy with sweeping, collar-length sandy-blond hair and a soft, warm look on his face.

"You look nice today," he says, setting down the *Calendar* section of the *Los Angeles Times*. "You're new here, aren't you?"

"Yes, I am," I reply as I pour a coffee for him, nervous and socially awkward as usual. As I pour I accidentally spill a little coffee.

He notices. With a smile he says, "I've been coming here for years. What about you? Did you grow up here?"

"Yes, pretty much," I say, not wanting to bore him with my story.

"Well, it's lovely to meet you. What's your name?

"Brook."

"I'm Jon, and I'll have the usual this morning. Pancakes with extra butter and bacon—crispy bacon. And a small orange juice. The coffee is perfect," he says.

"Thank you, sir. I'll put it in."

"Call me Jon."

"Yes . . . Jon."

Back at the coffee station another server says, "You know who that guy is, don't you?"

I look over at the tall, mildly familiar customer, now back to perusing his newspaper. "Not really. Is he in the movies?" I loved watching films but I couldn't quite place him.

"Yeah, that's Jon Voight. He's a big star and always tips well. Ever seen *Coming Home* or *The Champ years ago?* He has many more movies now, but those two are classics."

"I saw *The Champ.*" I enjoyed the tear-jerker about an alcoholic ex-heavyweight boxing champion and single-parent dad who must return to the ring to provide for his eight-year-old son, played by scene-stealing Ricky Schroder.

I glance up at him sitting there reading his paper. I note his kind face.

That night, I peruse the aisles at Blockbuster for other films starring Jon Voight. When I find one with him on the jacket cover, I think, *Yup, that's Jon.*

The actor turned out to be a regular at Hamburger Hamlet. I notice that he makes eye contact when he walks in and generally takes the same booth in my section or sits at the counter. I find him to be genteel, cerebral, and inspiring.

We slowly and responsibly build a relationship—and he becomes my very first mentor. He never speaks in off-putting overtones or utters double entendres. He is like family, treating me with a rare respect in this bizarre La La Land. I can sense a bad guy like the garlic fries adorning every hamburger entrée we serve, but Jon has an uncanny ability to lift my self-esteem when I need to find equilibrium in my life. He gives me air when I need it the most.

When my breakfast shifts are over, I move on to my other job —hairstyling. After leaving Las Vegas and moving back to my home state, I take the California state board exam and continue working as an apprentice until I can get in enough training hours at a salon. It helps that Los Angeles is the epicenter of the beauty industry in the U.S., and Hollywood has always been a place where fashion trends are born, and beauty icons are made. Some of the most renowned hairstylists and salons are located within a ten-mile radius of my Studio City apartment.

One of those is Umberto's Beauty Salon on North Canon Drive in Beverly Hills, where Janet Zeitoun, a leading celebrity hairstylist to the stars, hires me as her personal assistant. Besides helping her out with her schedule, I also work as a "shampoo girl." My duties included setting up the shampooing area, applying color, washing hair, applying relaxers—a chemical treatment that makes curly hair straight—and so on.

I witness a steady stream of A-listers and wannabes enter Janet's salon, which is situated within Umberto's. Janet— beautiful, talented, and Black—did the hair for all the famous Black entertainers and lawyers, including her longtime clients Denzel Washington, Natalie Cole, and Janet Jackson. She also styled the hair of Janet's brother, Michael Jackson, but he is too famous to come to the studio on North Canon. She works on his curly locks at his house.

So, between slinging hash at Hamburger Hamlet and running my fingers through a lot of wet hair at Janet's salon, I have full days that help me feel like I am getting back on my feet. I also apply color and assist Steven Smith, another talented stylist there. I squeeze in workouts and jog on the beach, leaving me fit and muscular.

I know it will always be a good morning when Jon Voight walks into Hamburger Hamlet. Sometimes he has breakfast with another actor or a producer. But mostly he is alone with his copy of the *L.A. Times*.

One time, he asks me if I have any long-term goals or dreams.

"Yeah, I'd love to become a full-time actress and singer someday," I say cheerfully.

"That's wonderful to hear," he says as if I were the first person waiting on tables ever to tell him that. "You certainly have a special look you don't see every day. You're interesting to watch, observe. Have you done any acting before?"

I gulp. "Yes, I have performed in two plays in high school. One was a musical, which brought me great joy. I also played characters with my mother around the house as a little girl and loved doing accents.[28] It was one of our special times."

"That's nice to hear. Tell you what. Let me invite some friends in the industry to come over to my place in Benedict Canyon. We can have lunch or dinner and talk about it some more. Maybe you can sing too. How does that sound to you?"

The invitation excites me—but I am wary. Is this a ruse that could lead to something else? Or is this famous actor sincerely wanting to share what he knows about the acting world with someone who has a dream?

My gut says he can be trusted. He has never said anything suggestive to me and seems genuinely interested in my welfare. Maybe Jon recognizes something in me that I don't see in myself.[29]

"I'd like to do that very much," I say.

My heart is in deep thought as I tour his home before dinner. I am thinking of my own father. Jon shows me photos of his son

---

[28] My mother was good at accents too. One of my best childhood memories was when she made spaghetti with meatballs and spoke to my older brother and me with an Italian accent, which I thought was funny.

[29] Jon was the first man I'd ever met besides my dad who was a father figure and didn't want anything more than for me to succeed in life. He was also the first to let me see that men could be safe and trustworthy. Jon also encouraged me to make peace with my own father, who would eventually become my main confidant.

and daughter, James and Angelina, who are also in the business, and a library filled with books and history. It is amazing to see the rooms of his children, now adults, still there for them. I find the home to be comfortable and lonely at the same time.

I love Jon, whom I will call "Uncle Jon." I sing for his friends and eventually feel a little better, though thoughts of suicide are still present, as well as feelings of depression and anxiety. I am thankful for intense workouts at the gym, jogging on the beach, and healthy eating. I have equilibrium.

Over dinner with a half-dozen friends, Jon tells me a bit about his backstory, starting with being born and raised in Yonkers, New York, a blue-collar city that is a half-hour cab ride to Times Square. He had caught the acting bug while attending Catholic University in Washington, D.C., and signed up for drama school. Then, as an apple-cheeked twenty-two-year-old with long blond hair, he played the part of Rolf, the telegram-boy-turned-traitor in the Broadway production of *The Sound of Music*. Jon got his big break in Hollywood when he was cast alongside Dustin Hoffman in *Midnight Cowboy*. Both were nominated for Best Actor in the Oscars.[30]

Then he turns the discussion toward me. "If you're serious about becoming an actor," Jon says "you have to go to acting school."

I have talked to some of my new friends about acting schools —or schools of drama, as they are called. There are a lot of them in Los Angeles, some reputable and some not.

"What's a good one?" I ask.

"Tell you what. Let me make a call for you."

Jon is a man of his word.

---

[30] *Midnight Cowboy*, rated X because it depicted gay and straight sex scenes, won Best Picture that year, the first and only time an X-rated movie won that coveted award.

Raymond Barry, who heads up one of the most successful acting schools in L.A., phones me within a few days. I enroll in one of his evening programs in Santa Monica to learn about the physical, vocal, and psychological aspects of acting.

I am introduced to Method acting, a technique in which the actor aspires to fully inhabit the role of a character by using one's own life experiences as the seed of the creative imagination. I love it. Actors must recapture a *once in a lifetime* event from their past and use those deep feelings to rise to an explosive moment in a scene. One couldn't *recreate* emotion but had to *relive* it.

To cut expenses while I pursue acting, I move into a smaller, cheaper studio apartment in Hollywood not far from Runyan Canyon Park, one of the most popular hiking destinations in Los Angeles. I run up into the foothills and jog from the Santa Monica Pier to Venice to stay in top shape.

I don't make a lot of money, but I do have a small savings, a nice Jeep and wardrobe, so people can't seem to figure me out. If they only knew all of the trauma I push down daily, often crying myself to sleep. Other times, I hold my head between my knees in terror. There are also occasions when I am on the brink of killing myself.

This is this.

I pull in air. I push air out. My chest rises. My chest falls. *Why am I suffocating?*

After only eight months of taking acting classes—and learning that I am very good at memorizing lines—I am ready for the next step: auditioning for roles. I sign with longtime showbiz agency Don Buchwald Agency and I'm sent to casting calls. Auditioning, I learn, is almost a full-time job.

Something has to give. I know I can't work at Hamburger Hamlet or Umberto's and get ready for an audition at the same time. I need a nighttime job—and one that pays well.

I see only one option to support my dream: becoming a server at a well-known high-end restaurant or supper club where I can generate way more in tips than what I pocket from a breakfast shift. I am beating the bushes when I hear about a pair of offbeat French brothers, Frederic and Nicolas Meschin. They have opened a French restaurant and cabaret on Santa Monica Boulevard in West Hollywood known as Po Na Na Souk.

This isn't any run-of-the-mill restaurant. The food is excellent and brings out foodies from all over, making this nightclub unique. Don't ask me how the Meschin brothers do it, but Po Na Na Souk becomes a favorite of Hollywood royalty ranging from creative film executives to celebrities like Mick Jagger, Tom Waits, and yes, even Madonna again, who has a craving for *haute cuisine* while seated among friends and acquaintances in the entertainment industry.

I hit it off with Frederic Meschin, an eccentric Frenchmen, and get a job waiting tables. Suddenly, I am making very good money —a couple of hundred dollars a night in tips amid a raucous, feel-good atmosphere that includes live music from a small stage.

And there are rowdy times. The French chef in the kitchen will yell and throw things at the servers, and the chef and Frederic will regularly shout at each other in French. Not all of us know what they were saying but watching them wave their hands at each other is funny.

On the plus side, our family meals for the staff are a fun, exciting time to learn about the evening's menu while sipping a glass of wine from an exceptional vineyard. We also learn about the entertainment for that evening. Acts like the Gypsy Kings and Youssou N'Dour play at Po Na Na Souk, and I feel like I am part of an international crowd of fascinating music artists, actors, authors, and journalists.

Everything feels *Old World*. I am good at my job, and I love it.

A group of French-speaking guys are seated in my section. They look a few years older than me, so it is easy to connect with them. The fact that they are speaking French isn't unusual since the restauranteurs come from the Bordeaux region of France, but I can immediately tell that these lively guests like to joke around and have fun.

One of the guys is super friendly. We connect when our eyes—the windows to the soul—lock onto each other. The attraction is mutual and immediate. Before the evening is over, he introduces himself as Guy Laliberté and says he is French-Canadian. When I ask him how to pronounce his name, my request induces more laughter from his friends.[31] Then he asks for my phone number.

Guy doesn't wait long to call me—less than twelve hours. We become an item quickly and see each other as often we can on lunch dates, trips to the beach, and meals at some of L.A.'s trendy restaurants. Our times together are intense and a ton of fun. I fall in love with Guy quickly—and he with me—but I am terrified to commit my heart fully to him.

Nonetheless, our relationship grows strong, and we share serious conversations over extraordinary meals. I tell Guy about the bad stuff that happened to me, and he describes similar things that happened to him as a small boy growing up in Quebec City in the Canadian province of Quebec.

The story of why he was in Los Angeles fascinates me. It began when he was eighteen and ditched college to hitchhike

---

[31] It's pronounced *Gee Lah-lih-bear-tay*. French was Guy's mother tongue, but like many Canadians, he was bilingual.

across Europe and play traditional French-Canadian folk on his accordion for passing change in tourist plazas. He met other street performers who taught him the finer arts of pantomime, fire-breathing, juggling, and stilt-walking. A year of busking in European capital cities and cobblestoned towns strengthened his passion for street performing.

Guy eventually returned to Canada, restless and wondering what to do next. He joined a stilt-walking troupe called Les Echassiers de Baie-Saint-Paul[32] and began thinking about bringing together a bunch of different street-performing acts under a big tent—a "circus without animals," he told friends. Instead of three traditional rings with clever clowns, lions jumping through fire rings, and dancing elephants, Guy envisioned a captivating show with highly trained artists and acrobats who could entertain audiences with performances that incorporated dance, theater, and gymnastics.

While spending a winter in Hawaiian busking and beaching it under a tropical sun, Guy says he was inspired to call his nascent show "Cirque du Soleil" or "Circus of the Sun." When he returned to Canada, he assembled a troupe of street performers and convinced the Quebec government to give him funding to produce a show that would celebrate the 450th anniversary of Quebec.

The proof of concept was successful, and Cirque de Soleil performed exclusively in Canada for three years until Guy decided to take a considerable risk and bring the show to Los Angeles. He tells me about business lunches with promoters and potential investors who told him he was crazy to think that a circus without animals could work. But Guy would not be

---

[32] Baie-Saint-Paul, known for its art galleries and restaurants, is a town of 7,000 on the northern shore of the St. Lawrence River in the province of Quebec.

deterred. He convinced the L.A. Festival to let his troupe perform on the edge of Little Tokyo in downtown L.A. for several weeks.

"We gambled everything," Guy says. "If the critics didn't like us, we wouldn't have had enough money to put gas in the trucks to get home."

The gamble paid off when reviewers praised the one-ring extravaganza comprised of high-wire stunts, thrilling acrobatics, and hilarious clowns, packing the 1,700-seat tent nightly. The show was successful enough that Guy could mount a six-city U.S. tour that included pitching the blue-and-gold Cirque tent in the Santa Monica Pier parking lot. His new show was called *Nouvelle Experience*, or New Experience, and Guy fretted about every detail.

To cover his bases, Guy made the rounds at places like Po Na Na Souk to talk up the show among L.A.'s star-studded "beautiful people." It was all about generating a buzz. When *Nouvelle Experience* opened, the glowing praise from the *Los Angeles Times* theater critic Dan Sullivan caught everyone off guard.

"Cirque du Soleil obeys our prime command as a circus audience: Astonish me. It also obeys our hidden command: Scare me," Sullivan wrote. "There's a moment when a female high-wire artist seems out of control, sixty feet up in the air, and oh, God, you can't look. But you do."

The next day, a three-block lineup snaked outside the box office. Sellouts became routine during the run. Jane Fonda saw the show seven times. People were saying the kindest, most complimentary things to Guy—how unique the performances were, how the complete lack of dialogue made it possible to cross every language barrier in polyglot Los Angeles, and how he had reinvented the circus.

I am overwhelmed when I first see the show with Guy. We sit in the middle center, his favorite spot. We even go backstage and meet the actors and artists, mainly from Eastern Europe and Asia.

Nouvelle Experience takes my breath away, as does Guy, but for some reason, I know we weren't destined to be together. I sense that all the travel he does, the jealous girls around us, and the drinking and drugs many of his friends do would get to me. I am also still on a search to find myself.

But all that self-reckoning is in the future.

Guy's success led to discussions with Las Vegas casinos about bringing a Cirque du Soleil show to their venues. I accompany Guy to Vegas a few times, rolling up to a casino entrance in a black town car—treated like royalty as we check into another penthouse suite.

A surreal experience. Just a few years earlier, I was a trafficked victim who moved in the shadows. Now I am being introduced to casino general managers and treated deferentially, but each time I think, *I wonder if they recognize me. I'm dying inside and not sure how long I can keep wearing masks.* I look different with my extremely short blond hair, straight and almost-boyish smooth cut, but I still wonder.

As my relationship with Guy deepens, we talk about being together. I am in love with him, but I am having commitment issues. I am on the verge of a nervous breakdown. I can't handle everything that is happening.

We agree to meet before a Cirque du Soleil performance at the Santa Monica Pier. I stand him up—leaving him wondering where I am.

Our romantic relationship ends.[33] My heart is crushed, and I need help to figure things out—I don't want to be a burden to anyone or lose face as some crazy person.

I have started much-needed therapy, which is going well.

Now, if I can just breathe forward.

Breathe.

After a while, a photographer who'd come into Umberto's when I worked there happened to call me. He had liked my look back then and he asks me to be a cover model for *Be*, a monthly publication targeted to "today's black women."

---

[33] Within a year or two, Guy began living with Rizia Moreira, a Brazilian supermodel. They had three children but never married during the ten years they were together. Then Guy married Italian model Cladia Barilla, and they have two children. Guy sold 90 percent of his stake in Cirque du Soleil in 2015 and the remaining 10 percent share in 2020 and is reputed to have a net worth of $1.2 billion.

My acting career is gaining traction. I star in a commercial directed by Ridley Scott with one of my buddies at Po Na Na Souk, Djimon Hounsou, the doorman at the restaurant.[34] I also do several other TV commercials and star in my first feature film. I do some theatre.

As I go from one audition to another and meet different producers and film directors, I notice a lot of similarities between certain parties in Hollywood and human trafficking: I see young girls and teen boys, I see drugs, I see money, and I see dirty men who only think about one thing. There is a system in the back shadows of Hollywood that needs the young, fresh, and new to satisfy the weirdoes, and plenty of drugs to get people to do things they usually won't want to do.

I see the underbelly of Hollywood. While there are also amazing times that have me pinching myself, I also realize that *crazy* is everywhere. If things are going to be different, it has to be on me.

Keenan Ivory Wayans invites me to the Beverly Hills home of Denzel Washington for a dinner party. The estate takes my breath away: a large circular driveway leading to a 29,000-square-foot home with eight bedrooms and fourteen bathrooms. The backyard is filled with lush gardens, gazebos, an Olympic-sized pool, and a tennis court. Eddie Murphy and Sylvester Stallone are neighbors.

Denzel and his wife, Paulette, are a delight as they greet us. We're led to a room filled with historical artifacts from America's darkest period—the years of chattel slavery of Africans beginning in Portugal and leading up to the Civil War in the first half of the 19th century with the kidnapping of Africans from the 17th and 18th century. There are iron ankle rings with three-inch radiating spikes, a neck collar with a ten-foot chain, and manacles of iron

---

[34] Djimon Hounsou would go on to become a huge success in Hollywood, including several films in the Marvel film franchise and *Same Kind of Different as Me.*

for the wrists. There are branding irons, a braided leather grip, and what looks like iron instruments of torture. Most striking is a wooden bench, well-worn and a bit warped, against a wall in the room.

"Slaves sat on this very bench, awaiting the moment of sale on the auction block," Denzel tells us.

Listening as a Black American, I am moved to tears. Denzel's passion and telling of the truth of Black world and American history takes me aback. While my mind races at how I have arrived at this moment, I feel a shadow of identity and complete sadness. My identity has come from my trauma during my upbringing, but part of it started long before I was born.[35]

I move closer and touch the wood that has to be 150 years old. I think about all the deeply traumatized souls that sat on this board, pondering their fate—their loss.

And then an epiphany: I see myself on the bench, realizing for the first time that I was enslaved and still am in bondage. I harbor hate for those who hurt me: Sabrina, Darnell, and Tabitha and their enslavement—enslavement that chains me to this day— *forced* to do awful things against my will, heart, and understanding. Knots, ties, and chains.

I am getting longer looks from various casting calls. One sounds right for me in the worst, triggering way. The audition is for someone who can play an attempted rape and kidnapping victim in the movie *The Silencer*, directed by Amy Goldstein. I grit my teeth and get the part—and my first feature film credit.

---

[35] I have since had DNA testing for my ancestry and learned that I'm 40 percent European from England, Ireland, Belgium, German, Norway, Sweden, Czechoslovakian (Jewish roots), Portugal, and Spain, and 60 percent African from all over Ghana, Mali, North Africa, Ivory Coast, Nigeria, Benin, and the Congo.

But I choose to step back from auditions after that. For the next couple of years, I attend an acting school with Black actors Wendy Davis, Hill Harper, and Taraji P. Henson in a special group on the Warner Bros. lot taught by actress Eleva Singleton. Then I land guest-starring roles in several episodic TV series, including a reoccurring role for a Fox production shot in Mexico City for a year called *Crystal Empire*.

I feel like I am getting somewhere, making contacts, getting call-backs, and meeting interesting people who promise me the world—if I can keep my place in line. I am no longer an aspiring actor—I am one. I just haven't gotten my breakout role yet, but I am booking all the time. But here's the funny thing: even though I am experiencing some measure of "success," I am falling deeper into depression and anxiety, except when I am working. Only then can I forget. When I Method act, I transform my pain into the role I am playing.

Any rejection, though, is hard on my psyche. There is also the casting couch to contend with.

I am invited to parties, and big-name producers come up behind me and whisper, "Do you want to fuck?" I receive phone calls at midnight from producers wondering if I am interested in doing a *reading* right then—at his place of residence, of course.

I lack the savvy tongue or quick response to handle them. All I was taught was to say yes, but I don't. I never learned to say no, so it doesn't come out very well whenever I say it. I am told I seem aloof, distant, and nervous. I am. If *nervous* is the right word.

I am invited to the home of famous producer Robert Evans to discuss a specific part in his new film. I wonder if it's a good idea, but he is a well-known celebrity from old Hollywood, so I can't imagine him doing something seedy or inappropriate.

Relationships are how things happen in Hollywood: people who know people. To meet and work with the great *Robert Evans* —maybe this could be my breakout role.

I drive to his big mansion in Beverly Hills. I am let in by someone who leads me down a long hallway. A door is partly open, and I step into an oversized bedroom with an enormous bed with an equally enormous bed-frame that goes up the wall. The walls are dark, and the bedding is red velvet. The red satin sheets have been turned down.

Bob is sitting up with his head resting against the headboard, under the covers. He is dressed in a silk robe that Hugh Hefner might have worn at the Playboy Mansion.

"I'm glad you're here to discuss my new film project and you're as pretty as your photos and audition tapes," he says.

I know immediately why he summoned me here—and it isn't to read for him or discuss the film. I start shaking—a panic attack grips me.

"No, no, no . . . ."

I run out of the bedroom, breathing hard—counting to ten as my therapist has instructed.

I don't look back.

I run. I get away.

I wonder if I am running from my past. Or my future.

Wings Over the Sea

Frightening incidents—like what happened to me at Robert Evans' mansion—are all too common with other male producers, directors, and production managers in Hollywood.

Part of my shock prompts questions: *Is this how life will be? Is this what women and girls or even boys have to endure to succeed in Hollywood? Or is this just me?*

I have already stopped wearing stilettos and heeled pumps because I am afraid of my body and sexuality. I want to be pretty, but whenever a male producer or movie executive comes on to me by entering my personal space without permission, I know I have to respond with a *yes* or lose that role that they are the door to. I am being pushed down into a dark hole and I can't play along—if I give in, I become just another Black girl in America looking up from the bottom scratching my way to my dreams. Lose, lose.

I honestly don't understand how my dream of acting—something I thought would be far from the hell I once lived in—doesn't offer safe harbor from some of the same characteristics of my past exploitation. When I learn there are men in the entertainment industry who share these attributes, my heart breaks again. Don't these male leaders in the film world know how powerful they are and that their position of influence can be used to build others up? Instead, some of them manipulate lives, rule, use, destroy.

I am barely holding on. I know how to work on my craft and memorize my lines with ease, but when it comes to how I feel most of the time, I am dealing with what my therapist diagnoses, and what we both know: PTSD, depression, anxiety—mental health challenges. I am struggling to think clearly about my life and past. The voices of anger in my head don't stop. I lose the ability to focus. I am lost in the shuffle of my own life and I do everything I can to avoid facing my past. I know, however, I need to uncover my past to discover my future. What am I to do? How am I to make it in this world?

Did I even want to anymore?

I clearly understand that there are ugly tragedies I can never share. The mere grotesqueness of what I witnessed sends chills down my spine. The sadness is asking how to cut away the dark memories of who I was. I wonder if I would ever truly enjoy lovemaking without the flashbacks of each buyer who purchased me.

I think I am a survivor, but then I suddenly realize I will be a victim—a victim until I believe and internalize that what happened to me was *not* my fault. I keep thinking there has to be many more actors and children caught in the same vise. How can I forgive? And if I do, can I forget enough to live an everyday life? Can I help others?

Fortunately, there are two people in Hollywood I can talk to. People I can trust implicitly: Jon Voight, my dear friend, and Donna Kinsler, who works at a movie studio production company and has become a big sister to me. I cherish these wonderful people who have my best interests at heart.

One day, Uncle Jon asks me to accompany him to a friend's house.

"Who's the actor?" I ask. "Or the producer?"

Uncle Jon smiles. "Let that be my surprise. It's a low-key affair, not too many guests."

We don't drive to Beverly Hills, Bel Air, or the Hollywood Hills this time but to the coast. Uncle Jon steers us onto Pacific Coast Highway through Malibu. I have the window down so I could stare out at the frothy, wind-whipped ocean the entire way. The wide, blue sea.

A steady breeze is blowing, softly brushing over my skin and through my hair. The cool draft feels like what I imagine could be wafting of air from mighty wings—like an army of angels soaring through the sky on my behalf, presenting me with a rare moment when I know something good will come from all the hurt.

Lost in the moment, I forget where I am. I disappear deep into my mind. The timing is perfect. No longer am I stuck down in a dark dungeon, under a trap door without a key to escape. Instead, I am free to experience pure joy in the middle of a raging storm. Forgetting about the constant pressure to be someone I don't know how to be, the weight of three hundred pound chains wrapped across my heart breaks and falls to the ground.

The angels turn to tiny specks of light on the horizon. The blue sea is fading to indigo. A mist of stars winking to life over the water makes me smile.

Turning from the freeing sight, we swing into a gorgeous neighborhood with custom contemporary homes perched on an outcropping reaching out into the Pacific. All the massive houses have postcard ocean views. This is prime real estate.

"Where are we?" I ask Uncle Jon.

"Point Dume."

We pull into a long, circular driveway and motor to the front of a stately two-story home, stylish and larger than life. I wonder who was living on the other side of the imposing front entry. A uniformed valet is waiting for us. *This get-together isn't as low-key as Jon suggested*, I think.

Uncle Jon rings the doorbell, and my knees weaken when Whoopi Goldberg flashes a warm smile and locks eyes with me.

"Hi, Brook," she says. "Jon told me about you. Welcome. Come on in."

Whoopi Goldberg knows my name? Feeling light-headed, I extend my hand for a handshake, but Whoopi will have none of it. The celebrity actress and comedienne opens her arms for an warm embrace. She guides me into the main salon, which is as big as my entire apartment. Feeling her hand intertwined with mine, I think what is happening has to be a miracle—that I have died and on my way to heaven—or maybe riding the backs of angels rushing out over the sea.

I spot all sorts of famous people milling about holding the yummiest small plates of food or champagne flutes. Some are perched on floral print couches, engaged in conversation with the white-capped Pacific Ocean beckoning from beyond the wall-to-ceiling windows.

"Relax and sit down," she says.

I don't see anywhere to sit. Shaken, I plop myself on the beautiful hardwood floor.

Whoopi chuckles. "No, not there, Brook," she says, extending a hand to help me up. "Tell you what. Let me show you around the house."

She leads me through her beautiful home, pointing toward the artwork on the walls. From her master bedroom, I stand on the balcony and look down as a series of Pacific swells crashes against the rocks—the sun dropping toward the horizon. I can't imagine what it would be like to wake up to this gorgeous seaside tableau every morning.

I also realize that very few Black actresses make it this far. I am in the presence of great talent. Unfortunately, I am so confused about who I am that I'm embarrassed to be here. Even though this intimate gathering of Whoopi's friends isn't an audition, at least not for a role, I don't do well meeting anyone new in a personal way—especially a global celebrity like Whoopi Goldberg. I feel like a rabbit peaking out of the ground to see what's around—and I scurry back down the hole if anyone is about. For me, it is easier to remain hidden in the shadows.

I do my best to deflect any conversation about me. I relax when Whoopi and I talk about her daughter Alex, born during her first marriage to Alvin Martin. After their divorce, Whoopi says she was a single-parent mom who hadn't yet made her big breakthrough in *The Color Purple*. She and her daughter slept in the same bed in studio apartments and barely got by while she was building her career. What strikes me about our intimate conversation is how kind and loving Whoopi is to me—a total stranger. Maybe she sees something in me that reminds her of her daughter or herself.

When Uncle Jon and I leave, several thoughts consume me: *Could my mother ever love me like that—or could I tell if she did?* I believe she wanted to, and maybe she didn't know how to do that for reasons I am not clear on. Can I experience the same type of breakthrough that Whoopi did? Is it possible to build a life from a dream? A life from a nightmare?

I think it is possible. Compared to the thousands of would-be actors living in Los Angeles, I am fashioning a budding career in Hollywood: guest-star spots in TV series like *JAG, Dangerous Curves,* and others; supporting roles in films like *Strange Days* and *Cover*; and a slew of prime-time commercials including McDonald's, Coca-Cola, Starburst candy, Honda cars.

Even though the right people say promising things about my work, I am not sure if I have the emotional stamina to deal with the pressure from the triggers I still experience. One shaky step, one bad smear, one busted relationship with a producer or director, and my acting career could be hurt by a Hollywood slice. This incident will later give me insight into the stories of Mira Sorvino, Ashley Judd, and other actresses following the revelations regarding Hollywood producer Harvey Weinstein and the *Me Too* movement started by Tarana Burke. I'm not speaking about young women who might have dated these men in hopes of a job, but those who'd been exploited, assaulted, harassed, raped, or blackballed because they said no.

Then a crack in the ceiling: I am up for a leading character for a prime-time TV series that would be shopped to one of the four major networks. There are auditions and callbacks. Meetings with the director and producers. One of the producers takes me on a tour of the Warner Bros. studio lot and told me flat-out, "You're the one."

What the producer says that day echoes what Reuben Cannon, the first Black casting director in Hollywood, had remarked to me weeks earlier. Reuben had cast Whoopi Goldberg *and* Oprah Winfrey in *The Color Purple*, one of my Top 20 favorite films of all time and winner of the Oscar for Best Picture.

During a visit to Mr. Cannon's office, he takes out a typed piece of paper from his desk.

"Here's a list of fifteen Black actresses that we think are destined for greatness." He presents me with the sheet.

I see names like Angela Bassett, Taraji P. Henson, Halle Berry —and mine!

Once again, my knees buckle.

So, this is where my life is going, I think. I should be ecstatic, and part of me is, but I have a problem: I am so emotionally jacked up that I feel awkward in my skin, except when acting on the set. But when I am not working, I am still working. The real auditions in life are all about relationships, meetings, and folks getting to know you. I have to talk to important people, to important strangers, and I am afraid they will see me for who I really am—a nothing, an unloved, unwanted bad seed.

I am still broken, hurting from years of being trafficked, and still a mess in disguise. I wonder if I am worthy of becoming a famous successful artist. When someone starts asking me personal questions about my life or my past, I turn nervous and aloof, act awkward and odd, and make everyone around me uncomfortable.

Sure, I can put on airs for a while—I am an actress, remember —but I crumble emotionally whenever questions of a personal nature are directed toward me. Thoughts of suicide rumble through my mind all the time. I feel like I am dying inside.

Why is this happening? I am not sure. I think I can push the profound pain in my heart deep down, but I am wrong. I have become a young lady who doesn't know her identity. I don't know who I am supposed to be. I don't know where I am going in life.

I think of the lit wings of angels over the ocean. I long to know where they land.

Since I settled in Los Angeles, I constantly explore my existence as an individual. The fundamental questions about life and who I am pop up when I have time to think—like when I am driving around L.A., stuck in another traffic jam. I tell myself that whatever is happening to me is part of the journey, that this, too, "shall pass," which is only true if I deal with issues head-on.

As I think about my predicament, another round of self-introspection prompts these questions:

What is the meaning of life?

What is my purpose?

Why do I exist?

And why does God allow such evil against so many?

These are undoubtedly well-worn spiritual and psychological questions. There is a spiritual hole in my heart. Something is missing. Instinctively, I know that landing a hundred breakout roles won't fill that void, and I don't think God can either. I don't know if I would be able to possess *faith*.

Besides counseling, which is a place to partially reveal my heart, I still lack trust. I decide to find some answers by visiting various churches and faith communities. I am invited to a Buddhist temple, where I find out that I like turning off the world by closing my eyes, slowing down my breathing, and remaining calm while I meditate on "emptiness" to "clear" my brain. Even though I find some measure of bliss, something is still missing for me.

After meditating one time, a fellow actor approaches me. "I shakubukued you," he says, turning the Japanese noun *shakubuku* into an English verb.[36]

By then, I had done enough studying of Buddhism to know that *shakubuku* was a technique of evangelism in which this individual—through the power of his mind—was attempting to mentally suppress any erroneous views I have about Buddhism to awaken me to the truth of Buddhist philosophy.

Hearing him say that he had shakubukued me makes me feel uneasy. Can he see into my heart as well? Does he know I am having doubts? That I harbor thoughts of killing myself? Because as much I like closing my eyes, slowing down my breathing, and meditating to reach a mental state of calmness, concentration, and inner joy, Buddhism isn't working for me.

I expand my search to find God. A screenwriter friend invites me to a meeting of those following the Baha'i faith, which is spreading through Hollywood like a brush fire in Topanga Canyon. I soon understand why the Baha'i faith appeals to so many searchers: a fundamental belief of Baha'i is that all peoples and religions, including Christianity, will one day unite into one faith—the Baha'i religion.

---

[36] *Shakubuku* is pronounced shah-koo-boo-koo. Japanese: "break and subdue," in which the resistance of the other person is destroyed by forceful argument.

While I warm to the Baha'i speaker's message of peace, love, and positive virtues, this "inclusive" religion feels like Islam. I do some research and discover that Baha'i originated in Persia (Iran) in 1844. Those in the Baha'i faith see Islam as the parent religion of their faith in the same way Judaism gave birth to Christianity.

Through my meditation practice and prayer, I hope I will find the one religion, one faith, or one way of life for me. I am not sure Baha'i is it. Since I have embarked on a very personal journey, I need the teaching and tenets of the faith to feel right.

Another religion popular in the entertainment industry is the Church of Scientology, thanks to a pair of Hollywood's biggest stars and proponents, Tom Cruise and John Travolta.[37] Several actors ask me to join them at the Scientology headquarters on Sunset Boulevard in Hollywood.

When I enter a crowded room one afternoon, the vibe is palatable and kinda weird. Some pastor-type guy begins delivering a sermon with the reading of the Creed of the Church of Scientology that sounds generic enough . . . *We believe that all men have inalienable rights to their own lives . . . We believe the laws of God forbid man from destroying his own kind . . . .*

The pastor quotes Christ as well, but the more he drones on, the more I feel like I am part of a hard-core indoctrination due to what I've been through before in the trafficking world. Seeing the same indicators give me an uneasy feeling, which frightens me.

I turn to one of my actor friends, a woman. "Excuse me," I say.

I gather my purse and find the powder room, feeling like I can't breathe. When I look at my wan face in the mirror, I know I can't return. I leave the Scientology building and find my Jeep. As soon as I get behind the wheel, I start hyperventilating.

---

[37] Scientology was founded by the late science fiction writer L. Ron Hubbard in the 1950s, who believed that a galactic overlord named Xenu expelled humans to Earth from another planet ages ago, and now their spirits live in everyone. Adherents were urged to seek spiritual fulfillment by "going clear."

I tell Uncle Jon what happened over the next lunch we share. He understands why I have embarked on a spiritual search—to find a higher meaning to life and make sense out of a crazy, chaotic world. Uncle Jon had told me one time he was on a spiritual pilgrimage as well, saying that he was studying Judaism even though he wasn't Jewish and was raised Catholic. His interest in the Jewish faith stemmed from his youthful exposure to an affluent Jewish country club in Scarsdale, New York, where his father, Elmer Voight, worked as the golf pro.

"Since you're on a search and checking out so many faiths, you should check out Self-Realization Fellowship because it's nondenominational. They're open to all religions. Maybe you'll discover something there," he said.

Uncle Jon is referring to the Self-Realization Fellowship Lake Shrine, also on Sunset Boulevard, but a good fifteen miles west in Pacific Palisades and a few blocks from the ocean. "I'll take you there," he offers.

The first time we visit Self-Realization Fellowship, I like what I see. The guru leading the Sunday service says the wisdom of the ages is metaphysical in its recognition of consciousness as the spiritual force behind all physical forms. He teaches that we are all fellow travelers on a spiritual path that should lead to self-initiated realizations free of ego-based masters and dogmatic religious doctrine—that we should be contemplative in approach via feelings beyond thought, emotion, and physical sensation.

He quotes Mahatma Gandhi, saying, "Happiness is when what you think, what you say, and what you do are in harmony." Then the guru opens a Bible and reads from the prophet Isaiah 40:31 in the Old Testament: "But those who wait on the Lord shall renew their strength; they shall mount up with wings like eagles." He also quotes from the New Testament scriptures.

Hearing him teach in this ecumenical way is for me like beginning to live for the first time. I felt I have been set on the right path—a narrow and straight one that will lead me to a place of sanity. At this moment, I need to know that my life can matter and that love is a real thing that I can grow to understand and believe in.

This is deep stuff. When the service is over, Uncle Jon takes me to the bookstore, where he buys me a copy of *Autobiography of a Yogi*, authored by the founder of Self-Realization Fellowship, Paramahansa Yogananda.

"Thank you so much," I smile. Then the speaker that morning walks by. I stop him and ask a question burning in my heart—a question pertinent to *my* life.

"I have to ask you something, and I'm looking for guidance here," I tell the SRF leader. "Is sex before marriage wrong?"

The SRF leader clears his throat, no doubt to give himself a moment to think. "It's not going to doom you to something eternally negative, but there are higher paths than that one can take that lead to commitment and peace. I urge you to seek the higher path."

I think that is a pretty good response and tell him so.

I become a regular at SRF and read the *Autobiography of a Yogi* from cover to cover. I not only love the book, but I find the life of Paramahansa to be special. The way he speaks of the Lord keeps Him before me, making me even more curious. Paramahansa shares how to believe in something, even when it isn't there yet . . . that faith makes it so. He quotes from Hebrews 11:1-6, which says that faith is what we hope for and assurance for what we do not see. Can it be true? Can belief help me overcome my lack of value? Help me to become what I am meant to become?

From my reading, I see that self-realization is a quest for freedom from worldly attachments and external coercion from the culture around us. I am taught that if I can get quiet and center myself, I can become one in body, mind, and soul.

Whenever I walk through the SRF garden, sit down on a bench in a meditation atrium, or stand next to a flower bed and contemplate my existence, I feel that God meets me and is drawing me closer. A sense of calm pervades as I focus on freeing myself from the trappings of the world and prepare my mind and my emotions to recognize self-realization when it occurs.

It is all about raising my consciousness that there is something greater out there than anything I can possibly imagine. More things than are dreamt of. . .

During this time of spiritual searching, I also seek to reconnect with my parents. My father, Norman Parker, has never left Los Angeles. We have spoken on the phone, but now it is time to see him.

Not only does he welcome me into his life, but we begin building a solid relationship where we like each other and each other's company. He proves to be an excellent sounding board, even allowing me to yell, fight, and express my hurt from him not being there for me. When he explains his side in his deep vibrato, my heart feels at peace. I understand as much as I can and love him for trying. I am glad my father opens his giant heart to me.

My mother and I also resume speaking to each other. Momma is still living in Las Vegas, so I visit her and Ricky and Stanton, my older and younger brothers. Connecting with my immediate family gladdens me, and I also spend time with my half-brother and sisters when I can.

When I call Momma to check on her, it always feels good to hear her voice, which has softened in tone sometimes, but there is still an uneasiness, too many occasions when her words have a bite and I feel Momma doesn't like me very much. But that doesn't stop her from bragging about my acting roles after seeing me in a McDonald's TV commercial or a guest role in a network TV series.

I believe Momma is proud of me for moving forward to make something out of my life. She still doesn't know about the rape when I was eleven—or the trafficking. She doesn't touch or hug me or let me speak whenever I visit—but sometimes I grab her anyway and even manage to get a word in. She keeps her arms down— but it never stops me from hugging her.

Nonetheless, I always feel weak in her presence, but there is nothing more I can do. I just have to wait and love. Her lack of acceptance cripple me, however. I was never sure of myself. I knew I had to break free from the fear of rejection because anytime someone looked at me in a way I didn't understand or didn't like, I was crushed.

Despite my mother's lack of displayed love, I am moved to embrace her because I have recently read *Awaken the Giant Within* by Tony Robbins, who teaches that the power of love is when you give it freely and don't let anyone control your love. The book also teaches about creating a value system for one's life —ten levels that I will begin to live by and refine as time moves on.[38]

I continue my quest to explore spirituality in a compelling way that appeals to my sensibilities. As part of my effort to better myself, I enroll in a six-month meditation program at the Self-Realization Fellowship in Pacific Palisades, where I make friends

---

[38] I gave my younger brother Stanton a copy of *Awaken the Giant Within*, which he loved and credits with beginning his journey as a successful chef.

with similarly minded people. When I hear the SRF leader say that meditation, brought to bear the power of the conscious mind and how the conscious and unconscious minds could come together in harmony, I become a devoted acolyte.

The leader also encourages the reading of cards about the art of forgiveness, patience, service, attention, and intention. I remember studying the following Scripture, which was derived from Matthew 6:22 (KJV): "If therefore thine eye be single, thy whole body is full of light." This got me thinking about the depth of some of the religions I am investigating, which are often seen in the Torah and the Old and New Testaments—and they were there first.

I learn from SRF that when thoughts and feelings came into my consciousness, like the times when I was exploited and controlled, it is up to me to choose to empower the positive ones and release the negative ones. The goal for me is the creation of a higher consciousness. This will be where my search for answers will reach fruition, but I still need to learn how to release the horrible memories of those times with Sabrina, Darnell, and Tabitha.

I find that it is easier said than done in practice. Those horrific times can be drudged up at any time. And all too often, my thoughts go to dark places in my past. How can I discover happiness if happiness comes from what I thought about throughout the day and night? I start reading and meditating for ten minutes in the morning and ten minutes at night, which soon grows to forty-five minutes to an hour each morning and evening.

It isn't easy sitting still in the beginning, but I get better as I learn to *disappear.* I focus on lessons from Paramahansa, scriptures from the Book of Psalms, and the words of Christ (Yeshua) in the Gospels because I have purchased a Bible at SRF, which I can't put down. I even have a small, sketched image with His name.

For some reason, I feel drawn to Him because of His push to seek justice for those who need it most, which is everyone— and certainly me. I appreciate His ability to push with love against those who hated Him. I also lean into wisdom, described as *she,* in the Book of Proverbs. I often ask for insight and understanding when my mind races with anxiety.

But the wind isn't under my wings. Sometimes it feels like a headwind pressing against my chest—pressing me to the ground.

I will ground. I will look skyward. I will fly.

Three months into my half-year course on meditation, I am working out at Bally's Gym in Hollywood. In a business where *how* you look is as important as who you are or what you say, I am willing to put in the hard yards to stay in top physical shape. I also like how strenuous bouts of exercise balance my mind. I float in an energetic bliss during workouts and for at least three hours afterward.

I also belong to Easton's gym in Hollywood. With my athletic background from running hurdles, the clomping sound of my Nikes on the treadmill is better than any cocaine or drug I ever had.

Running hurdles back in the day was like running over my fears, even when I fell and scraped my knees in practice. It was always easy to get back up because I knew the payoff. Sports have an order and structure that give me wins by following strategic plans that are always clear to understand. After competing in track and field and playing baseball, basketball, and volleyball, the gym is a happy place for me, just like those times when I am in the ocean off San Clemente, riding cleansing waves on my boogie board and spreading a towel to lay out on the warm sand.

Both gyms are filled with actors with the same goals—to look our best in person and on the screen. One morning, Rudy McCoy and I strike up a friendly conversation. Rudy, a good-looking guy, is an aspiring Black actor and singer.

I don't feel like Rudy is on the make. We remain friendly the next few times we run into each at Bally's. After one workout, we order protein smoothies at the club and sit down to chat. He is totally friendly and seems like the brotherly type.

During a lull in our conversation, he asks me an unusual question, at least among actors: "Do you go to church?"

I am not sure how to answer. "I go to SRF," I reply.

"SRF? What's that?"

"It stands for Self-Realization Fellowship. There's an SRF in Pacific Palisades, right by Malibu."

"What do you do there?"

"I meditate, read, pray, and pass through a vegetarian buffet afterward or go have fried fish at Gladstones. I really love it."

Rudy's eyes light up. "Do you ride your motorcycle to this fellowship? Because I saw you pull up on a Honda Rebel. Cool bike. Looks like a little Harley."

"You saw me ride up?"

"Yeah. Love the saddlebags too."

"Thank you."

Then Rudy turns serious. "That's awesome hearing that you're pursuing God. You should come to my church with me sometime. It's uplifting as well. Have you ever been to a church-church?"

"A little bit. We went to the West Angeles Church of God on Christmas and Easter when I was a kid. It was the same church my mom's side of the family attended."

"Then I think you'll like Bible Enrichment Fellowship Church in Inglewood. Pastor Bam Crawford heads it."

I don't think I hear him right. "Who's Pastor Bam?"

"Dr. Beverly Crawford, but everyone calls her Pastor Bam because of how she teaches—bam, bam, bam. She's famous for saying, 'Good, better, best—never let it rest till your good gets better and your better gets best.' She's a brilliant teacher, and we definitely dig into the Word."

I smiles. No actor has asked me to go to a church like this before, so his request touches me. But going to a "Bible Enrichment" gathering feels out of my comfort zone. Although I have good memories of going to church on Christmas and Easter when I was six and seven years old—and witnessing the beautiful choir in their burgundy robes, the loads of friendly faces in hope, the shouts of "Amen!" and "That's right!" from the congregation —the experience was so long ago that it doesn't seem real. I have found something at SRF, and I don't want to get thrown off the horse.

"I'm good," I declare. "Thanks a lot, though."

Rudy accepted the rebuff with a smile. "That's fine," he says.

But that doesn't stop him from asking again. The next time Rudy and I chat, he tells me he is one of the "worship leaders" at Bible Enrichment.

I have no idea what he is talking about.

"I'm part of the team that leads us in worship and song before Pastor Bam teaches a sermon," he explains. "The worship songs are fantastic. You really should come to check us out."

"Maybe I will," I heard myself say. "Maybe I will."

Becoming

A few nights after Rudy asks me to go to church with him, I am in my apartment stir-frying a mixture of shrimp, tofu, and veggies in my new wok. After plating my delicious meal, I dig in with chopsticks and enjoy every morsel. When I finish eating, I place a pot of green tea on the stove. I've been collecting various teas, bulk herbs, and adaptogens for several months to make health tonics to cleanse my body. The scientist in me likes discovering new and exotic blends.

With a cup of pungent Ashwagandha tea in my hand, I decide to meditate on the floor near my bed. I have closed my eyes and I'm trying to clear my mind when suddenly I feel a cool, water-like sensation flow over my body. Surprised by the coolness, my mind flashes when a strong, loving presence fills the room.

I begin to cry. I can't stop weeping as I beat my breast. I know who has come down to touch me—God, the Holy Spirit, Jesus . . . Yeshua . . . the Messiah. It is confusing. It is real.

"I believe it's you, Heavenly Father. I believe it's you."

My spirit soars as I look to the heavens. I cry out to the God of the Universe—at that moment, at that time. My lips form words as I start singing, but I have never sung these words before. Still, I worship and I continue to sing to my Creator, who I suddenly realize loves me with a deep, incredible love that I can't wholly fathom.

Since He is speaking and listening and I am hearing, I become aware of the bad things that happened to me—darkness is still on the attack. But if I can discover God's purpose hidden within me, then I can grow beyond it and maybe come to discover why such horrible things are allowed in a world with so many complexities.

I have lived with a fearful, foreboding presence for many years. But in in this single moment, I know God loves me and wants me to be on the other side of pain and grow as a person. I believe for the first time that I can become who and what I am meant to be.

Then I hear a whisper: *Go to that church. Go.*

The following Sunday morning, I find myself in Inglewood, several miles away from where I grew up and attended elementary school near Baldwin Hills. Pastor Bam's church, Bible Enrichment Fellowship, is a fortress-like one-story building that used to house the city's utility company. It doesn't look like a church.

The service has started when I walk into the foyer. A dozen or so people are bunched up at the entrance, waiting to enter. I move in closer and ask someone why we are all waiting to walk into the sanctuary.

"Because they're praying," he says.

I strain for a look inside. The place is packed. And that's when I hear the singing . . . the same singing I heard when I was in my bedroom. I get goosebumps again.

"What are they praying?" I ask the man.

"They're praying in the Spirit in song," he replies.

Eventually, we take our seats as the service continues. Pastor Bam isn't there that morning; her associate, Pastor Gerald Lee, is in the pulpit. I can't keep my eyes off him as he talks about the bound being set free and the despaired receiving hope when they turned their lives to the Messiah, the Son of Man and Son of God. The soft-spoken Pastor Lee talks about being a *true worshipper,* both biblically and personally.

"It's as natural to worship as it is to live," he says. "When we thank God, we acknowledge His love and omniscience. True worship transcends style, culture, genre, and ethnicity. God has called all nations to worship, not merely sing, but as a way of life. His Word says, 'I will bless the Lord at all times; His praise shall be continually in my mouth.'"

After forty-five minutes in the pulpit, Pastor Lee invites those in the congregation who want a new beginning to come to the front and make their hearts right with God. "We all make mistakes and sin every day, and often it's done to you," he says. "Whatever the case, come up now, this morning, and leave it all here. Cast your burdens upon Him and give your heart to the God."

I practically run to the altar; I am the first one there. I don't feel as awkward as I usually do. I know that I have already received the Lord when I had a conversion experience following my stir-fry meal. During a long meditation and prayer, God met me where I was at. It was done that evening at home. Still, I want to make an open, fearless show of my faith.

I kneel at the altar, reverent. Pastor Lee approaches, his kind eyes gazing into my soul.

"Welcome," he says. "Do you believe—?"

I don't let him finish. "Yes, I already believe in Him," I say.

"Then let us pray," the pastor says.[39]

During this special moment, I realize that I am loved well by an eternal Father—which is an insane thought. I have sought and found a Father, one of the most important things I longed for besides my identity.

The music is powerful, her voice calms me and I know I won't be like others. The bad seeds—like religious zealots who judge their neighbors, use the Lord's name for bad things, or stand

---

[39] I realize, especially now, that each person's search for God is personal to every human being. We cannot judge or force or ever use what we believe to try and control others. Exploiters do that all too well, including those who enslaved others for centuries and those who allowed it. Maybe that's why it happened to me like it did, but I didn't know at the time.

outside of abortion clinics calling confused girl *sinners* rather than loving, listening, and providing for them the counseling and resources needed. I personally know what that is like: when others think they know what I've done but fail to ask who or what made that happen. I realize such judgement is not God but the error of people—ignorance, and I feel free from what others have thought of me or how they reacted to my horrible plight. If I can feel this in every area of my life, I know I can make it. Empathy. I will have empathy.

Just breathe, Brook. Breathe forward.

That is the breath of freedom.

I don't keep my newfound faith in God a secret because I want everyone to see how my life is changing. But you try going around Hollywood as a young and up-and-coming actress, talking about the love of God. Sometimes being bold like that is welcomed, and sometimes, not so much. I will eventually have more wisdom and understanding of how to best share my story.

If I think the moment is right, though, I'll say things like:

Have I told you that I love God with all my heart?

Have I told you that I love a heavenly Father who has shown me an acceptance of my right to pursue my destiny and purpose?

Have I told you that I cannot believe that He loves us so much?

Do you know how loved you are and that we're not alone? Isn't that amazing?

I am in love with God, and this will eventually help me love others and fill me with a reason for being. Imbued with fervor, I woo a dozen or more famous actors of all ages to church with me, including Rockman Dunbar, Keenan Ivory Wayans, Kahlil Kain, Clifton Davis, and others.

I had chosen to be abstinent months before attending SRF and out of a need to get to know myself. The desire to be celibate grows stronger as I realize I possess the power to say no. After years of programming, I discover now that I have a choice.

I am now able to share my heart on the second or third date—or the first date. "Why create a past if there is not going to be a future?" I ask.

If a guy asks to come in when he drops me off at my place, I say, "Yeah, you can come in, but just remember that I'm not going there, if you know what I mean. When and if I'm married one day, and I do want to be married, then that will be the beginning of a deeper physical romance for me. Please don't take it personally. It's about living an authentic life—or at least I have to try. Besides, I'm still a wreck."

I love the looks of astonishment I receive, especially from well-known actors—who are supposed to know how to act, *right?* Most are cool about it, but here's the thing: informing them that I am *not* going to have sex until I am married seems to make me *more* attractive to them. I've had guys tell me, "You don't know what this means to hear you say this. I've been in Hollywood for years, and I've been looking for a poised and sweet woman who's not going there."

"Thank you," I reply, in shock, but thinking the entire time, *Oh, my gosh, if you only knew my past.*

I am secretly ashamed about my body, that I am not a virgin, and that my virginity was taken from me. Purity meant blameless, and I can't take that back, at least on some level. I will eventually learn by understanding, listening, and praying that I can own my purity again on my terms.

Here's the exciting thing: I probably received a dozen marriage proposals over a couple of years. I'm talking about the bended knee and the open velvet ring box.

But these sincere marriage proposals haven't come at the right time.

I am not ready.

Knowing the divine is a process of understanding the kind of life I longed for. I don't withdraw from activities like clubbing all the time nor do I think having an active social life is terrible. It really depends on what I am doing when I'm out there in the moment. But on the personal side, I end a relationship with an actress.

I wasn't born gay; I know that. But I came through so much violence from men that when I was raped by them and their wives and girlfriends, at a young age, it changed me . . . and confused me. It took me a while to realize that my desire was not for women but for their friendship; I was on autopilot.

That doesn't mean I hated the intimate times with them, but it also doesn't mean I liked it either. I loved the false sense of love I felt. But man or woman, a passionate affair can exist without any love whatsoever and I didn't know the difference. Nowadays, my gay friends ask me questions about it, and my response is quite simple: "I had to figure out my life and journey. We all do. I'm just trying to do me."

Another thing I can't shake is the subtle cloud of bewilderment and sadness that follows me. I still feel hollow at times with a heaviness on the inside. There are occasions when I am in a very dark place, and nothing tastes, smells, or feels right.

Meanwhile, I get a break in my acting career when I land a solid role on a TV series that requires me to live in Mexico City for almost a year. The experience is mind-altering, character-building, and downright life-changing.

I am the only Black girl in the cast—I seem to be the only Black American woman in Mexico. Taking European Spanish classes, along with Mexican history, reveals the African, Arabic, German, and, of course, Spanish influence over the Mexican culture and language. Eating new foods that are nothing like tacos and enchiladas back home create a foodie out of me. Going to areas like Chiapas, which border Guatemala, move me with compassion when I see hundreds of homeless Mexicans living in tents.

During a short break from shooting the *telenovela* drama series filmed in English, I decide to take a three-day trip to the seaside resort of Zihuatanejo, northwest of Acapulco. I find myself in the international terminal at Mexico City's airport when I should be in the regional terminal. My Spanish isn't good enough to communicate or understand the flight announcements since they speak too fast.

A security guard comes up to me, his eyes concerning, odd, different. I become immediately afraid. He speaks rapid Spanish and keeps trying to get me to go down a hallway and into a room that he is pointing at. I refuse in broken Spanish, saying that I am an actress and work for Televisa, owned by Emilio Azcárraga Sr. and 20th Century Fox, but he won't let up.

Thirty minutes go by with me sweating and others staring at our standoff. Then he eventually lets me go. I find the right terminal and board my flight, barely in time. I happen to sit next to a Spanish-speaking U.S. investigator who was a former Marine general and I tell him my story. He is shocked and amazed.

"You're lucky," he says with a serious tone.

"Why's that?"

"We've been investigating rapes, robberies, and murders of young American women in Mexico," he replies evenly. "I'm glad you're okay."

He gives me his card, and in a very fatherly way, several tips on how to remain safe and asks me to stay in touch. I thank him.

So much for traveling alone anymore. Upon arrival, I check into my hotel and make sure not to venture beyond the resort's pool and beach. I don't order a drink without seeing it poured and keep my head on a swivel for any lurkers.

Later, I hear that our English-speaking *telenovela* might not air because of the completion of only sixty-plus episodes and not one hundred due to the different way U.S. episodic shows are shot as opposed to a novella's. Lighting each scene took one hour longer, and our cast's lack of desire to use an ear-prompter that keeps feeding us our lines creates challenges.

Eventually, I get good news and another big break when I learn I will be cast in a Fox Network sci-fi series called *Stargate SG-1*. It is about a team of explorers who travel through a Stargate, an ancient portal to other planets, where they explore new worlds.

A producer tells me that I am perfect for the role of Drey-auc, a strong, authentic woman. I am excited and completely ecstatic to be in this position.

"This show is gonna do well for you," he says. "You're gonna do great things. I see a lot of good is gonna come out of this."

On the last day of the first season's shoot in Vancouver, Canada, I am hanging out at the production trailers with some of my co-stars, feeling like a true artist, when one of the actors gently pulls me into his dressing room trailer to say goodbye. His girlfriend and her two children periodically travel to see him, but they aren't here today.

I have no sooner stepped into the trailer when the door shuts. I have a sinking feeling of *No, not now, please.*

Then the actor grabs me around the waist quickly. I hope the move is for a typical cast-hug goodbye—until he shoves his tongue into my mouth. I nearly shout and push him away, managing to wrestle from his grasp—wiping the back of my hand across my mouth.

"What are you doing?" I seethe, careful not to raise my voice so others could not hear us, as though what has just happened is no big fricking deal.

He is lost. So very lost. A lost joker.

We wrap up the shoot, and I return to Los Angeles. Not too much time has passed when I receive an interesting phone call from one of the producers.

"Brook, we've decided to go in a different direction with the role of Drey-auc. We're going to kill her off at the beginning of the next season."

I am upset, but not surprised. I am being written off the show because of one of the oldest dictums in Hollywood: I rebuffed the sexual advances from someone in a position of power. In my case, that someone is a male star on the show.

The lost joker.

I didn't report anything because I was too afraid. When filming resumed in Vancouver, I *died* from an explosion in a rebel Jaffa camp for refusing a new larval symbiote—whatever that means.

Dealing with this sort of sexual attack in my work affects me. Losing my job because I don't like being abused by an actor is a reminder that there are sick people no matter where you go.

Ever since I was a young girl, I had a dream of becoming a serious actor. In many ways, I've succeeded. I'll never forget what actors like William H. Macy and Laurence Fishbourne said to me—that I am destined for the acting world, and that one can't be taught the kind of gift that they saw in me.

Not only has the abuse stolen my dreams, but I feel like it has stolen everything. I know that I have to leave Los Angeles sooner or later, or at least for a while, if I am going to survive. I have to rethink what comes next.

I pray about what I should do and have more sessions with my therapist. I also seek wise counsel from Pastor Bam and a pastor at Church on the Way in Van Nuys, where I start sometimes attending since my move back to nearby Sherman Oaks. I also reach out to casting director Peter Wise, a Church on the Way member and a friend. He says there may be something more important for me to do with my life and that I can return to acting later when I'm not struggling from the assault on my body and dream. He tells me to follow my heart and that God will lead.

During this time of introspection, Pastor Bam hires me to co-produce one of her TV ministries as part of the media team, which is special. I also take a role in a local stage play with Ted Lange, a Black actor moonlighting from his role as the bartender Isaac on *The Love Boat* TV series.

During our run in North Hollywood, something strange starts happening to my body: I notice blue bruises all over and hundreds of tiny red dots called petechiae, which are caused by bleeding under the skin. I immediately visit my doctor. Blood is drawn. Then a lab technician calls me at home over the weekend, which I think unusual.

"Miss Parker, I'm glad I reached you," he says. "I'm afraid you don't have any platelets in your blood. You need to rush to a hospital immediately. We left a message with your doctor, but this can't wait."

"How come?"

"Platelets help your blood clot, which stops bleeding. You could be at real risk if you got a cut."

I thank the lab tech for the call and sit down, astounded by the turn of events. The tech tells me to go to the Hematology Oncology Center at Cedars-Sinai Medical Center, the top hospital in L.A. and the place where all the celebrities go. Fortunately, I have Screen Actors Guild medical insurance, the best kind you can have.

I see a hematologist-oncologist, a Dr. Heitzman, who reviews my lab work.

"I see you're crossing your legs," he says. "Please uncross them."

"Why?"

"Because you have no platelets in your blood. You should have a few hundred thousand, but you have only six. Circulation is key. You could be bleeding internally, which could be fatal. Your blood work tells me you have an autoimmune disorder known as ITP or idiopathic thrombocytopenic purpura. It's treatable, but I'm afraid it's not curable."

I am getting freaked out. "So, what can be done?"

"We'll give you a treatment of gamma globulin, which is blood plasma to build up your platelet count. We may have to remove your spleen, but medication such as steroids is something you will take for the rest of your life, as well as receive blood treatments. We'll start by putting you on prednisone, a steroid often used for this disease. Then we'll monitor how your body reacts. In addition, I'm admitting you immediately, so you'll need to cancel your entire calendar. You'll be here for three to five days so we can monitor you. You need to rest."

I tell Dr. Heitzman that I have faith things will work out. This Jewish doctor says that is great to hear, adding that he has read *The Road to Damascus*, the story about the apostle Paul's conversion. When he says he also believed, I feel good being in his skilled hands.

Several hours later, I receive another bedside phone call, this time from Pastor Bam.

"Hey, Pastor Bam! Great to hear from you!"

"Well, you sound upbeat. I guess I don't even have to pray for you."

I chuckle as I explain what has happened and the treatment plan. We close the phone call with her praying for me anyway. My spirits are also lifted when my father visits a couple of times.

Once I am released after just under a week at Cedars-Sinai, I want to see my family in Las Vegas. I've been in touch with my mother, and she has been nice, even sympathetic about what's happened. I can tell she is trying to be pleasant. I start to see that she may have had her own mental health issues; I know her mother did, stemming from some form of trauma. I want us all to be together.

I make arrangements to stay with my older brother, Ricky, and his wife. But I know I can't—or shouldn't—drive myself there. That's when my half-sister from my father says she'd drive me across the desert to Vegas.

After we arrive I receive a phone call from my agent with exciting news: "You got a callback. You gotta be there!"

"When?"

"Tomorrow."

"But I'm visiting family in Las Vegas. I just got here!"

"Yeah, but they really want you. You must come back to L.A. This could be big."

I am in the running for a significant role in new TV series with the working title of *The Last Patrol*. If I get the part, I'll have enough money to make a down payment on a home, a financial goal that I'd told my agent about. But going to the audition meant disobeying my doctor's orders not to travel and canceling any appointments.

I've already taken a risk by having my half-sister drive me to Las Vegas. Now I am being asked to hop in the car first thing in the morning and drive myself back to Los Angeles for a role that I may or may not get. Can I do it in my condition? Was it wise?

"Let me think about this," I tell my agent, who doesn't know about my illness. After hanging up, I have no idea what I should do.

That late afternoon, I lie down on my brother's sofa, full of prednisone, wondering if I will have to have my spleen removed. My brother and sister say they will support me in whatever I choose to do.

My Bible is on the hardwood floor next to the sofa. The weirdest thing happens: when I put my hand on the Bible to pray, my hand goes through the Bible, way down deep. Then I hear the Lord's voice clearly and distinctly: *Go!*

The supernatural event is absolutely jolting.

I tell my siblings what has happened and feel that it is a sign for me to drive to L.A. for the audition as soon as the sun comes up.

"I'm gonna be okay," I promise. "Then I'll drive right back." They can tell something good will happen, so they let me go.

When I wake up at dawn the following morning, instead of a bluebird sky and waves of summer heat rising from the desert floor, the air is filled with dark thunderclouds. Motoring across the Mojave Desert, I get hit with a deluge: the heavy rain and a bizarre hailstorm result in flash flooding.

I slow to a crawl on Interstate 15 because I can barely see anything in front of me. I am driving my second car, a white Volvo four-door sedan with a tan interior and sunroof. Although I feel sluggish and swollen from the medication, I marvel as BB-sized hail pelts the Volvo.

Quickly, though, I become worried. The wiper on the driver's side is losing its rubber strip. I have to pull over to the shoulder every ten minutes to slide the rubber strip back on the windshield wiper. It is crazy. The semis driving by shake me and my car on the narrow shoulder.

I finally pull into the production studio in wet clothes and runny make-up. I change in the car, wipe the moisture off my face, and put on new make-up. Then I walk into the audition like a springtime daisy. I feel scared, shaky, and ready all at the same time. Part of me wants to skip the callback, but another part of me also wants to knock it out of the ballpark.

One of the assistants speaks up. "Welcome, Brook. You ready?"

"Yes," I reply.

I am handed a script—a script I've already studied. Then I read with another actor for the next half-hour, acting with brio and confidence. When we finish, the producer says I did great.

The director has a request: "Brook, now we need you to speak in another language. We don't care what the language is. There's this rainstorm, and you're an oracle—you know things that no one else knows. We want you to speak in a foreign language that no one knows. Can you do that?"

I don't know a foreign language except for some Spanish, but I suddenly think of praying and singing in the Spirit, in tongues, when I was in my apartment alone at my moment of conversion. I start singing in the Spirit with force and power, and everything comes together in one moment. When I finish, one could hear a pin drop.

"That was amazing, Brook, just amazing," the director says.

"Thank you," I say. "Thank you for allowing me to be here today."

When I leave the room, the casting director runs after me. She holds me tight when she catches me and says, "You were wonderful."

Two days later, I receive the welcome news that I am booked for a role that will pay me enough to make a down payment on a home. The series will be shot in Israel, however, which means international travel.

At first, my doctors say I can't go to the shoot, but when I promise to take my medication and check in with a doctor over there if I feel ill, she gives me a release to travel to the Middle East. I don't feel that pretty, though, because I am getting red from prednisone. I eat less. I ice my skin to bring down the swelling.

As expected, the month-long production in places like Tel Aviv, Jerusalem, Jaffa, and Eilat on the southern extremity of Israel on the Gulf of Aqaba is transformational. The Scriptures come alive, seeing the towns on the shoreline of the Sea of Galilee, retracing Jesus' steps as He carried the cross along the Via Dolorosa in Jerusalem's Old City, and praying at the Wailing Wall, where I place a note with my family's names and my prayers for them into the cracks of the Temple wall. Diving in the Red Sea, eating new foods, floating in the Dead Sea filled with salt and sailing to Egypt is life changing.

As with all my travels, whenever I check into a hotel, I am thankful to enter my room not to be sold or purchased.

When I come back from the shoot in Israel, my challenges with depression creep in like never before. I am tired of it.

Can't I just be normal? What is wrong with me?

I question everything, especially my future and where I am going in life.

I eventually reach an emotional tipping point where I feel I need to shake things up by getting out of L.A., which will force me to put my acting career on hold. That means moving back to Las Vegas, where I have family and know I can get a well-paying job in a fine-dining restaurant based upon my previous work experience on the Strip. I am sure that my acting career credits will bolster my resumé.

I decide to go for it. I return to Las Vegas, where I purchase a home and get a front-of-the-house serving position at Rumjungle, a high-end restaurant that caters to high rollers and the in-crowd at the Mandalay Bay casino. I figure I'll go back to what I used to do and lay low for a while.

One evening, a few actors I know arrive for dinner, including Black actress Sanaa Latham. Their response seeing me is surprise and shock: *Brook Parker, what are you doing here serving? It's a happening place, but why? You were the girl to beat. Everyone was saying you were the next big star.*

I don't know what to say, so I smile and say something about needing to be closer to my family.

Within a few weeks, though, I am stressed. More despair clouds my thinking. The darkness gets so thick that I can't see a way out. I am living a futile existence, unable to feel optimistic about my future. I cry out for hope. When I don't feel any better, I decide to end my life by taking half a bottle of sleeping pills.

After swallowing the last of the capsules, I am out of it, feeling the moorings slipping away—I receive a phone call from Shirley Hogan, a member of Bible Enrichment Fellowship. She is checking up on me.

"How are you doing?" she inquires.

I slur some response that includes something about taking a bunch of pills because I want to die, my life is worthless, and if it all ended today, I will be . . .

"Brook, you gotta get it out. You need to throw up—immediately!"

I can't think. Outside a tree limb brushes against the window. The plastic bottle is tipped on its side on the counter. The lid is on the floor. I am dizzy. I began to vomit. Shirley stays on the phone with me for over three hours until she convinces me to call my family and my mother. Momma comes rushing to my place, and she sits there while I sleep. When I wake, groggy and out of it, we have a sort of a heartfelt conversation. There's no way I'm going to the hospital.

"I'm sorry about everything, Brooky."

Momma is trying, and I appreciate it. And she tells me she loves me. I see her dark beautiful eyes. There is a tender smile seated behind her usual mask.

I tell her about the rape when I was eleven years old —Uncle Mike. She doesn't respond—as if she doesn't want to hear about it. I decide not to press the issue or tell her about the trafficking.

Our conversation is still a major turning point in my life—a crossroads.

A start.

Moving forward, what else can I *really* do? Pastor Bam and others have said I that have a gift of speaking, teaching, and motivating. I have been taking community college classes on and off, working toward a bachelor's degree. I realize that I can't be an actor at the moment because I am not whole and don't have the savviness to pretend anymore, but I have to become the person I am meant to be. But how?

Why the Caged Bird Sings

After the suicide attempt, I am ready to move forward to make my peace with God.

I don't want to die.

I read *I Know Why the Caged Bird Sings* by author Maya Angelou[40] and I love how her memoir takes readers on a journey through her compelling life. I see myself in the pages. I am enthralled by how she connects her experiences of growing up in the Deep South with those of a caged bird.

I am sitting under a fig tree. It is a hot desert evening. A light breeze hisses in the leaves. I think of that caged bird. I imagine being that bird, knowing I can fly—I'm trapped in a cage, unable to do what I am born to do. Since I can't get away, I hop around my wooden perch, imagining I am flying—but I am powerless to spread my wings.

If only to rid myself of the metal bars surrounding the cage and be free to do what I believe I am destined to do—mend the wings of the wounded and help others discover their wings for the first time.

Then I hear God's voice speak to me: *That's right, and on the other side of pain, My will for you will be revealed all the more, and you will know exactly who you are, Brooky.*

Peace fills my cup. I know the healing process won't happen overnight, so I settle in for the long haul and listen, wide open—

---

[40] Maya Angelou is perhaps most famous for reciting her poem, "On the Pulse of Morning," at the presidential inauguration of Bill Clinton on January 20, 1993, which resulted in more fame and recognition for this esteemed author.

as if for the first time. I am aware that I am dealing with unresolved issues, a history of brokenness, and an abundance of mental, emotional, and heart anguish. God touches me beneath this fig tree. Now it is a matter of waiting for the divine winds of destiny to move in my life.

I am seeing a therapist again. It is difficult sometimes. I sense a new confidence as I work with tools to live and connect with my family. I visit Momma more often, and we manage to spend a little time together here and there. Sometimes I feel she is merely tolerating me, that is good enough.

My therapist suggests that my mother acts that way because she doesn't love herself and that she has been through a lot without any resolution from her mother's mysterious death a very young age. There is also all the physical and verbal abuse she suffered at the hands of her husbands, including my father, when they were married.

My point of view has changed: I now regarded Momma as a survivor, even though she doesn't know it herself. Later on I will discover a key aspect of my program: to become a survivor one must know and accept they have been a victim of a crime in order to crossover into a survivor—with no victim mentality hidden or otherwise. I'm not sure if Momma knows. She is a mystery and never, ever speaks about her feelings or allows herself to admit her pain.

Meanwhile, I find my footing at Rumjungle.

As a server, I never write down guest orders. I remember everything each person says around a four-top: *I'll have the Jamaican Spice Chicken Skewers to start and then your Maminha tri-tip, cooked medium rare . . . I'll take a baseball cut of your*

*Fraldinha steak, cooked medium, but hold the chimichurri sauce .
. .*

Prominent family dinners, raucous bachelor parties, or girls' night out—all the verbal orders go into my head until I walk back to the kitchen and punch them onto a ticket. I also have a knack for suggesting the right wine—always expensive—after having assisted a master sommelier at another fine dining establishment two nights a week. I receive extensive training on the history of winemaking, its varietals, and the difference between Old World and New World wines.

I am good at selling $700-plus bottles of champagne and wine by "pairing" them with just the right appetizer and entrées. My Mandalay Bay managers are impressed, especially after they tell me that my table tickets are the highest among all the servers, male and female. I am promoted to lead server, responsible for training others and monitoring their work. I do such a good job there that I am offered the best gig of all—lead server over one of Rumjungle's "bottle rooms."

Here's the background: sometime after 11 p.m., when the dance floor opens on the top tier of this three-story establishment, Rumjungle transforms into one of the hottest nightclubs on the Strip. Decorated with a Latin flair, the club's interior mixed rhythmic fire and melodic waterfalls—sheets of glass dripping with running water—it is the place to be.

On a stage above the dance floor, several DJs and a live percussionist get the feet moving with throbbing salsa music that carries a pulsing, energetic rhythm. Go-go dancers entertain the crowd from podiums around the dance floor and from suspended dancing cages. Acrobats moonlighting from the latest Cirque du Soleil show perform in the air. The 144-foot-long, nineteen-foot-high main bar—billed as the world's largest rum bar—has a twenty-foot-high liquor display. Everything is high class, including the dress code: no hats, sports attire, or ripped, baggy clothing.[41]

Rumjungle has private areas—known as "bottle rooms"—for VIPs and high rollers. After really hard work this can be the mother lode for landing big tips to make a decent living since a bottle room's exclusivity is reserved for Mandalay Bay's most affluent, wealthy patrons; a place where they come eat and drink without having to rub shoulders with the masses. To maintain a high-class ambiance, I have a dress code as well: a tight black bodice that pushes up my breasts; black patent leather shorts that barely cover me; beautiful black stockings; and patent leather, knee-high Doc Martens boots.

Access to each bottle room is restricted by a security guard who keeps one hand on a red velvet rope. He isn't lifting the rope if you aren't on his list—unless you happen to get invited in. Regular patrons can see into the bottle room, so it is a bit of a fishbowl. See to be seen, right?

I am good at upselling. I can talk our top, most well-heeled guests into purchasing a bottle of Macallan 18 scotch for $500 or even spending $4,000 for a bottle of Louis XIII cognac. If vodka is their thing, I suggest Grey Goose, Belvedere, or Ketel One.

If they are wine drinkers, I come across as a sophisticated sommelier as I wax eloquent regarding the bouquet of a particular French wine from Bordeaux. Each shift is fun, and my heart feels lighter. I don't have to prove myself.

Like sports competitions, success is clearly defined when I work hard. Yes, I love filmmaking, live theatre, writing, and acting, but those are pursuits in which many people hold things over me, and I have to contend with rejection between victories. Like tennis, I feel I am only as good as my last match.

---

[41] Rumjungle consistently made the *Nightclub & Bar* magazine list of the Top 100 nightclubs in the United States and was one in the Top 20 of *Restaurant & Institutions'* Top 100 Grossing Restaurants.

Watching the nightclub scene at Rumjungle unfold, however, reminds me of how those who violated me would allow male buyers to choose us, as kids, based on our hair, race, hue, eye color, and body type. All these things still trigger me, but not as bad.

Inside the bottle room, I play bartender and security. I am also on the lookout for guys *and* gals who are criminal pickpockets clipping wallets, purses, and watches from unsuspecting guests. Vegas can get crazy, and we have to watch out for each guest. My bottle room is my house. Then there are the slime guys who slip a Mickey into girls' drinks so they can take advantage of them. Keeping my eyes open is a part of the job.

I am paid well to manage this bacchanal. Most evenings, I pocket $1,500 in tips for my expertise behind the bar and for keeping everyone happy. I often don't get home until four or four thirty in the morning, my clothes smelling of sweaty perfume.

Because of my past, I am different from other servers: I see more than most— I have other priorities. Witnessing the rich and wannabe rich people get plastered each night, watching them go from one level of drinking to a whole other level becomes tough to stomach, but most times, its fun.

As a "bottle room hostess," my attractiveness and knowledge of our products are a good foundation because our clients love running thousand-dollar tabs on themselves, their families, and their guests for a night on the Strip. That's why they come to Rumjungle: they want to spend well and be taken care of, so it is a fair trade.

All of that being said, being part of the club scene is hard and most of the time doesn't feel good. There is too much temptation to drink, and the drugs I see . . . let's just say I know it will soon be time to go.

What keeps me going is the nest egg I'm building for the next chapter of my life.

The bartender I work with the most is Jenny, a tatted-up super chick.

One morning, around four o'clock, Jenny and I are straightening up inventory and wiping down the bar area when she touches my hand.

"I had a dream about you," she announces.

"Really? What was it about?" I am naturally curious why I'd be in one of her dreams.

"I'm not religious or anything, but this dark and evil monster was chasing me. I was running and sweating and couldn't get away. Eventually, I was led to this giant slayer—so tall that I could only see the knees. I looked up and saw that it was a female giant. I grabbed her leg and hid behind her so the monster dragon wouldn't find me. When I looked up again, it was you—you were the huge giant slayer, ten times my height. You were fierce, and I felt safe. Do you know what my dream means?"

I stare at her. I am stunned. Did her dream mean that I will become a giant slayer on behalf of others who can't defend themselves one day?

"I'm not sure," I reply, "but I'll keep you on my mind."

"Thank you. I've been through a lot, so thanks. Really."

"No problem."

Our hands touch; we have a moment. Then go went back to cleaning up.

All sorts of other interesting things are happening to me, like when I am in crowded spaces and inadvertently touch a man's or woman's hand, I'll sometimes get a horrific flash in my mind's eye of that person touching a child or grandchild or even being caught up in an actual child rape. But there are positive, celebratory things, too. When I touch other people inadvertently, I'll see someone's good heart or their future success. Whenever weird, supernatural things like this occur, I think: *What am I supposed to do with this?*

I think of Momma and her former magic, and realize it has nothing to do with that—she left that behind along time ago.

I also have my own dreams and visions that I never tell anyone about, like my dream of walking in a green field on a sunny day, laughing and singing—the sun moving quickly across the sky. I stroll into an orchard of orange and lemon trees. I notice the sun begins laughing with me and descend until it drops down between a row of fruit-bearing trees. The sun, laughing and joking, then lays on his back and giggles as I squeeze the fruit juice in his belly. Then he bids me to join him in grooving to the beat of energetic music before it takes its place back in the sky—smiling at me. The dream is beautiful.

That isn't the only technicolor dream that seems to defy explanation. I figure that whatever I am dreaming about is preparing me for the next chapter in my life, and until I figure out what to do next, Rumjungle is an excellent place to park myself. I have my days free and stay out of trouble by working in my garden, reading by my oversized fig tree, and writing poetry and short stories. The beautiful, mature tree filled with golden figs is the main reason I bought the house.

Since I no longer have to support a drug habit or give money to most of my friends (who ask because I seldom say no), the extra cash gives me the funds to decorate my three-bedroom, 1,500-square-foot house in a beautiful, tasteful way. I transform my backyard with new landscaping, a built-in barbecue, and patio furniture—the pride of homeownership propelling me. It is a different kind of fun, and I love it.

Away from the Strip, I don't mind being alone and hearing myself breathe.

With all these good things happening, I am ready to turn a corner—but what waits for me? I speak with my father about my future, he tells me that I don't have to figure it all out. "It was good to step away from Hollywood and take stock, baby girl," he says. "You don't have to make any lifelong decisions right now. Just move forward little by little."

One thing I know: Las Vegas isn't where I want to spend the rest of my life. Los Angeles—Santa Monica, Sherman Oaks—is and will always be my hometown. But if I return to L.A., what will I do? I know I will write since I have already composed short stories and poems and have published a book of poetry, *To Soar Without Leaving the Ground*. While I think I might still act here and there, I need something real for now.

I remember how good it felt to give by feeding the homeless while attending Pastor Bam's church. These weren't "one-offs" in which I showed up on Thanksgiving morning and ladled gravy on the plates of the homeless as they filed by. I participated in several food drives and regularly volunteered. Then I kicked things up a notch when I enlisted a few of my actor friends to help me set up food stands for those in need in different neighborhoods in Van Nuys and Sherman Oaks when I was living in the Valley. We purchased high-quality meats and produce and prepared delicious meals that we shared with the hungry.

Helping others feeds my soul and makes me feel alive. Helping others makes me think of old movies where someone could be there for others and expect nothing in return. That's why I became an actress—and watching movies saved my life.

It also feels like I am living inside a good song, sometimes with my favorite notes. The minor notes depict the joy of life I hope for while telling the story of the soul, which can be deeply sad. But every time an unaccompanied teen girl or young woman in her twenties passes by with a paper plate in hand for her next meal, questions nag at my heart: *What's her story? Is she being exploited?*

Within a twenty-mile radius of our food stand, I know that there has to be hundreds, if not thousands of girls, boys, and young women living in the shadows, under the thumbs of pimps and bottom girls. They are in bondage, held against their will, and commanded to satisfy the lustful desires of tricks—or else.

Knowing what they are up against, I formulate a thought while working at Rumjungle: Can I help others escape their oppressors and guide them in rebuilding their lives? Because I am certainly feeling a call on my heart to help those who have been exploited, raped, or suffering bondage and have nowhere to go.

Other thoughts crowd my consciousness: Did God rescue me so that I can come to their aid? Are all the horrible, abusive things I have endured leading me to start an organization to help those I understand? I can hear TD Jakes, in my ear saying, "get ready, get ready, get ready."

Something tells me that I need to go to Los Angeles to find out.

Denise calls, out of nowhere. She finds my number through my agent.

"I can't believe it's you." I'm happy to hear from her. "Denise, I wondered where you were. I know you don't even know all that happened to me. But we can talk about it some other time. I'm just glad you're six feet above ground."

She laughs, "Remember that time helicopters took us for other people and were chasing us kids through some complex?"

"Oh man, I totally forgot about that." We both laugh. Pause. Only we know the unspoken breath between us, the non-verbal communication piercing through the phone. We could be like this for hours and understand every unspoken word. I love her, we're family and she loves me.

"Well, see you again."

"Yeah, see you."

I decide to talk with my father to seek advice on what I should do. He is a brilliant man and has become one of my closest confidants. There is something about hearing his voice, the voice of a father who hasn't always been there but is trying to make up for lost time. We've been getting along well enough for me to tell him my story in bits and pieces, but not everything. He was devastated to hear how much I suffered. Our father-daughter bond, which had been nonexistent for many years, has now strengthened considerably.

"Hi, Pop," I begin. "I think I've been in Vegas long enough. I'm ready to come back home to California. I don't know exactly what I'm gonna do, but I can't get this idea out of my mind—the one about starting an organization to help exploited children and women and assisting in homelessness prevention. What do you think?"

I hear his deep, reassuring voice. "That's good, baby. You're very smart and can do anything you put your mind to. You're also strong, very strong, Brooky. Even as a little girl, you loved helping others. You used to talk to adults like you understood them—and they you. You understand freedom from bondage, even if you're not there yet, you will be, which is what our people have fought for. All people need to be free—the men, this labor trafficking, domestic violence, and young people, just angry because of what they're faced with. I know you can do it, baby."

"Thank you, Pop. Wow . . . I need to finish school and get a degree at some point," I say.

"That's always good, li'l Parker."

I chuckle. My dad either called me Brooky or Parker as terms of endearment. I loved them both.

"I also want to do more writing and travel," I continue. "I'll figure it out."

"More of that beautiful poetry of yours?" he says. "What was that poem you wrote that I love so much, the one about how you find joy and the miracles of life?"

"Yeah, I'm glad you liked that," I smile. I feel like my creative side has more things to say.

"So, what are you going to do about your house?" My father is being practical.

I've been giving that some thought as well. "I'm debating whether to sell my home or turn it into an income property." I don't know anything about leasing a home, but someone has suggested that to me. "What do you think, Pop?"

"Well, if you rent it out and something goes wrong, will you feel like driving back to Vegas and dealing with it?" my father asks. "If you hire a management company to do that for you, they'll take an easy 10 or 15 percent off the top. It makes more sense to sell the property if you want to move forward and not worry about it. You really don't want to be concerned with taking care of a house in another state."

"You're probably right. Thanks, Pop."

I put down my mobile phone and go out to my fig tree, pick a few figs, and bring them into the kitchen. I put on a pot of water to make green tea.

I settle into my sofa, cup in hand, I feel a sense of direction, a fire, an inner drive that I haven't felt since I started acting. This is different, however. I have always dreamed of acting and helping others—like many actors do—but I have to do this first, which feels good because it isn't about me. It is freeing to take my eyes off my own life for a change.

I run some specs on the real estate market and pray about what to do. In the end, I feel led to sell the house, which turns out to be a good decision.

When I leave Las Vegas, I am debt-free with some money in the bank.

I move into an apartment in a familiar area on Rossmore Avenue in Hancock Park and sign up for a full load of classes at College of the Canyons, a two-year community college thirty miles north in Santa Clarita. I don't mind the drive to the high-desert valley. I like getting away from the city.

At College of the Canyons, most of the student body is eighteen, nineteen, or twenty years old. It's an adjustment for me since I am more mature and have certain life experiences— experiences I wouldn't wish on my worst enemy.

I am told that my classmates think I am mysterious and interesting because I provide insight they don't see during classroom discussions. My thoughts about psychology and the way the mind works impresses my professors.

It's a good feeling to be in school. I have missed getting an *in school* education. I can see how this environment is a wealth of knowledge, community, and discovery. Several professors tell me I should pursue a degree in psychology. That is my mother's field, and I begin to see the gifts I have from her and my father.

Hidden behind the pain my destiny is slowly being revealed.

While the compliments for my academic acumen raise my self-esteem, I haven't lost sight of why I returned to Los Angeles: to launch a 501(c)(3) nonprofit organization. The desire to do something for others hasn't lessened at all—it has grown. I feel this is something I have to do.

The most pressing need for those in trouble living on the streets, besides shelter and clothes, is food; intense hunger crowds out every other necessity, except for those struggling with substance abuse. They need far more, and I will assist them as well.

I approach a local grocery store and ask if my team of friends can distribute their unsold, almost-expired foodstuffs, day-old bread, and perishable fruits and vegetables. The market manager says he will work with me.

The logistical work is formidable, organizing the food deliveries and preparing meals and sandwiches. Once we are ready, we caravan to different places in the city and set up food tents, or hand out meals and items that we have prepared.

My church, Bible Enrichment, also has a food drive pick-up day each week, and my team and I will sometimes provide chicken, steaks, fish, and ground beef. Seeing the overjoyed faces of families receiving good-quality, healthy foods is a bright light. The conversations with lost fathers and mothers speaking about families and children in other states are heartening: I can see, feel, and sense that we are on the right track.

I talk with a bright young woman, nineteen or twenty years of age, looking me in the eyes.

"I was six years old when my father started to come to my room," she says while holding a bag of food. "He also went to my sister's room, and she was five. The abuse stopped when I was thirteen and he shot himself. My mother doesn't admit that the abuse happened. She doesn't speak to us, barely. I feel like she blames us, I know she does."

She pauses and gives me a penetrating look. "How did you do it, get better?"

"Me?" I ask. "I don't know if I have yet. I'm still a work in progress. Sometimes I can barely breathe, but we just have to keep moving forward."

"Wow," she says softly. She asks if she can call me sometime.

"Yes, sure. Here, take my number. And call me or text me. Thank you for sharing your story. I know it's not easy."

With tears in her eyes, she reaches out and hugs me. When we say our goodbyes, she looks a little lighter walking away. I know what she is going through. My eyes fill with tears.

How and why do some men do this? What can I do to stop it or at least lessen the impact? I feel like this has something to do with the legacy of fatherhood as a root cause. I have to find out more.

Another problem is that the girls' mother never believed this happened—not even after the father shot himself. She is probably racked with guilt and shame.

It is surreal how doing this kind of volunteer work has allowed me to discover a different side of myself. I no longer want to be focused on my pain or how to get rid of it. When the world is saying: *Look out for No. 1* or *Become all you can be*, God is showing me the importance of losing my life so I could find it.

He is saying, *Don't worry—don't torment yourself any longer and just trust and move forward, assist others, and allow the layers of doubt and shame to fall away, little by little.* That's what I do for myself and the lives of others, allowing them to see how it's done.

By sharing my story with others who have been exploited, I realize what I have gone through can help those in pain. Adopting this attitude allows my brain and heart to mend, as I see my life in theirs and their lives in mine.

In my College of the Canyons psych classes, I learn about egocentrism, which is the inability to distinguish between self and others or accurately understand any perspective than one's own. At one end of the spectrum are the narcissists who feel the world revolves around them. At the other end are the broken— those stuck in self-pity about themselves. That was me at one time. As I ruefully remember, I fretted and brooded so much about my brokenness that I developed suicidal thoughts that nearly killed me.

After moving back to L.A. and getting involved in street outreach, something clicks in me: *I can live for something greater and far beyond myself.* Not only that, but my life experiences from years of being exploited gives me a unique understanding of what it means to be imprisoned and treated as less than a human being—like a property owned by someone else.

I speak with Pastor Bam to hear her thoughts. We've grown closer after she asked me to be part of the church's media team that produced her TV series.[42] Pastor Bam knows my desire to help victims and change the hearts of men who allow it.

"I know just the person you need to speak with—Willie Jordan."

"Who's he?"

"She. Willie and her husband, Fred, have served the homeless and been helping women get off Skid Row for decades. Fred died a few years ago, but the ministry is still going strong."

---

[42] I learned important skills being on Pastor Bam's media team: how to operate a camera, edit video, and put together a sermon episode.

When I visit Willie at the Fred Jordan Mission in downtown Los Angeles,[43] I am impressed by how this gracious woman welcomes me with open arms. I sit in her office and pour out my desire to come to the aid and identity discovery of women and children in bondage while sharing with men in preventative ways. Not only does Willie prove to be an empathetic listener, but she offers to let me do some on-the-job training by hanging around the Mission and observing how they do things.

Willie shares the nuts and bolts of starting a nonprofit—what it costs, helps me to draft the bylaws, file the articles of incorporation, and apply for federal and state tax exemptions. I soak in all her words. Now it is a matter of pulling the trigger by filing an application for a 501(c)(3) nonprofit, which will exempt my organization from federal and state taxes and allow donors to make tax-deductible donations, the latter being the lifeblood of any nonprofit.

I share what I learn at Fred Jordan Mission with a good friend, Donna Kinsler, whom I've "adopted" as a big sister. She is well aware of my goal to save girls and boys, women and men, from all forms of human trafficking, exploitation, and rape. Donna is full of encouragement. She suggests that I meet with a CPA named Ruth, who owns Corporate Minute Books in Pacific Palisades.

Ruth walks me through all the steps of starting a nonprofit, which includes the compilation of articles of incorporation and all sorts of paperwork. She assists with everything and charges me only $1,500.

"What do you want to name your nonprofit?" she asks.

---

[43] Fred Jordan Mission was started in the 1940s by Fred and Willie Jordan, who poured their lives into ministering to the needs of the lost, the homeless, the poor, and the hopeless. When Fred died in 1988, Willie stepped into the leadership position. I'm not sure how or why Mrs. Jordan went by "Willie," but that's what everyone called her.

I was ready with an answer. "More To Life," I say.

"That's interesting. How did you come up with that?"

"When I was trying to discover my identity for the first time, my hurt in Hollywood, and was distraught about life in general, I'd tell myself, 'There has to be more, so much more to life.' Then I realized this would be the name of the organization."

Ruth nods. "I can appreciate that. It's a nice name, and you seem very certain, which is a win," she says.

A week later, however, she calls with some news: some other nonprofit already has the More to Life name.

I am bummed—until a lightning bolt of an idea strikes me: I can name my nonprofit More *Too* Life—*too* instead of *to*. Grammatically, it doesn't make sense, but sometimes you need to tilt a light hanging on a wall to make it shine brighter. I am doodling a few designs when I have an epiphany: the two "o's" can represent the chains of trafficking, symbolized by the dash holding them together. Opening up the second "chain" or "o" represents freedom.

And *More Too Life* is born.

I start small, just myself, a small board of directors, and several volunteers. Early on, a pastor and a friend tells me about a couple of exploited victims who need a place to stay. They are being forced and prostituted by a sex-trafficking pimp and want to escape. They have just turned eighteen, and no one seems to care or understand that they are victims. I have them move in with me in my apartment because their need is immediate. I told them living with me isn't a long-term solution, but I understand that they need to get away from their oppressors. Together, we can figure out the next steps.

Word of mouth about my venture circulates. Once people hear what I am doing, several want to help by writing a check. The amounts are modest initially—a few hundred dollars and then a few thousand dollars. Those funds are enough in the early days to allow me to feed, house, and clothe these victims and survivors.

I assist one victim in getting her child back.

I am referred to a case in Kentucky where an uncle had repeatedly raped two girls between the ages of eight and thirteen while babysitting them. He hung them from the ceiling, cut them, and stitched them back up. When the parents came home, he told them the girls fell while playing outside.

Only the beginning of the sick realities I would face daily.

They say Hollywood is a small town, which explains why word gets around about my fledgling organization. Actors send their support. Others tell me they love what I am doing. I also start receiving requests from the media and community groups to speak about trafficking and its root causes when they hear of the important work I am doing.

I recognize that I need an outlet to counterbalance the tough stuff I am dealing with as More Too Life gets off the ground. As the author of a book of poems, I start participating in "poetry slams" at various coffeehouses that combine performance, writing, competition, and audience participation elements.

Random audience members judge performances on a scale of 0 to 10. The "slam" part comes from how the audience reacts: they have the power to praise your spoken effort or destroy your poem.

I share the floor at these poetry slams with some exciting people: actress Lisa Bonet; actor Malcolm-Jamal Warner (*Suits, The Resident*); funk artist Ronald "RonKat" Spearman; a poet called D-Knowledge; and even Cedric the Entertainer, a comedic actor and one of the funniest guys alive.

Although I rarely go to audition calls, I satisfy my acting itch by starring in a play I wrote called *The Rabbi and the Lady*. Uncle Jon gives me the seed money to get it produced. In this story, a young Black girl—that would be me—runs away to Hollywood to become an actor. In the foyer of a high-rise building one day, she steps into an elevator with a retired Jewish rabbi who's there to visit his son, an entertainment lawyer. She's there because she's going to audition for the part of a prostitute. Subsequently, she's dressed like a street corner girl: short gold lame dress, deep-V top, and spiked stilettos.

When the elevator gets stuck between floors, the rabbi freaks out, and that's when the fun begins. (The rabbi was played by Jewish actor Abraham Kleiman, who told me his life mirrored the fictional one I wrote about.)

All twelve performances sell out. After the final staging, Ron Spearman—my buddy from the poetry slams—holds an afterparty at his house with food and music. While filling up on hors d'oeuvres, I meet a white guy my age. He introduces himself as Teddy Bello. Curly brown hair. Nice build. Ready smile. Doesn't put on airs. Says he was a musician—and a worship leader at a church.

He catches my attention. I don't often meet many sincere men like Teddy in Hollywood or anywhere, especially an Italian

American who plays bass at an all-Black church. I think he is an adorable guy and feel safe with him at the party. I love how Teddy talks about how God is working in his life.

There is a spark between us—a spark I haven't felt in a long time. Before the evening is over, he asks if I want to have a coffee with him sometime. My face lights up and I say yes. Teddy suggests Buzz Coffee on Beverly Boulevard near the Powerhouse Gym and Erewhon Market, a health food store where I love ordering smoothies and shopping for groceries and healthy treats.

When we meet a few days later, we have both come down with colds—but neither of us cancel the coffee date. As we sit down and share our backgrounds, my jaw drops when I learn that Teddy had grown up in . . . Las Vegas![44]

His father is Al Bello, a drummer, comedian, and entertainment director at a bunch of casinos on the Strip—places like the Aladdin, the Thunderbird, and the Dunes—he even played on a calypso album with Maya Angelou recorded in the late 1950s.

Teddy's mom is April Ames, a big band singer back in the day. When Teddy was a little tyke, his father would dress him and his brothers, Timothy and Todd, in tiny tuxedos and bring them onstage. Hanging around backstage with scantily clad dancers was normal as a kid. So was having celebrities like Sammy Davis Jr., Telly Savalas, and Don Rickles over for dinner. Frank Sinatra was a family friend.

Teddy grew up playing a lot of baseball and had aspirations of making it to the Major Leagues one day. While competing for the University of Nevada, Reno, he hurt his Achilles tendon, which ended his dreams of pro ball. Teddy, who'd grown up playing the piano, guitar, and bass guitar, turned to music. He started playing

---

[44] Ted also grew up in Reno and Lake Tahoe since his father performed in casinos there.

in numerous bands and revues, usually a bass guitar, which meant frequent travel. I could tell he was a thoughtful, creative guy.

I am circumspect about my background, but I talk about my acting career and how I am taking some time off to figure out what God has waiting for me. We talk about our spiritual journeys, and I speak of my heartfelt desire to help others. Teddy listens and speaks softly. He isn't full of himself—unlike more than a few actors I've dated. I like him immediately.

The next time we see each other, we meet over Chinese food. We both can tell there is a chemistry between us—a sexual energy—entirely normal between a single adult man and a single adult woman—but to me, this is different.

Our meal was yummy bites of Szechuan tofu with brown rice and broccoli, Moo Goo Gai Pan, egg rolls, and jasmine green tea. While we share the courses and conversation, I think I am falling in love. At the end of the meal, when the fortune cookies are brought out, I lay my cards down on the table like a Vegas dealer. "There's something I have to tell you," I begin. "I've chosen to abstain until I'm married, at least that's the goal. I hope you're okay with that."

A warm smile comes to Teddy's lips. "Me, too. And just so you know, I decided to be abstinent more than a year ago. I'm willing to wait as well."

My heart melts.

I am like, *Wow, wow, wow.*

I've never gone out with anyone who feels the same way as I do.

"I would like to know what it feels like to go on a walk, holding hands and bumping shoulders on accident," I share. "I want to know what it feels like to embrace and kiss each other, allowing everything to be what it is meant to be and build from there. True romance. I've never known that."

We have a whirlwind courtship. Teddy lives in Playa del Rey, a beach town near LAX known for its wide, sandy strip of sand along the stunning coastline. He doesn't have to twist my arm to jog on the beach, swim in the ocean, or take long sunset walks in the sand.

Six months after we start dating, Teddy bends his knee and holds out an engagement ring. This proposal is different: I know I have met my future husband. Tears fill my eyes and immediately say *yes*.

We don't want a long engagement. There is a hitch: Teddy is leaving with his latest band on a two-month tour of Europe. While we are still willing to wait, we don't want to wait *that* long.

We have been talking about getting married barefoot on the beach at Playa del Rey in front of friends and family, with the reception catered right there. As Teddy and I go through our calendars and talk through various dates, we decide to elope before Teddy's trip to Europe and have a formal wedding upon his return.

Two close friends say they'd help. Donna Kinsler offers her gorgeous home in Encino. Michelle Rashida Turner, a production manager in Hollywood who'd directed me in my play *The Rabbi and the Lady*, says she knows the perfect caterer who'll prepare a special "first meal" for us—organic and yummy, including a flourless chocolate cake.

Teddy's pastor and close friend, Lonnie Hinton at Press Christian Fellowship Church in Los Angeles, officiates the exchange of vows. Donna and Michelle are our two official witnesses.

Just seven months after we met each other, Teddy and I promise to have and to hold, from this day forward, for better, for worse, for richer, for poorer . . . as long as we both shall live.

After Pastor Hinton pronounces us husband and wife, the five of us share a few hors d'oeuvres. Then they excuse themselves so that we can enjoy a special dinner at Donna's house.

Our first "husband and wife" meal is as unique and intimate as we both hoped it would be. Donna and Michelle have prepared her dining table solely for us and worked together to prepare the special wedding dinner. As Teddy and I enjoy each course, we giggle like school kids on a first date because we both know there is a "wedding night" ahead.

We drive to Teddy's apartment in Playa del Rey, unable to suppress our laughing and tittering. Teddy make a show of carrying me across the transom. After showering and cleaning up, we hop under the covers, knowing what will happen next.

My heart is racing, and I am afraid of how to act. Teddy is all thumbs opening a bottle of champagne, prompting laughter. We read to each other, share our deepest fears, and fall asleep only to wake up in the early morning with a passion that frightens me— in a good way.

We don't tell our families or our friends that we have eloped. After all, they were invited to our "wedding" in Playa del Rey in a month's time, so don't see a need to let people know.

While Teddy is in Europe, his mother calls with concern in her voice. For various reasons, she says, "I hope I'm not stepping out of line here, but I've been doing a lot of thinking, and I don't think you two should get married."

I don't have the heart to tell April that we are already married.

But all of this will work out in the end. I know it will.

The wedding ceremony on the sands of Playa del Rey is memorable. I wear a white ensemble with flowing chiffon. My hair runs past my shoulders, the longest it has been in a long time. The sun is bright and high.

My entire family are there: mom and dad, and my brothers and my half-sisters and half-brothers. Uncle Jon Voight is in attendance. White fold-up chairs are set up in the sand, and a generator powers the PA system, set up by Teddy's best friend, Kenny Hoff.

Teddy's entire family joins us. His father, who I affectionately called Alzie, is the best man.

When it comes time to walk down the aisle, I follow a walkway on my own in the sand outlined by beautiful ceramics and bottles.[45] I look at my dad, my brothers, my family, and my friends, and then I focus my gaze on my husband, flanked by his father. Waiting for me to arrive is Pastor Bam, who will lead us in reciting our vows.

For Wedding No. 2, my future unfolds—and I arrive.

More Too Life

Where do I start?

Or asked another way, where does one person attempt to tackle the enormous problem of exploitation? How do I raise awareness about this scourge against humanity, this modern-day version of slavery that began centuries ago? How do I spread the message

---

[45] My father did not walk me to the front. He still felt bad but worked so hard for us that day, and did much to ensure the wedding was a success.

about its root causes and collateral damage to our humanity and our world?

These are pertinent questions that demand answers because the exploitation of persons is happening right now—today, where you live. My message is that anyone could be vulnerable to trafficking.

Keep in mind that the word *trafficking* means to merchandise. It doesn't mean a human being has to cross a jurisdictional line or a country's borders. It ultimately means that a child, boy, girl, woman, or man has been taken and moved away from how they were meant to live to do something they were never meant to do. Or do something they are proficient at—like farm labor or domestic servitude—and not get paid.

That's what trafficking is at the end of the day—an extreme form of violating someone's human rights by coercion, fraud, or force. Many are unaware that only a few percent survive sex trafficking while those who escape bear lifelong scars from this type of exploitation.

As I get More Too Life up and going, another penetrating question fills my consciousness: How can I make a difference in a cruel, distracted world that not only allows these cruelties to happen but, in some instances, condones this behavior?

There is only one place to start: to use my voice and my presence—two characteristics that I have to build up by overcoming my fears—to speak for those sidelined to the margins of society. I am confident that I am well suited for the role because I have lived on those margins for years.

Many victims and survivors are stigmatized by the past crimes done to them, but hope is not lost. I've seen firsthand how many survivors are late bloomers and filled and overflowing with treasures waiting to be discovered. All it takes is a little digging.

Let me illustrate this by telling a story about the San José, a sixty-four gun, three-masted galleon belonging to the Spanish Navy in the early 18th century. The ship, laden with 200 tons of gold, silver, and emeralds and bound for a return trip to Spain, was intercepted by the British Navy off the coast of Columbia on the night of June 7, 1708. A mighty naval battle ensued, which ended with the San José being sunk to the bottom of the Gulf of Mexico. Six hundred sailors lost their lives.

A little more than three hundred years later, in 2015, the shipwreck was discovered by an unmanned underwater vehicle known as the Remus 6000, which found the remains of the San Jose and its treasures 2,000 feet below the ocean surface. The treasure was calculated to be worth $22 billion.

The Remus was a tool used to discover what lay hidden for three centuries. Similarly, I want to be a tool—a Remus 6000, if you will—to show victims of exploitation how they can survive and then thrive to become champions. I want to be a tool to explain to victims who they are and why what happened to them, primarily as children and teens, is not their fault. That's the beginning. From there, they can begin the healing process in a whole new way.

I remember speaking to a group of survivors in my home one time about this topic. "Being a victim of a crime doesn't make you weak," I stated. "It simply means you understand it wasn't your fault; it was a crime. This leads to you no longer be in bondage to those that hurt you; that you were born for greatness, and are worth far more than all the treasure in the world. I say this because you possess attributes and characteristics no one will ever have.

"You must realize that on the other side of pain is a wealth of life experience, information, and intelligence. Nothing you go through leaves you empty-handed, so you must ask yourself:

What have I learned about life, other people, and myself in all this? Because the answers will help shape your identity, yourself, and your purpose in life."

Before a recent talk in New York, a woman I admire named Marilyn reaches out to me. The message she shares knocks me off my feet. Here are some excerpts:

> Dear Dr. Bello:
>
> I told a therapist in one of the group homes about how you were a light from God and showed me I could make it back from what happened to me. You helped me see that it wasn't too late to get an education and fulfill my dream. Now I've graduated from nursing school! Can you believe it?
>
> There was so much abuse from all the men in my early life. I was sex-trafficked from a young age. I didn't have a chance growing up and lost all my youth. I think of the self-disrespect I felt.
>
> My case is moving along, but the people alive back then who are now either deceased or the records are splotchy. The abuse started before I was nine years old when I was in foster care operated by the Catholic Church. I was abused terribly: I was beaten, molested, trapped, traumatized, and moved to so many Catholic schools that I can't remember all of it in sequence.
>
> But God knows everything that happened, and He will make it right for me and all the others. I will live and tell others how your help gave me hope.
>
> I had a life that no child should have. That's why my heart is for young people and children, for hurting people. People that do great things without recognition show us they are human with hearts that still care. That's you, Dr. Bello.

Marilyn takes my breath away. On top of her story, her two granddaughters are in our program for four years after being trafficked in the worse way by their father before they were seven years old. They are cognitively challenged because of this abuse.

We offer these girls love, therapy, mentoring, tutoring, and mock court settings. We are able to see one of the violators get beyond life prison terms. As for these two young girls, they are now graduating high school.

But their grandmother Marilyn, in all her passion and care for them, has never lived out her dreams either. When I tell her not to give up, she goes back to nursing school. This family of survivors is the reason I do what I do. I'm grateful that we get to stay in touch.

I love them deeply.

In the first few years of More Too Life's existence, I address any audience I can find or who would want me. I do dozens and dozens of speaking engagements in the early days, sharing intel and information without charging, because I want everyone to understand what trafficking is. I relish the opportunity to speak the unvarnished truth on trafficking and how it will continue to exist until there is a willingness to change among those inside and outside the world of exploitation.

Whenever I get up before audiences or I am interviewed by the media, I say provocative things like:

• "We need to change the myth that prostitution is the world's oldest profession. It has never been a profession."

• "There's no such thing as teenage prostitution. It's called rape."

• "This may surprise you, but I'm going to challenge the term 'sex trafficking.' I think it should be referred to as 'rape trafficking. Sex is meant to be intimate.'"

• "Even if you escape your traffickers, you're still in bondage in your mind."

It doesn't matter how big or small the audience is. If there are community groups, service clubs like Rotary or Lions, Junior Leagues, PTAs, or legislator offices and they are willing to hear me speak directly on trafficking, I am there. If an interested person wants to meet me at a coffeehouse, I meet them at the appointed hour. Whenever I am in public, be it a social event or business mixer, and I'm asked what I do, I use that opportunity to share my heart because it is all about getting the truth out and building social impact. When asking for financial support, I remind friends and acquaintances that I've put together a board of directors to provide guidance and accountability for what I am trying to do.

I let them know that one of More Too Life's goals is to prevent exploitation, to work with men and boys, and to educate others, like telling people that African American women, who make up only 6 percent of the U.S. population, account for over *half* of the prostituted persons, based on current data.

Which raises this question: Why are Black women and girls disproportionately at higher risk for trafficking?

My take is that social inequalities in this country, the history of chattel slavery, and the high number of fatherless homes in rural white families and urban Black families are some reasons why too many Black girls and women end up being trafficked. They grow up in poverty without fathers, either because their fathers abdicate their parental role, or they are incarcerated. The pressure to make rent and put food on the table puts many of these women in a position of being providers—a tough spot to be in and one that traffickers and pimps take advantage of.

Historically, African American women have been treated less than human ever since the days of slave ships. Crew members routinely raped Black women in the vessel's holds. When the captive women were led to the auction block, they were stripped of their clothing, oiled down, and ogled by potential buyers, who poked and prodded them like prized steers on the hoof.

Once they were purchased, their "masters" felt they had a claim to the slave's bodies—they owned them.   Rape was common on the plantation, and the perception among slave owners and many whites was that African women were hyper-sexual and therefore *wanted* it.

Throughout colonial times and into the 19th century, the myth persisted that it was "socially okay" to sexually abuse African American women and girls of various hues, such as Native American women. Since rape was used to assert power and authority, a narrative was built around the intersection of ethnicity and rape in which the law treated white men accused of raping African American women with proverbial high-fives. Black defendants accused of raping white women, however, were murdered either by being beaten and tortured to death, lynched, or executed in some other way.

During Reconstruction and into the early 20th century, this status quo remained. White rapists were seldom prosecuted, especially in Southern states like Mississippi and Alabama. On the flip side, the stated attempted rape of a white female by a Black man was a capital crime resulting in death. During the Jim Crow era, white men used the pretext of a Black man even *looking* at a white woman as well as rumors of rape to justify violence against them. Each lynching or court judgment reminded Black men that they had very little control over their lives and put African American women on notice that their bodies were not their own. Years of low prosecutions for rape make it easier for traffickers to assume that not many care to report or care about women and children enough, which is true and only 6 percent of rapes against all women—white, black, or brown—resulted in convictions in the U.S. You see, most never make it to trial because victims underreport and child victims hardly ever tell, if they survive.

Even do-good intentions like the passage of the Mann Act in 1910 failed to move the needle. Also known as the White-Slave Traffic Act, the legislation made it a crime to transport women across state lines "for the purpose of prostitution or debauchery, or for any other immoral purpose."

The Mann Act came out of the "white slavery" hysteria in the early 20th century. It seemed that women, predominantly white, were moving to the city and entering the workforce as this country was changing from an agrarian society to one of manufacturing during the Industrial Revolution. These single women, who worked in garment factories, textile mills, or offices in clerical roles, were no longer "protected" by the family-centered system of courtship. They could date on their own, a new notion.

In response, rumors traveled up and down the Atlantic seaboard that young women were forced into prostitution by white gangs and white immigrants arriving at Ellis Island. Muckracking journalists wrote titillating stories about innocent girls being kidnapped off the streets and secreted into brothels. Suddenly, exploitation was shown to be something that affected white women. The trafficking of African American women did not merit a closer look.

The Mann Act did nothing for African American women coerced, forced, and duped into prostitution against their will. Not only did the Mann Act fail to protect women and girls of color, but the law was used for racial purposes *against* Black people.

Jack Johnson, heavyweight boxing champion of the world in the 1910s, was arrested for bringing a prostituted person "across state lines" from Pittsburgh to Chicago and served a year in prison at Leavenworth. Today, historians agree that public outrage over Jack Johnson's marriages to white women motivated the prosecution.

While the way Jack Johnson was treated was wrong and regrettable, the one constant over the last century is that African American women have been subjected to a disproportionate risk of sexual violence.

Black historian Danielle L. McGuire[46] contends that the start of the civil rights movement can be traced to an incidence of rape against an African American woman. The event occurred on a Sunday evening in September 1944 when Recy Taylor, a twenty-four-year-old married woman and mother of a three-year-old daughter, was walking home after attending services at Rock Hill Holiness Church in rural Abbeville, Alabama. She was accompanied by a friend, Fannie Daniel, and her teenage son, West.

Six white men in a green Chevrolet sedan circled and then pounced. Brandishing knives and guns, they pulled Recy into the car and blindfolded her. She begged them to let her go back to her husband and daughter, saying, "Don't shoot me. I got to go home and see my baby."

Instead, the men drove the frightened woman to a secluded area and ordered her to take off her clothes. The six men took turns gang-raping her. One of the men told her, "Act like you do with your husband, or I'll cut your damn throat."[47]

Danielle L. McGuire is the author of the 2011 book, *At the Dark End of the Street: Black Women, Rape, and Resistance—a New History of the Civil Rights Movement from Rosa Parks to the Rise of Black Power.*

[47] Recy Taylor was violated to a degree where she could no longer bear children following the assault by six men.

When the men were finished, they left Recy on the side of a deserted two-lane road. Her father found her at 3 a.m., staggering along the highway.

Later that morning, Recy reported the crime to the county sheriff. There was only one green Chevrolet in town, which belonged to Hugo Wilson. When confronted by the sheriff, he confessed to the crime and gave the names of the other five men. "Sure, we all had intercourse with her," Wilson said, but he contended that they paid for it, making the rape a form of consensual prostitution.

The county sheriff filed no charges, but for daring to report the crime, Racy and her family were terrorized. White vigilantes firebombed their house. Recy and her husband and daughter had to move in with her father, who sat up all night on his porch with a Winchester rifle on his lap.

The unmistakable injustice outraged the Black community in Alabama. The NAACP sent their best investigator, a woman named Rosa Parks, to get to the bottom of the atrocity.[48] Justice was never served, but the outcry resulted in the formation of the Committee for Equal Justice, which would later become known as the Montgomery Improvement Association.

If the names Rosa Parks and Montgomery look familiar to you, they are one and the same. In 1955, Rosa Parks made history when she refused to give up her bus seat to a white man, launching the Montgomery Bus Boycott by 17,000 Black Americans.

The boycott, often heralded as the opening scene of the Civil Rights Movement, "was in many ways the last act of a decades-long struggle to protect Black American women like Recy Taylor

---

[48] Mrs. Parks was the perfect pick: she had firsthand knowledge of what sexual assault was like. In 1931, at the age of eighteen, a white neighbor who employed young Rosa in his home tried to rape her until she successfully fought him off.

from sexualized violence and rape," said historian Danielle McGuire.

Here we are, nearly eighty years removed from Recy Taylor's horrific story, and violent rape is still a problem for many women and girls, especially those of color. Girls as young as six months old and even little boys are not immune to sexual assault. Given the impact of historical trauma, racism, and oppression, Black women will seldom tell anyone about the abuse. For every Black woman who reports being molested in this way, at least fifteen Black women fail to inform the authorities.

Here are some quick stats from the National Center on Violence Against Women in the Black Community that are only based on what has been reported. Therefore, I believe these numbers are low:

• One in four Black girls will be sexually abused before the age of eighteen.

• One in five Black women are survivors of rape.

• Forty to sixty percent of black women report being subjected to coercive sexual contact by age eighteen.

Next, let me paint the bigger picture:

• One in four of all women are raped.

• One in five women on a college campus is raped.

At More Too Life, the amazing young women and girls we serve are white, black, and brown, although I will note that 50 percent of the survivors we serve are white. Ultimately, color is irrelevant. We care about protecting any woman, girl, or boy being trafficked or exploited and work with all people to prevent incidents. And that goes for young men and all others, such as LGBTQ persons. My point is race, ethnicity, and sexual orientation should not be an issue, and I refuse to make any of them one. It's my goal to do something about exploitation in the clear and present.

When I look into the eyes of victims and survivors, I see their pain, whether they know it or not. I know I can feel it. I haven't forgotten the fear I felt in the pit of my stomach, but my focus is on the possibility and potentiality of their futures. I tell every overcomer that they are born to be the best possible version of themselves, and together we're going to do something about it.

I'm fully aware that *talking* about the problem of trafficking is a lot different than *doing* something about it. I'm not surprised that some still don't realize that trafficking exists and how it happens, while others find it too harsh to hear. That's why we are here—because victims can't wait. They can't hope for everyone to understand because their lives are possible today. That's why More Too Life offers extensive programs and resources that help survivors.

Eighty percent of prostituted persons of all ethnicities have been violated, raped, or exploited as children, so, it's easy for many prostituted persons to look at themselves and believe they got there by their own decisions.

Brick by brick over the last eighteen years, I have built More Too Life steadily and continuously—but not alone—through developing framework models and curriculums to reach victims and high-risk youth. We provide "direct services," meaning housing, counseling programs, mentoring, court advocacy, education, and independent living support for those trafficked and exploited. We also provide mentoring for high-risk youth and work with buyers and human traffickers post-incarceration.

Over eleven years ago, I felt that the best place to expand our work was in Florida, beginning with the Tampa Bay region with offices in Tampa and Sarasota.

I chose Sarasota because of its proximity to Tampa Bay, Orlando on the East Coast, and the Interstate-4 corridor, which has been buried in human trafficking, sex and labor trafficking, and domestic servitude. In addition to our new offices in Miami Dade county where our staff focuses on victim services, court appointed prevention programs. Florida also has over 60 percent of all farm labor trafficking in the U.S. and is third in the nation in sex trafficking.

I believe we've put together excellent community programs in which a key component is focused on prevention. That's what we pursue every day at More Too Life.

While prevention is at the core of what we do, identity discovery is also urgent. Our direct-care services to hundreds of victims each year are done through various programs, including residential support and food for sustenance. We also provide therapists, substance abuse counselors, and staff to help victims stay on track through career guidance, parenting help, and assistance in helping them shape their destinies. All victims must deal with the trauma of abuse, or their wombs that were damaged and need medical attention.

Here's a quick but comprehensive list of what we can do for victims of exploitation:

• safe shelter
• mental behavioral health
• healthy food
• medical and dental health
• legal support, such as court advocacy in human trafficking cases
• career, work, and job-training programs
• educational services for GED, college, and vocational programs
• life coaching

- mentoring
- transportation
- crime victim compensation support

We also partner with national and global leaders on the root causes of trafficking and do our best to help shape public policy debates.

But if you had to put the work of More Too Life in a nutshell, it would be these three words: mentoring toward identity. Everything we do—our programs, our life plans, and our team building—is all based on mentoring and behavioral mental health-care framework model and curriculum.

Technically speaking, More Too Life is a nonprofit organization that operates independently of any government, making us a non-governmental agency or NGO. Our NGO status means we can apply for and receive private and government grants. We do this for three reasons:

1. Federal and state agencies have budgets with monies earmarked to "fight" trafficking, and we can help.

2. When prostituted persons are arrested, it's cheaper and more effective to put them into one of our comprehensive counseling programs with housing than locking them up in a state or local prison.

3. Federal grants are the most complex and most challenging to manage. The cost to manage these grants is often more than what an organization is usually awarded. Federal grants are never the first choice for this reason.

What we are doing these days astounds me. More Too Life serves hundreds of victims each year while working with global campaigns, the U.S. Department of Justice, the Bureau of Alcohol, Tobacco, Firearms and Explosives (ATF) on sting ops, and victim support for difficult cases that place their traffickers behind bars.

More Too Life also works with over one hundred organizations globally, including think tanks, supporting the collective work against human trafficking. I was named the executive ambassador for AuthenticIDs' All for Humanity Campaign and partnered with the Carlyle Global Group, one of the world's premier social impact investors.

All too often, abusers give their victims a false sense of their identity so that they can have an easier time controlling their lives. That mindset has to be turned around. The A4H campaign by AuthenticID, partnered with the Carlyle Group, embraced the framework that we developed at More Too Life to help victims through identity discovery, which we believe is the foundation of life and allows victims to discover their purpose.

Furthermore, I'm a Google Next Gen Fellow who's had the opportunity to learn from some of the top executives in the tech world about how technology can play a role in exploitation prevention. I've also met with federal, state, and local leaders and worked as a consultant on the Jeffrey Epstein case, and I've consulted with the HHS Health and Human Services Population Affairs office with Global Centurion. This work has also been instrumental in teaching about the urgency of womb health.

More Too Life is also a member of the Florida Children's Campaign's Open Doors Outreach Network, a network of providers in more than thirty-one Florida counties. We're working together on behalf of survivors in an innovative way, led by founder Roy Miller, who has done more for children than many men I know.

I am also building an incredible Metaverse virtual reality technology for mental healthcare while also working on mobile apps and case management systems to support victims and those that serve them with another company. The social impact of the tech companies' work drives what we are doing and positions More Too Life at the forefront of future prevention and services.

I've been fortunate to help thousands of trafficked victims over the years, and everyone has been unique. Some you never forget. Like when I got a call to help a fourteen-year-old girl who'd become pregnant by her trafficker. I'll call her Gina, who was from Florida.

Gina was a beautiful girl who'd been in 120 foster homes. She often ran away after being raped and trafficked while in foster care. No one knows better than me that traffickers prey on foster youth, the vulnerable, and runaways, and Gina was no exception. Many foster kids are raped by foster parents, while more than 70 percent have been trafficked in the U.S.

The state referred Gina to More Too Life. She came to us on a frantic night when we were searching for her because she was on the National Center Missing & Exploited Children list. She called me in hysterics, saying that the trafficker—a Mexican national—was going to drive her from Florida to Mexico. He was connected to a cartel whose connections in Mexico were extremely violent and dangerous. She said she heard stories on the streets about what happened to underage pregnant girls like her—they were shot or beheaded by cartel members. One less problem to deal with. Actually, two fewer problems since she was pregnant and carrying an unborn child.

When I asked her where she was, she said she was near Okeechobee, roughly in the middle of the Sunshine State between Fort Myers and West Palm Beach.

Teddy was listening to my conversation with her, as concerned as I was. I called the police and stayed on the phone with them for over two hours as I drove toward Okeechobee. Gina told me the street she was near and handed the phone to the trafficker.

I spoke in broken Spanish and begged him to let her go. He said *de ningún modo*—no way. The back-and-forth was exhausting and turned into a shouting match. I lost my voice.

We knew we didn't have much time. I drove like a maniac to get to a café in the area, arriving after midnight. I was scared but okay. Then I saw Gina and the truck drive by and pull into a parking lot, where he dumped her on the pavement. I rushed to gather her while they argued in Spanish. Teddy helped me get her into our car, and we drove back to our place in the middle of the night.

She stayed with us for a spell. I treated her like a daughter because I don't have any daughters or any sons, for that matter.[49] Gina ended up staying five years with More Too Life. I witnessed the transformation from a very hurt and upset teen to a smart, studious young woman who got an education, could hold on to a full-time job, get married, and do so much more in life.

While Gina became someone special to my heart, many others have as well. Two others come to mind: Lisa and Joanne, white women in their late twenties. One was blonde-haired with blue eyes; the other was a brunette with brown eyes. They both came to us in a federal case; I had to go in and grab them.

This was a federal case because their trafficker also ran guns, which put him in the crosshairs of the ATF. When I got them to a safe house, Lisa was wearing a $200 pair of Nike high-tops that her trafficker bought her. Lisa loved those shoes and wanted to wash them.

---

[49] One of the consequences of me being trafficked in my teen years is that my womb really got messed up for all the times I was forced to have sex with men. In addition, I had to undergo two more abortions. Even though Teddy and I tried to have children, it was never going to be in the cards.

I had to show her and Jo how to do laundry or Washing Your Clothes 101. I explained all the dials on a washing machine, how and where to add laundry detergent, and how to tumble-dry their clothes and shoes in a dryer. They *loved* learning how to do their own laundry and felt a sense of great accomplishment, as it had been so long that they had forgotten.

One time, I dropped by the safe house as they were putting in another load of clothes. They were laughing and giggling, but it was like a light switched when I arrived: they started crying.

These were not tears of sadness but tears of joy.

"You have to understand, Dr. Brook, that we didn't know diddly about doing laundry when we arrived here," Lisa said. "When we were trafficked, we didn't do our own laundry. All that was done for us. But the fact that we're going to get a warm meal shortly with our sweats on, just hanging out and doing our laundry . . . you don't know what that means to us!"

I was taken aback by their joy. I thought of all the things most take for granted, like the simple task of washing your clothes, eating when you want to eat, sleeping when you want to sleep, or calling whom you wish to call. That even extended to the kind of scent in laundry detergents. Lisa and Jo were bewildered by all the different scents found in brands like Tide, Cheer, and Glade. But they both loved choosing the scent that pleased them because they could. They didn't have a trafficker telling them what to do and where to go during their waking hours.

One more story about Lisa and Jo, who represent what we're doing at More Too Life: one of our close supporters, former Green Bay Packer Donald Driver, hung a "Giving Key" around their necks. These were old keys were inscribed with words like Believe, Strength, Faith, Dream, and Daughter.

I got misty-eyed when Donald placed a chain with a key around each of their necks and then hugged and hugged them, reminding Lisa and Jo how special they were.

The world would say that we at More Too Life "rescued" all of the survivors from the horrors of trafficking. While I've heard some people say they don't like the word *rescue*, I will argue that technically what we do *is* some kind of rescue from a place, person, or state of mind. Our rescues are an opportunity to provide care and assist someone with discovering their identity, something I know something about.

While in bondage to Sabrina, Darnell, and Tabitha, I wanted answers to the following questions about my identity:

- Who am I?
- What is my purpose?
- What is God's purpose for me?

To find answers, I *needed* to be rescued from my old way of thinking and the situation I was in. And so do the women, girls, and boys who need someone to rescue them, and that's where we come in.

I do not underestimate the difficulties of traveling on the road to recovery. So, let me ask this: Have you fully addressed the trauma you've experienced? Have you acknowledged that you need help to deal with unresolved issues?

If you're in this spot, the best place to start is by answering the question, "Who am I?" As I have shared in *Shame Undone*, I grappled with that fundamental question for way too long, but I did.

Having the ability to define yourself plays a huge role in your recovery purpose. Don't be afraid to ask for help from counselors and therapists who have experience in this area.

If you do, you can be transformed from victim to survivor, from survivor to thriver, and, finally, from thriver to champion.

And then your shame will be totally undone.

Sidebar:
More Thoughts on Trafficking

When I speak before conventions or large groups or when I'm interviewed on television, I often start with a description of what human trafficking is and how pervasive this problem is in this country and around the world.

While cold-blooded statistics don't begin to relate the tragedy that befalls real living and breathing victims, they are instructive. These declarations stand out to me and should to you:

• **Human trafficking is way more prevalent than anyone would think.**

The data on human trafficking is nowhere near what the actual numbers are. What we need to remember is that hundreds of thousands have died, and many family members never knew they were missing.

The Covid-19 pandemic generated conditions that increased the number of people who experienced vulnerabilities to human trafficking and interrupted existing and planned anti-trafficking interventions. Governments worldwide diverted resources toward the pandemic, which hindered investigations and prosecutions of traffickers.

Here in the U.S., school closures didn't do our young women any favors as traffickers took advantage of a situation that precluded many from having a main source of shelter and nourishment.

• **The ongoing crisis at our southern border means that the drug cartel and gangs like MS-13 can take advantage of**

wandering migrants and prey on their desperation to get to the United States.

Coyotes—those who smuggle illegal immigrants over the border—and human traffickers view these migrants as highly vulnerable individuals who will do whatever they can to cross the border. In addition, those who recently migrated to the United States are highly susceptible to adult and youth human trafficking because they need to earn money.

According to a United Nations Human High Commission for Refugees study, many undocumented Mexican migrants and perhaps the majority of all Central American migrants are trafficked as they head north. These immigrants may be forced to smuggle drugs into the U.S., enter the sex trade, or work for gangs to deceive unsuspecting travelers. They are often raped repeatedly throughout their arduous journey and even murdered if they refuse to carry out the wishes of their captors.

• **The phrase "human trafficking" also refers to compelling or forcing adults and children to perform labor.** "Trafficking" is often thought of as exploiting others to engage in commercial sex—and profiting from those acts. But forced labor, also known as "labor trafficking," is becoming more and more widespread in this country, especially among recently arrived migrants.

The language barrier is formidable and leaves foreign domestic workers vulnerable to being taken advantage of. For instance, a trafficker—a coyote, a gang member?—will require the victim to work in a private residence, where the employer often controls every aspect of their lives—their food, how they get around, and their housing. What happens in a private residence behind closed doors makes it difficult for authorities to intervene.

In rarer instances, traffickers force children to work for them, sometimes to settle a parent's outstanding debt. Anyone who thinks child labor isn't happening in the United States is either naïve or unaware of what's happening these days. But the majority of victims in the U.S. are Americans.

The Legacy of Fatherhood

Now that I've introduced the work of More Too Life, I want to take a moment to talk to the men reading my book about the issue of fatherlessness and the importance of committing to a higher standard when it comes to sexual conduct, consent, and intimacy.

First, a few words about fatherlessness, which can be associated with nearly every societal ill facing our country's children, including:

- poverty
- drug and alcohol abuse
- poor physical and emotional health
- inadequate educational achievement
- crime rates
- early sexual activity
- teen pregnancy

We can add trafficking to this list because 90 percent of all homeless and runaway children come from fatherless homes. They are the children that traffickers target, just like Sabrina,

Darnell, and Tabitha did with me. When traffickers look for the vulnerable to exploit, they scour the streets and home in on teens and young children in peril. Don't ask me how they know, but they know. They are practiced at understanding that young peoples' brains are not fully developed, which puts them in jeopardy.

Traffickers also comprehend that the primary structure for protecting children is the family and that stable homes are essential to establishing a stable community. I believe that family is the foundation stone of society, a social institution created by God. Whether by marriage, common law, consummation, blood relation, adoption, or a deep connection between very close friends, families look out for each other with unconditional love as a core value. Families come in diverse cultures, creeds, and sizes, but they have remained the heart and soul of human existence for millennia.

The most common building blocks of a family are two parents, preferably married or in a healthy relationship that demonstrates a deeper level of commitment. By every metric, children do best when raised by their two biological parents who have low-conflict relationships. That doesn't mean that single-parent moms aren't up to the unique challenges of raising children: they clearly are, but it's also been said they have the toughest job in the universe and should not have to bear the rigors and expense of parenting alone.

My point is that children are more likely to flourish when raised in an intact co-parent family unit, followed next by a single mother. The transition to stepfamily living presents several risks for children: boys and girls in stepfamilies exhibit more problems than do children in two-biological parent households, according to a study published in the *Journal of Marriage and Family*. Data also shows that children are better off living with single-parent moms than in homes with stepfathers who have a hard time embracing children not their own.

From my experience, many of the victims we have worked with were sexually violated by their stepfathers and were on the receiving end of harsh, even violent disciplinary treatment.

Let me directly speak to the men reading this: there is no more significant role you can have in life than being a father. Unfortunately, according to the U.S. Census Bureau, too many biological fathers are AWOL since mothers head 84 percent of single-parent homes.

I speak from the perspective of one who was never able to bear children but has been a parental figure to thousands of victims over the years. After Teddy and I married, we wanted a son and daughter badly, but maintaining a pregnancy never happened. We have been thrust into parenting situations when trafficked girls lived with me when I was single and then when I was married, so I learned a few things.

I'm think of the times when I've been in homes where I've seen Dad walk through the front door at the end of a long workday and seen the faces of two preschoolers light up and scream in delight, "Daddy, Daddy!" It never ceases to amaze me how fathers can just show up after being gone all day and the kids flock to him like he's a superhero. Adoring kids want to swing from his biceps or "play horsey" by riding on Dad's back while he moves about the living room on all fours. Working moms that walk through the door or stay-at-home moms can tie shoelaces, wipe noses, change diapers, cook meals, and run a vacuum cleaner throughout with nary a reaction from the little ones all day, but all it takes is for Dad to walk through the front door and the kids go ballistic with joy.

Men underestimate their impact on children and young people in general, but they shouldn't. Involved fatherhood is linked to better outcomes on nearly every measure of child and young adult wellbeing, from their brain development to educational achievement to their self-esteem. Families are strengthened and benefit from positive father involvement. I say this as an *equalist*—someone who celebrates the unique differences between men and women, boys and girls, as I have experienced with every victim I've had the opportunity to serve.

I love how the nature of men is described in one of my favorite plays, *Othello*, penned by William Shakespeare in 1603. Talk about a play that was avant-garde for its time: the lead protagonist is a heroic Black general named Othello who is in the service of Venice. In the production, he has recently married Desdemona, a beautiful and wealthy Venetian lady, against her father's wishes. And no wonder there is opposition: Othello is a black Moor, and Desdemona is as white as an alabaster jar.

The antagonist is Iago, a deceitful, rich, and evil ensign. He's also the jealous type who deceives Othello into thinking Desdemona is cheating on him.

In Act 5, Scene 1. Desdemona is having her hair stroked by her maidservant, Emilia, setting off this exchange in which Emilia does not condemn a woman for having an affair:

> But I do think it is their husbands' faults
> If wives do fall: say that they slack their duties,
> And pour our treasures into foreign laps,
> Or else break out in peevish jealousies,
> Throwing restraint upon us; or say they strike us,
> Or scant our former having in despite;
> Why, we have galls, and though we have some grace,
> Yet have we some revenge. Let husbands know
> Their wives have sense like them: they see and smell

And have their palates both for sweet and sour,
As husbands have. What is it that they do
When they change us for others? Is it sport?
I think it is: and doth affection breed it?
I think it doth: is't frailty that thus errs?
It is so too: and have not we affections,
Desires for sport, and frailty, as men have?
Then let them use us well: else let them know,
The ills we do, their ills instruct us so.

There's a lot to unpack in this section of Shakespeare, but I will be brief. I think Emilia is saying that the idea of men having a *right* to play around while women are to stay faithful and subservient is ridiculous. Emilia's saying, "Let them use us well, treat us well." She's instructing us on how the world should work.

The key line in this passage of Shakespeare is this: *their ills instruct us so*. Emilia puts men and women on equal ground in her speech by stating both sexes are capable of human fault and that women are not necessarily the weaker sex. She declares that the adulterous traits displayed by women are often and perhaps actually learned from men, and therefore women are not solely to blame. Her speech serves as a threat to men to be faithful to their wives. Or at least honest.

I've shared this bit of Shakespeare over the years with audiences and point out that her soliloquy can be viewed as awareness to men regarding the power of their decisions on those that love them. I fear that today's hook-up culture reflects how young men and women don't want to get married—and sometimes not raise the children they produce from these unions.

Consequently, the legacy of fatherhood is a dying art because of the massive changes in how families form these days. The two-parent family has fragmented into single-parent households, children going into foster care, or children living in chaotic situations in which different boyfriends and husbands come into the picture for a short time and then leave, which was my situation.

As many as 25 percent of all children in the U.S. live in households with a mother alone. That is over 20 million children who do not live with a father figure. Broken down by race, 72 percent of African American children are born to unmarried mothers, followed by Hispanics (53 percent), whites (29) percent, and Asians (17 percent), according to government statistics.

For the most part, I grew up in a fatherless home. I often wonder how my life would have been different if I had my biological father living under the same roof as me when I was growing up. Unfortunately for millions of young girls and boys, fatherlessness elevates the odds of daughters—and sons—getting raped or exploited. The U.S. Department of Justice says that daughters are 900 percent more vulnerable to sexual abuse and rape in the absence of biological fathers.

We know that children who grow up with absent fathers can suffer lasting damage. They are more likely to end up in poverty or drop out of school, become addicted to drugs, have a child out of wedlock, become juvenile delinquents, or end up in prison.

Fatherless boys are fourteen times more likely to become rapists when they grow older. I heard that the rapists in my life— Uncle Mike and Mr. Singh—were raised by single or divorced mothers.

The sobering statistics on fatherlessness go on and on, but this one stood out to me: an overwhelmingly vast majority of mass shooters grow up in fatherless homes.

Here's why I'm so concerned about absent fathers. Fatherless homes mean a lack of role models, less family income, more children on the street, more children and teens getting into trouble, and more opportunities for traffickers, exploiters, and bullies to contribute to teen domestic violence and identity crisis.

Worst of all, when teen girls get pregnant, the cycle of fatherlessness continues, and sometimes they deal with the shame of a forced or chosen abortion.

If you're a father but not living with your children, I encourage you to do everything you can to be more involved in your children's lives. I understand there are many issues to overcome, but your children need you. A father brings unique contributions to parenting that no one can replicate. A father's involvement will make a positive difference in a child's life. It will matter. Be there.

It's never too late to pick up the reins of parenting. I speak from experience with my father, who made a considerable effort to be a loving dad to me after I reached my twenties.

With that being said, here are some compelling ways that fathers are vital in a child's life:

• **Fathers parent differently.** Fathers have a distinct style of communicating and interacting with children, a diversity that provides children with a broader, richer understanding that men and women are different and have different ways of dealing with life.

• **Fathers play differently.** I mentioned earlier how kids love to hang over Dad. It's because fathers tickle more, like to wrestle, and throw their children into the air.

• **Fathers build confidence.** Dads have a way of encouraging kids to push the limits. If you go to a playground, watch how fathers encourage their kids to swing or climb a little higher while mothers remind them to be careful. This balance is essential and beautiful.

• **Fathers discipline differently.** Fathers tend to enforce rules and be sterner in teaching children the consequences of right and wrong, while moms tend toward grace and sympathy.

- **Fathers provide a look at the world of men.** Guys eat differently, dress differently, and go through life differently. Boys can learn about masculinity and how to channel their strength in positive ways. Daughters can know how men should appropriately act toward women.

Fathers are far more than just another adult in the home. When they're involved in their children's lives, they can leave a legacy that impacts their offspring's lives for generations.

Every day at More Too Life, I have to deal with the fallout of those who fail to parent their sons and daughters—and it's not good. In response, I created a three-to-twelve-month educational curriculum called Living Above the Noise (LATN) that gives participants the tools they need to transform their lives and discover their identities.

The purpose of LATN is not just to foster a champion mentality but also to teach leadership with a high purpose by educating and empowering young men—and women—with various ways to build and live a sustainable lifestyle. That's how they can become champions, no longer pained by their past but fighting forward, not only for themselves but also for remembering they can be the difference for someone else.

I mentioned earlier that I had to find or discover my identity. We help those in our program discover their identity, which is something that took me so long to do after I escaped my traffickers because I had my own mental bondage. We help survivors learn to think critically and ask the essential questions:

Who am I?
Why am I here?
Where am I going?
How do I forgive others?
How do I forgive myself?
Does my life have value?

The goal is to educate, inspire, motivate, and empower survivors with ways they can live a healthy, sustainable, and purposed lifestyle. And another way we do that is through a phone app that I developed called Coming Home.

Let's face it: young people do life through their smartphones, so I felt we needed to develop a secure interactive mobile app and digital case management system that gives all youth or adults as well as human trafficking victims a reliable means of finding and receiving life coaching and mentoring, along with other services and resources. Victims now have a place where they can:

• communicate with counselors and health care providers

• make appointments for mentoring sessions

• set goals for themselves, like eating healthy, exercising regularly, or learning a new job skill

• check out resources like local family health centers

• look for jobs

• complete tasks given to them by their counselors

• tap into online videos on topics like "The Power of Vulnerability and Overcoming Shame"

• and keep a personal journal where they can keep up with their dreams, thoughts, and feelings in one place

Every time we hear how the Coming Home app is changing lives, I'm gratified that we're reaching victims in innovative ways.

For more information, check out *cominghome.app* on your phone or browser.

I want to wrap up this chapter by talking to my male readers about male sexual integrity. I'm not going to get in your face, but I will be blunt: Sex trafficking would disappear overnight if men fled from sexual and identity proclivities. Be inspired by this quote from the Italian Renaissance philosopher Niccolo

Machiavelli: "The wise man does at once what the fool does finally."

Or I could say, "A wise man does at once what the fool does when it might be too late."

Sexual indulgence, infidelity, and addiction begin with lustful attitudes fueled by our sex-soaked culture, which often has nothing to do with what sex really should be about—intimacy. Men's eyes have been likened to heat-seeking missiles searching the horizon, locking on any target with sensual heat. Since men draw genuine sexual gratification through their eyes, they are turned on by nudity in any way, shape, or form. That's why pornography is such a huge problem today: guys have difficulty taking their eyes away from curvaceous naked women on their smartphones or videos of couples engaging in sex acts. Sadly, I speak from the experience of witnessing it firsthand.

Sooner or later, sexual thoughts can become all-consuming, causing men to sense a powerful urge to orgasm. When a pressure valve releases a rush of feel-good chemicals to the body, a sense of control is delivered to their psyches. This short description explains why men tell themselves they *have* to get that release. If that means purchasing a trafficked young woman, girl, or boy to get that orgasm, then so be it.

This compulsion to have an orgasm drives the sex trafficking world. It's why some men will embark on "sex tourism" trips to places like Germany and the Netherlands, where prostitution is legal, widespread, and highly organized. Other popular international destinations are Bangkok, Thailand, Nairobi, Kenya, and Bogota, Columbia, where children as young as five are brutalized. While traveling to these foreign cities may sound exotic, it must be noted that homegrown sex trafficking is happening right in our backyards in large cities and small towns in the USA.

The foundational problem is that the demand for trafficked sex is high, which grieves my heart. In a perfect world, no demand for commercial sex would result in no victims of sex trafficking or incidents of rape, incest, and so forth.

But we don't live in a perfect world, far from it. There is evil everywhere, led by wicked people enslaving others against their will to line their own pockets. I mentioned earlier that trafficking is the third-largest criminal industry in the world. Unfortunately, human trafficking is practically a risk-free opportunity to make boatloads of cash, so the practice is prevalent here in the U.S. and worldwide. Because of its clandestine nature, it's nearly impossible to know how many victims there are, but I can assure you that it's way too many.

In response, I have developed a curriculum known as Restorative Justice End Demand Education, which is a restorative justice program called the Legacy of Fatherhood and available at RJEDE.com. The goal is to educate men and boys.

Our mainstream court-appointed or volunteer Demanding More with RJEDE Legacy of Fatherhood program in Florida, in partnership with the state's attorney offices in Miami/Dade County and the Advocate Program, is the first state-approved course of its kind. Geared toward men who have been violated, are incarcerated, or are in recovery, this comprehensive education is directed toward men who have committed sexual violence or are addicted to porn.

Our RJEDE Legacy program sets out to ignite honor among these men and educate them on how they can make changes in their lives. They do this by reducing their demand for porn, prostitution, and human trafficking while being encouraged to engage in mutual respect and social responsibility.

I actively participate in these sessions with men willing to confront their behavior and/or participate in counseling regarding their actions. Many of the men are businessmen, fathers, pastors, and former gang-related human traffickers who are former victims themselves. It has always given me pause to know that 28 percent of the men in my program were victims themselves when they were even young, meaning they are victims of child sexual battery and other abuse, sometimes at an age that would mean their fathers, grandfathers, or others were pedophiles.

The definition of pedophilia is important because not all male sexual violators are pedophiles. We need to be consistent in understanding what pedophilia is, which is a sexual perversion in which children are the preferred sexual object specifically. The classic definition of pedophilia is a psychiatric disorder in which an adult has sexual fantasies about children or engages in sexual acts with children ranging in ages from nine to fourteen years of age.

Of course, children much younger than that are sexually abused. Personally, I've seen children as young as three be victims. What I want to address are the men who pay for commercial sex with fifteen-, sixteen-, and seventeen-year-old girls, which is a sickness as well as dark, ugly, and seedy—but it's not always the actions of a pedophile. It's the actions of a child rapist because sex between an adult and anyone seventeen and under is never consensual. It's flat-out child sexual battery rape. When money changes hands, food, drugs, or a place to sleep, it's human trafficking.

But anyone who fantasizes or engages in rape or sexual molestation toward a child that is fourteen and under is and should be classified as a pedophile. Let me be crystal clear on this while I make this distinction: if we throw every guy under the bus by declaring that he is a pedophile when he should be called a child sexual batterer or a rapist, it's been my experience that they will be more resistant to receiving help or participating in programs such as ours in order to stop it.

Prevention and education and truth are where restorative justice starts. I'm proud of our work alongside the criminal justice system and NGOs that educate men to begin to understand the damage they've done and what restorative steps they need to make to turn their lives around.

Human trafficking doesn't happen in a vacuum. The fight is huge. Here are some ideas for fighting trafficking—or lowering its incidence:

- **Increase awareness.** Data shows that a vast majority of trafficking victims have historically faced discrimination. We know that people of color, indigenous communities, and immigrants are disproportionately victimized. People living in poverty or struggling with addiction, trauma, abuse, or unstable housing are more vulnerable to trafficking. We need to have conversations about human trafficking to raise awareness and prioritize education about this insidious practice.
- **Look for ways to intervene.** Providing trauma-informed, victim-centered training to health care and social service professionals who can interact with victims and survivors can go a long way toward restoring shattered lives.
- **Urge authorities to enforcement of current laws.** Prosecuting traffickers and seeking justice for survivors is vital.
- **Become a trained mentor to a young person or someone in need through a vetted organization.** We train mentors at More Too Life, and we've seen firsthand how mentoring provides the boost that victims need to change their lives.

• **Change hearts to end demand.** So, where do we start with this blanket statement?

Perhaps we need to start with you. How is your heart in this area? Do you understand that trafficked women, girls, and boys hate what they're forced to do? Do you need to flee sexual immorality? Because it is a crime and immoral to engage in rape (sex) this way.

One of the issues that must be brought to bear is that many young men believe their ticket to manhood is by having sex. Sometimes the only ones available to them are trafficked women. Or they will cajole their dates or casual friends into having sex with them or commit date rape when non-consensual sex takes place.

Ending demand often means a change of heart, which means a moral, spiritual, or thought-process transformation. I was fortunate to experience God's personal touch when I was in my apartment and experienced a cool, water-like sensation come over my body, and God's presence filled the room. I believed in the Creator God that day and haven't looked back.

Since then, I've met tons of guys who have made major changes in how they treat and look at women. A "purity movement" is making waves among young people from all walks of life. Some men of faith are looking to replace their sexual addictions and infidelity with a different destiny—a destiny to walk in the divine nature, well above the fray. They are diligent in maturing their precious faith so they can establish self-control and perseverance in their lives and be found blameless and at peace with God in their sexuality.

The power of the legacy of fatherhood is bubbling over in my heart all the time. So much so, I can tell you that my father used to floor me with his voice when he encouraged me. One sentence from him was like a thousand winds that caused me to feel as though I could do anything. That is all I ever wanted—to know and understand that he was crazy about me.

After he died in 2018, I was told I was his favorite. Now, maybe all his children heard that, which would be amazing. But the fact that I felt it is what mattered. When he died, he had no money to give me, no inheritance of property, no stocks, but what I received was extraordinary. He gave me his felt love and the knowledge that my identity was part of his, which became my heritage and the strength of my ancestry. He gave me his name, and most of all, he gave me himself. He was and will always be my dad.

So, your destiny awaits. Will you now make every effort? That question hangs over the head and heart of every man.

By this point of the book, I hope you've learned where you stand today, and you know the choices you must make to be a man of purpose and sexual integrity. It all comes from the hearts that are changed.

Wrapping up, one of the best descriptions I've read about the make-up of the male heart comes from author John Eldredge in his book *Wild at Heart*:

> There are three desires I find written so deeply into my heart that I know now I can no longer disregard them without losing my soul. They are at the core of who I am and who I yearn to be.

> I gaze into boyhood, I search the pages of literature, I listen carefully to many, many men, and I am convinced these desires are universal, a clue to masculinity itself. They may be misplaced, forgotten, or misdirected, but in the heart of every man is a desperate desire for a battle to fight, an adventure to live, and a beauty to rescue.

That's the heart of a man—a desperate desire for a battle to fight, an adventure to live, and a beauty to rescue—that must be called out of you.

Are you up for it?

The Treasure Box

Gripping the podium at the White House Forum to Combat Human Trafficking on an April afternoon in 2013, I allowed waves of applause to wash over me. I was humbled and deeply moved by the standing ovation I received from government leaders, knowing that my words and delivery had reached this audience on a topic that affected all of us. Inwardly, I hoped this extraordinary moment would result in significant changes.

As the conferees and I worked throughout the rest of the day, we set forth ideas, discussed curriculum, and debated ways to find government funding, which would bear fruit later that year when the Obama Administration announced a major outlay to fight the scourge of human trafficking.

What we did that day didn't merit much coverage in the media, but my colleagues and I felt we were doing our part to change the world's attitudes toward human trafficking. Our progress was incremental, but we were moving in the right direction.

As I think back to that day among many at the White House and that experience, I ponder a quote I heard one time: "Three things cannot be long hidden: the sun, the moon, and the truth." Regarding the latter, there's no greater truth than self-discovery and identity discovery. Without those things, one's purpose is never found.

This is something that I personally have had to be resolute about in my work, which is framing and constructing the building of traffic-free communities across the United States and globally. I'm trying to do this through something known as "first principles thinking," which looks at age-old problems with new eyes.

First principles thinking is a way to reverse-engineer complicated problems by actively questioning every assumption you think you know about a given issue or sequence of events. I'm referring to taking something complicated—like life itself or the trauma we suffer—and breaking it down into essential elements and reassembling it. Then you go to work creating new knowledge and solutions from scratch.

I've been employing first principles reasoning in areas of technology innovation that I've been working on, specifically around mental health. What I've seen so far unleashes creative possibilities that are insanely beautiful and promotes critical thinking, something we need when tackling something as big as human trafficking and mental healthcare.

First principles thinking, which I use in everyday life and my work, is about building and genuinely living a life of purpose, especially after you've gone through horrific trauma and the foundation you thought was there is being chipped away. You must build as if it's for the first time without being crushed, but looking forward to the excitement that life can bring.

Critical thinking gets lost in the hearts and minds of those who have been traumatized, which is exacerbated by being plugged in too much to social media. But when we think about first principles, it's really about constructing new sails to pass through life, an idea that I teach survivors and others I work with.

First principles thinking is vital for those who provide care and for all of us. Take the topic of life after death. Life after death is a concept that no one wants to face because it speaks to one of the most profound questions anyone can contemplate: What happens when we die?

I'll let you decide if heaven is for real, but I feel that life after death happens among the living. Life after death occurs to anyone who's been traumatized, abused, exploited, trafficked, or beaten down. When a part of you dies, you have to find life on the other side of it.

Let me share how life after death is happening right now and not just happening in the clouds.

When I think about life after death, I think about a miraculous treasure box that my mother mailed me around seven years ago. When this treasure box arrived at my home, I wasn't expecting it. Honestly, I couldn't remember the last time Momma said anything really loving to me, hugged me, or even sent me a card on my birthday. She was the mother who didn't come to my games very often or watch me practice my favorite sport.

When I opened the treasure box that day, however, I had a rush of emotions. Tears began to flow when I saw childhood items and replicas or symbols of who I was or what I had accomplished as a child. There were also handwritten notes wrapped in ribbon for me to behold and read.

The first item took my breath away when I reached for it inside the box. I held up a pair of ankle sports socks, gray and pink, with an initial capital B high up on the ankle of each sock.

Then I remembered: Momma bought those socks for me because the capital B was for Brook, she said. I took off the ribbon around the note and saw her distinctive cursive handwriting. Momma had penned this:

> *To my daughter, the ribboned athlete, the hurdler, the*
> *basketball star, the volleyball player, I saw you*
> *and still do.*

I was crushed—in a good way. I had no idea my mother even cared about me after all those years of calling me the bad seed, all the times she was so rude to me.

Then I saw a face to hang on the wall, a face made of wood and gold and red cloth—the classic comedy and tragedy face that symbolizes the acting world of filmmaking and theater. The note said this:

> *To my daughter, the brilliant actress, the beautiful poet.*

The box was filled with other symbols representing important moments in my life and a dozen notes relating to those times. There was a photo of me dressed in my Little League uniform, wearing a mitt, with a message that said:

> *To my daughter, the first girl pitcher in an all-boys Little*
> *League in California, who took her team to the All-Stars*
> *championship but couldn't go to state because she was a*
> *girl. I'm proud of you.*

There was a school ruler with this note:

> *To my daughter, the straight-A student.*

And a little compass with this note:

To my daughter, the brilliant and wise explorer who will travel the world.

I was in shock, floored by the sentiments. I had no idea that she thought these nice things about me or cared enough to put the treasure box together.

Then, a couple of years ago, Alzheimer's disease descended upon my mother, taking her into the dark world of dementia. During the height of the Covid pandemic, I was not allowed to visit her. However, a nurse made it possible for us to FaceTime each other, which was great fun even though there were gut-wrenching moments.

I would remind her of her accomplishments and other celebratory moments in her life, like when she went to high school and university. In response, she would speak with passion, but she'd get so mixed up that it sounded like she was speaking gibberish. I could feel what she said, though, which was the most important thing.

I will never forget the FaceTime occasion when she started crying midway through a conversation in which she was the only one who could understand what she was saying, but I nodded and said, "Yes," and "Uh-huh, I get it." Then, mumbling through tears, she said, "You know, my Brooky, my Brooky, my Brooky, I was never mothered. I was never mothered. I was never mothered."

She had a look of terror, and I could feel the sorrow and shame as she struggled. Even though she only said my name and that she was never mothered, this is what I felt was unspoken: *I was heartbroken my entire life. That's why I didn't mother you. I am so sorry, Brooky.* That is what I heard, and it was overwhelming.

After hearing her sob a little longer, I wept for twenty minutes. She did too. I understood that even though she had shown me vivid hate and a lack of love for many years, deep inside her was a great reservoir of love for me—and pain for the past. She had treated me like she had been feeling her entire life—unloved because her mother wasn't there for her. My grandmother had died when my mother was very young. And I understood.

Momma passed away in the late summer of 2021. Whenever I think of her, which is always, I focus on the treasure box of memories she sent me and what it took for her to do that.

And now, I would like to share a small treasure with you—one of my favorite Scriptures. Typically, I dispense with something from the Torah, which is the first five books of the Hebrew Bible or what Christians call the Old Testament.

But this time around, I'd like to visit one of the Gospels, and I'm referring to the story in which Jesus teaches the parable of the hidden treasure. Matthew 13:44 (NIV) says this:

> "The kingdom of heaven is like treasure hidden in a field. When a man found it, he hid it again, and then in his joy went and sold all he had and bought that field."

I've come to realize that the field in this parable is the world—the world of chaos and pain and beauty and joy and confusion and struggle. Yet this man sold everything he had to buy this field so that he would have a place to plant and harvest.

That man is my God. That man is my savior. He bought a field so that I could be harvested with hope in a crazy, mixed-up world. But we are all the treasure hidden in the field. Never forget that you are the treasure, too.

When I began to understand this parable better, I was enlightened, again. These days, I teach victims, over-comers, and others that not only are they a treasure, but there's a treasure waiting for them on the other side of the pain they're dealing with right now.

After they hear this and are receptive, seeds of hope need to be watered. We stay beside victims until they become survivors, then thrivers, and then champions as they discover they are worthy of life and all the love in the universe. We remind them that their potential will line up with opportunities to live the life they dream of, and that is changing the world for the better.

I don't believe our greatest economic assets are gold, cryptocurrency, or land, which I can appreciate. Nor are our greatest assets unknown galaxies or other forms of money. The greatest asset we have, our greatest treasure, is human beings. When that notion becomes a palatable and powerful realization to everyone, you and I will be able to live a life of true freedom that's crisp and filled with the type of sobriety, unity, and humility required to lead and allow others to lead extraordinary lives.

Listen, I know there will always be evil and pain in this world, but what we do on the other side of it and how we help others get to the other side is what makes our lives valuable, especially if we can prevent as much evil and pain as possible.

Tomorrow's not promised, and no one knows what the future brings, but as we move forward to fight the various forms of exploitation, sexual violence, rape, trafficking, physical violence, bullying, and other trauma, please realize that a political party can't fix this problem. The Democrats can't do it. The Republicans can't do it. The Independents can't do it. It will be up to you and me to do it.

When survivors understand that they are their greatest treasure to discovering who they are and walking in that, greatness is around the corner. I say this even though I know our world is in deep trouble and largely unaware of what human trafficking is all about, including research showing that almost 30 percent of those exploited are boys, mainly used for forced labor but also sex too. That percentage has increased five times in the past fifteen years.

Human trafficking is not a woman's issue— it's everyone's issue. Let's come together across party lines, gender lines, cultural lines, and age lines and be grounded in purpose and destiny, doing good and being on the right side of history. We are armed and dangerous—armed with the power of love and compassion and dangerous with wisdom, knowledge, and a unified voice.

I close with a plea: Will you join me in this fight? Will you support our efforts?

Because it's that important to have shame undone.

Shame Undone and My Mental Health

Shame is defined as a painful feeling of humiliation or distress caused by the consciousness of wrong or foolish behavior. As I was staring out through a crack in a window during one of the rapes I endured, I felt ashamed. I was sixteen. I was conscious that wrong was being done and I thought it was all my fault. Now I realize it was because I didn't think I was loved enough to be protected and that I must have deserved it. Mental health challenges is something that I've struggled with. My mother and grandmother suffered similar challenges but that didn't mean I had to. But after all these things I thought were my fault, what I faced was my burden, and I had to make heathy decisions to transform. I also realized that in all I do and all my work was all centered around mental health, and I needed to continue to focus on mind. One root cause for me was shame.

This shame had crippled me for much of my life. It was like another person, with another voice that lived within me was deeply rooted in the fear and profound pain I felt of being rejected.

As a child, teen, and young adult, the shame I felt was because of crimes others and those I loved committed against me. This shame formed my identity. I carried that emotional bondage into adulthood, but the shame I felt needed to be undone.

Ultimately, the shame I experienced caused me to focus inward and view my entire self in a negative way. I was up, then allowed myself to be shot down, up and down, on a moment by moment or daily basis. Depression, anxiety, and stress were like three different enemies that lived within me fueling shame; they were an assassination team out to end my life.

Psychologist, Annette Kämmerer writes: "We feel shame when we violate the social norms we think we believe in. At such moments we feel humiliated, exposed, and small, and are unable to look another person straight in the eye." I know this very well. My self-sabotage was born in my shame because I owned it, it was a part of me. Who doesn't want to be accepted on some level within society? When I was not, I felt I was breaking a social norm and therefore— I didn't belong.

Shame because my mother didn't know how to love me.

I felt shame when she was hurt, or cried and there was nothing I could do to comfort her.

I felt shame because my father didn't love me enough to see me, raise me or take care of me and my big brother.

I felt shame because I was told my nose was too big—unlike the rest of the family.

I felt shame because all the reasons I've written about in this book.

I felt shame when I told others I love that I'm a late bloomer, and they didn't understand what I meant.

I tried to explain that when I went to college in my 30's and early 40's and I stopped having suicidal thoughts and the shame that preceded and followed—I no longer felt overwhelming depression or anxiety. I no longer felt socially awkward and filled with the kind of fear that stunted my ability to speak, share my thoughts, or be clear with strategic planning for the vision and ideas given me.

I had bad days. I was often crippled emotionally and had to find help like, exercises, self-talk, therapy, working out, eating healthy —timing it all well enough to get through each day. I appeared normal to others, but inside it was once a constant implosion. I felt ashamed that I didn't achieve my goals at a certain age and had to walk away from my passion and career as an actress and filmmaker.

Once I woke up from the deep well of remorse and pain found in shame, little by little, everything was better. Prayer was everything. Without God, nothing works for me. Food tasted better, colors were brighter, being with others was exciting, thinking clearly was profound. My thoughts bright, I can truly imagine what a healthy twenty-one year old college student might feel, filled with life and possibilities.

Though, I'm not twenty-one. So, I even felt shame for not knowing all of this until now.

Hopefully this is my last bout with shame. I'm still working on this one, but it is almost out the door. Today my life is filled with love, passion, desire, energy, and unshakable fearlessness and joy. Mental behavioral health feels good. It is not perfect; it's not supposed to be. Things are getting better all the time. I've made peace with my past and I am close with God in ways that make me giddy and myself.

What about you? Are you dealing with shame? Do you feel ashamed for things you've done or horrible crimes and trauma committed against you? Well, it's your time to let it go, to forgive yourself and others and to finally allow your shame to be UNDONE. Please go to shameundone.com and click on my "letting go of shame" tab—and as you write about it, let it go, into the river of forgetfulness. Know that I and my team will personally be thinking about you, praying for you—knowing that you are letting it go, and in doing so, are looking forward and desiring the things of value and virtue that shame stole from you to be restored.

Acknowledgments

To all those that hurt me, beat me, raped me, and tried to rip out my soul, you almost killed me, but you didn't win. What I found on the other side are a thousand oceans that keep me going. You gave me that. To my brothers, your love and affection guide me. To my other siblings who share the same father, thank you for loving me. To my mentors, Dr. Barbara Williams-Skinner, actor Jon Voight, and Diana Rowan Rockefeller, thanks for being there when I really needed help. To James Haven Voight, thank you. To my pastor John K. Jenkins and Trina Jenkins for covering me in prayer. To Dr. Beverly Crawford for seeing me and giving me the first opportunity to share my story. To Pampa Thompson, for words of direction and hope. To my dear friends, Shanna Biedron for words of prophecy and prayer, Chanelle Patrice Hardy for seeing me and Donna Kinsler for years of listening and all of you for making me laugh, loving me unconditionally, and allowing me just to be a girl. To my team, leadership, and board of directors at More Too Life, you make the work on behalf of so many extraordinary, Shavon Reed-Agard for your dedication and trust. To big sister, Mechelle Wilder, for reminding me not to take myself so seriously and to love on myself while I love on others. David Arkless, you know exactly who you are and you were there when no one else was on behalf of so many victims.

A special profound gratitude to Dan Spalding for giving me such a gift, seeing deep into the reservoir of my soul's journey and painting my portrait for the cover—which took my breath away and what my friends say is a masterpiece of authenticity. Thanks to, Will Dreamily Arts Publishing and their entire team for believing in my book and working hard to get it out to the world.

To my friends, Chance Glasco, Sean Pinnock, Carlos Wallace, and Mark Ervin, for believing in our Mental Health Tech for

Good Project that will change the world, and for allowing me, a survivor, to be taken seriously. To my managers, Victoria Fisher and Andrew Frances, and film producer J.D. DeWitt, for encouraging me to write, and Mike Yorkey and his wife, Nicole along with Michael B. Koep for guidance. I would also like to thank Jeff and Jill Jani, Kim Moore, Doug Plank, Kimberely Clarke and Matt Hosteler from Mission3A for being part of my future and all at AuthenticID and All for Humanity Alliance family for hearing me and allowing me to join the team to be able to turn the tide on exploitation, human trafficking while working to prevent it.   To all my mentees, you are my reason and to my survivor sisters, you know who you are, as well as my survivor brothers and those in this fight. Because of you, we are dangerous to those that hurt and harm.

About the Author

Dr. Brook Parker-Bello is the author of several successful books and digital and copy educational curriculum platforms aimed at the prevention of sexual exploitation and gender-based violence as well as the Legacy of Fatherhood, including the author and curator of a new book "Fine Heart Table book "Monaco Edition" a collection of paintings by survivors, supported by the Caryle group, Picasso family with Authentic ID, Mission 3A and Skies Fall. Dr. Bello has spoken alongside presidents, prime ministers, and fellow change-makers at universities, large conferences, and federal agencies. Aside from holding a PhD in Pastoral Clinical Counseling, she was recognized with the Lifetime Achievement Award from President Barack Obama and the White House, the Advocate of the Year Award from Florida's Attorney General Pam Bondi and Governor Rick Scott, named by

United Way Worldwide as a Hero on the Oprah Winfrey Network, for her work, and most recently named by Google as a Google Next-Gen Policy Leader2017-2022 and 2019 Department of Justice ATF Division Victim Advocate of the Year. She is an expert consultant for the US Department of Health and Human Services (HHS) Title X Clinics and Population Affairs National Human Trafficking Training with Global Centurion and the US Department of Justice having consulted on federal cases. She holds a US Patent in technology and is the creator of groundbreaking software in mental healthcare, case management, AI, and machine learning virtual reality chosen by Techstars Founders Catalyst Program. Her new book SHAME UNDONE comes out in 2023 and has been optioned for a limited series and a motion picture, Brook is also an alumni of the Master's Series of Distinguished Leaders.

Mike Yorkey is the author, co-author, editor, or collaborator of more than 115 books. In the past, he has worked with:
• Elishaba Doerksen, who grew up as the oldest of fifteen children with an abusive father in *Out of the Wilderness*
• Casey Diaz, a Latino gangbanger, in *The Shot Caller*
• ex-NFL wife Cyndy Feasel in *After the Cheering Stops*
• paralyzed Rutgers defensive tackle Eric LeGrand in *Believe: My Faith and the Tackle That Changed My Life*
• Ron Archer, who was sexually abused as a child in *What Belief Can Do*
• Walt Larimore, who shares the heroic story of his father fighting in World War II in *At First Light*
Mike is also the co-author of the best-selling *Every Man's Battle* series and two World War II novels, *The Swiss Courier* and *Chasing Mona Lisa*.

Michael B. Koep has been called an Inland Northwest Renaissance Man. He is the author of the Award Winning *The NEWIRTH MYTHOLOGY: The Invasion of Heaven* (2013), *Leaves of Fire* (2015) and *The Shape of Rain* (2018). He is an avid world traveler, swordsman, educator, accomplished visual artist, and touring rock musician. He is the drummer and lyricist for the progressive rock group KITE, as well as the percussionist for the variety power trio The RUB. His latest book, *GIGMENTIA: A Drummer's Love Song to Rock Shows, Fatherhood, Writing, and the Passing of a Beloved Mom* releases in the summer of 2023. He lives in Coeur d'alene, Idaho with his family.

Ask Brook Parker Bello to Speak at Your Community Event, Business Gathering, or Conference

Brook Parker Bello is a gifted communicator and an inspirational international champion against trafficking and gender violence. She holds a Ph.D. in Pastoral Clinical Counseling and believes in the power of changing the trajectory of people's life by discovering their pure potential through identity discovery that can be used to catapult them forward and be a blessing to others.

If you would like to book Brook for a community event or conference, call her through the More Too Life offices at 941-227-1012 or contact her through the More Too Life website at moretoolife.org. You can also call her agent at Kjar & Associates at 818-760-0321.